THE BOOK OF THE YEAR 2019

THE WORLD'S WEIRDEST NEWS

James Harkin, Andrew Hunter Murray, Anna Ptaszynski
and Dan Schreiber

Illustrations by Adam Doughty
Graphic design by Alex Bell

HUTCHINSON
LONDON

1 3 5 7 9 10 8 6 4 2

Hutchinson
20 Vauxhall Bridge Road
London SW1V 2SA

Hutchinson is part of the Penguin Random House
group of companies whose addresses can be found at
global.penguinrandomhouse.com.

First published in the United Kingdom by Hutchinson in 2019

www.penguin.co.uk

A CIP catalogue record for this book is available
from the British Library.

ISBN 9781786332011

Typeset in 9.5/13pt ITC Cheltenham Std by Jouve (UK), Milton Keynes
Printed and bound in Great Britain by Clays Ltd, Elcograf S.p.A.

Penguin Random House is committed to a sustainable future
for our business, our readers and our planet. This book is
made from Forest Stewardship Council® certified paper.

INTRODUCTION

The biggest news of 2019 was that the UK would definitely, 100 per cent be leaving the European Union on ~~29 March 2019~~, ~~22 May 2019~~, 31 October 2019. And that's the last you'll read about ▓▓▓▓▓ in *The Book of the Year*. (See ▓▓▓▓▓ for a comprehensive list of all the places you won't see it mentioned.) Instead, the mission of this book is to champion all the other weird and wonderful stories from 2019, that, unjustly bumped from the front pages of the newspapers, failed to have their day in the sun, or indeed the *Sun*.

What a year it has been . . . Three new lawnmower records were set (see **Lawnmowers**); the first winners of the Heavy Metal Knitting Championship were crowned (see **Competitions**); and the world was introduced to 'meat carrots', aka 'marrots' (see **Vegans**). It was a year that saw an abundance of new scientific discoveries, bizarre inventions, animal exploits and holy news (see **Bless You!**), as well as a whole lot of hole-y news (see **Holes, Black; Holes, Glory**; and **Holes, Pot**).

To those returning to our series for a third time, thank you for joining us once again. We promise there will be much less news about boars than there was in the previous two volumes. And to those new to the series: Hello! Thank you for buying this book. We are Dan, James, Anna and Andy, four fact nerds who host a weekly podcast called *No Such Thing As A Fish*. Being compulsive readers ourselves, we fully understand how intimidating jumping into the third book of a series can be, and so we thought in order to quash any concerns you might have, we'd provide a short Q&A to help you get to grips with what lies ahead:

Is this book simply a collection of amusing but useless facts?

Absolutely not. You must be thinking of *The Book of the Year 2017* or *The Book of the Year 2018.* In fact, if used correctly, you'll actually find this is the most useful book in any book store. It can make you rich (see **Killing, Making A**); help you find a job (see **Eternal Employment**); help reduce your tax bill (see **Kelly, Lorraine**); save your life (see **Booze**); and even tell you how to unglue someone's bottom from a window (see **Extinction Rebellion**).

The news can be depressing. Was there anything you were unwilling to write about?

Nothing (apart from ▮▮▮▮▮) was off-limits. That and mushroom-based news, which James has a strict veto on (see **Fungi, Not Such A**).

Much of the news these days is fake. Can you guarantee that everything in this book is true?

Yes. Except for the bits written by Dan. All factual inaccuracies in the following pages are most probably his. The guy actually believes that after you die you might come back in your next life as 'sexy lichen' (see **Reincarnation**).

Why does this book contain less boar news this year?

Because it was time for Andy to move on with his life. Unfortunately, all he did was replace one addiction with another (see **Sausages**).

This is absolutely not the right kind of book for me.

No problem. Buy it anyway, and you'll see that Anna has some excellent suggestions for alternative reading materials (*see* **Mueller Report**).

That last one wasn't a question.

Sorry. But the point still stands.

I'm still not sure. Are there at least some fun games to be played in this book?

If by fun games you mean: 'Will I get the chance to decode Nigerian political party promises that have been translated into Emoji symbols?', then yes, you've come to the right place (*see* **Emojis**). There's also a crossword, a spelling test, a spot-the-difference challenge, and even some hidden Easter eggs to find.

Did you find out all this stuff yourself?

No. We are merely the messengers' messengers.
This book would be nothing but a pile of blank pages were it not for the tireless work of all the incredible journalists working around the globe – from the *Birmingham Post* and *The New York Times* to *Meat Management* magazine and the *Uranus Examiner*. Once again, we dedicate this book to them. In particular, to the journo who reported that a man called Bud Weisser had been arrested for trespassing at the Budweiser factory (*see* **Unusual Suspects**). What a find.

Okay, I'm sold. This book sounds fantastic.

Great, now pop us into your basket, head to the till, and get stuck into *The Book of the Year 2019*. Rather than being an A–Z, it's an A–Å (*see* **Aa**) of the world's news – a full round-up of yet another year when real life was stranger than fiction.

Dan, James, Anna and Andy
Covent Garden

THE BOOK OF THE YEAR 2019

IN WHICH WE LEARN . . .

Which motorists were disappointed to see the Aa, who had Noah luck insuring their boat, which world leader turned down a $5 note, who didn't want to be sent flowers, and who absolutely shouldn't bother flying up a supervillain's bottom.

AA

Two tourists planning to visit the Norwegian village of Å ended up 1,310 kilometres away, in Aa.

The pair of bewildered Chinese travellers were spotted by the region's deputy mayor, literally in her front yard. She realised they had mistakenly put Aa into their satnav, and that they'd actually intended to go to Å (Å is a letter at the end of the Norwegian alphabet, so just like the tourists, it's in a completely unexpected place). Aa is in a village called Hyen, more than 1,300 kilometres south of Å. Since the tourists didn't speak Norwegian and the deputy mayor didn't speak Mandarin, she was unable to help them. In the midst of this confusion, it can't have helped that the deputy mayor's surname is Aa-Berge. The tourists disappeared without a trace shortly afterwards.

ADVENTURING

A 71-year-old Frenchman crossed the Atlantic in a barrel without a paddle. Or an engine. Or any sails.

Jean-Jacques Savin, a 71-year-old former paratrooper and sailor, wanted to become the first person to rely solely on currents to make the crossing – so he built a 10-foot-long plywood barrel. It was designed to be killer-whale-proof, weighted to stay upright, and his bed had straps so that he wouldn't fall out in the night.

Savin cast off from the Canary Islands on Boxing Day last year and hoped to make it to the Caribbean within three months. However, things didn't quite go to plan: he was blown 600 miles off-course almost immediately, and the weather remained against him for five weeks. On the upside, as there was no need to spend time maintaining an engine or the sails he didn't have, he was able to dedicate himself to writing a diary, playing the mandolin and looking at passing fish through a porthole in the bottom of the barrel – although he also had to spend three hours a day replying to emails forwarded to him by his secretary. As any good Frenchman would, he celebrated his 72nd birthday with foie gras and a bottle of Bordeaux.

Finally, after 2,930 miles and over four months of bobbing around on the ocean, Savin made it to the Caribbean Sea. He was then given a tow by a friendly oil tanker to the nearest land – the Dutch island of St Eustatius – some 230 miles away (he had been hoping to end up on a French-owned island because 'That would be easier for the paperwork'). For his next challenge, Savin is thinking of crossing the Pacific in a barrel. His friends are trying to dissuade him.

AIRPORTS

For the American president who says there were airports when there weren't, *see* **Fourth of July**; and for the Russian president who says he's an airport when he isn't, *see* **GPS**.

AMAZON VS AMAZON

Amazon attempted to bribe the Amazon with $5 million worth of Kindles.

Twenty-five years ago, Jeff Bezos decided to change the name of his nascent company, Cadabra.com, after a group of people participating in a conference call misheard it as 'Cadaver'. He finally hit on amazon.com: the Amazon is the largest river in the world, he said, and he wanted to build the largest bookshop in the world.

Amazon.com *is* certainly now the world's largest bookshop, but Bezos still wants it to expand; so to help him meet this ambition, he hatched a plan to create websites that, instead of ending .com, end with .amazon. Unfortunately, the idea didn't go down well with the governments of Bolivia, Brazil, Colombia, Ecuador, Guyana, Peru, Suriname and Venezuela, all of which argued that because the River Amazon runs through their countries, they should own the rights to web addresses that make use of its name. At one stage amazon.com offered these countries $5 million worth of Kindles to try to break the impasse. The gesture was rejected, and the matter was eventually turned over to the Internet Corporation for Assigned Names and Numbers (ICANN).

After five years of wrangling, ICANN finally judged in favour of amazon.com, but with the proviso that the eight countries through which the Amazon runs will be allowed to divide amongst themselves nine domain names ending in .amazon (it's unclear how they'll decide who gets the ninth one). These countries will also be allowed to request a veto for up to 1,500 web addresses proposed by amazon.com. What the ruling did not reveal was whether or not those countries still get the Kindles.

APOPPYLYPSE

The population of Lake Elsinore tripled, thanks to the popularity of its poppies.

Heavy rain this spring meant that the hills around the Californian city of Lake Elsinore (pop. 68,000) became covered with a 'superbloom' of millions and millions of poppies, so extensive it could be seen from space. Unsurprisingly, their beauty attracted eager selfie-seeking poppy tourists; more than 150,000 arrived in the city in a single weekend to admire them. At first the local mayor declared the phenomenon 'Poppypalooza'. Then it became the 'poppy apocalypse' and finally the 'Apoppylypse'. Other officials described it as a 'poppy nightmare'.

All this might sound histrionic, but the fact is that the superbloom was a disaster for the people of Lake Elsinore. Local services were overrun. Medical assistance had to be offered to the many tourists who fainted in the heat. The authorities had to watch out for those who cut through barbed-wire fencing to get at the flowers (one couple even illegally landed a helicopter in the middle of the poppies, to skip the queues). And then there was the problem of rattlesnakes, which were

As well as captivating hundreds of thousands of influencers, the superbloom attracted around a billion butterflies – good news for a state that has seen numbers of some butterfly species decline by 97 per cent over the last 20 years.

5

On 20 July, the world celebrated the 50th anniversary of the Apollo 11 mission, which landed the first humans on the Moon. But few remembered the crew of Apollo 12 – Pete Conrad, Alan Bean and Richard Gordon – who arrived there just under four months later...

Immediately after Apollo 12's Saturn V rocket launched, it was struck by lightning. Twice. This garbled the on-board equipment and the mission would have been aborted, had it not been for the quick thinking and excellent memory of a crew member who recalled an obscure piece of training from a year earlier and managed to reboot the system.

When Pete Conrad became the third person ever to stand on the Moon, his first words were 'Whoopie! Man, that may have been a small one for Neil, but that's a long one for me', making fun of his own 5' 6" height. He said it in order to win a $500 bet with a journalist who believed the government scripted everything the astronauts said up there.

Unbeknownst to ground control and the astronauts themselves, backup pilot Dave Scott had secretly smuggled nude *Playboy* pictures in amongst the checklist sheets attached to their spacesuits and added captions underneath each photo. Conrad and Bean discovered the pictures two hours into their first spacewalk. Conrad's checklist included a full-frontal picture of Angela Dorian, aka Miss September, accompanied by the words 'Seen any interesting hills & valleys?'

The Apollo 12 Moon landing footage was faked. When Alan Bean, the fourth man to stand on the Moon, accidentally pointed the mission's only video camera directly at the sun, its components promptly burned and broke. Left with only the audio, news channels on Earth were forced to improvise the visuals. CBS showed two actors in spacesuits acting out what was happening, while NBC used astronaut marionettes that they happened to have on hand, made by the puppeteer who performed 'The Lonely Goatherd' in *The Sound of Music*.

When Conrad and Bean returned to the command module after their spacewalk, they did so in the nude. Command-module pilot Richard Gordon was so worried about the impact of the moon dust on the spacecraft systems that he made them strip off all their clothing before letting them pass from their lunar lander back onto the main ship.

As they returned to Earth, Bean was knocked unconscious on splashdown when a 16mm camera was jolted out of place, fell through the command module and smacked him on the head. He needed six stitches.

Pete Conrad died on 8 July 1999, after crashing his motorcycle while riding through Ojai, California. Ojai comes from the word *'awha'y*, a Native American word from the Ventureño language. It translates as 'moon'.

coming out of hibernation at the time, and which bit at least one visitor. Eventually the town felt it had no choice but to bar access to the main poppy site, Walker Canyon, and plead with people to stay away. 'This weekend has been unbearable,' said the city's officials, adding that it had 'caused unnecessary hardships for our entire community'.

Once the poppy nightmare was over, the city posted on Instagram: 'We survived the poppy apocalypse!' The *LA Times* recommended that poppy fans should not thank the city authorities by sending them flowers, 'as that would be horrifically insensitive'.

APPOSITE

A shark that had just eaten a shark was caught by a man called The Shark.

Former professional golfer Greg Norman is known as 'The Shark' because he's from the home of the great white shark, Queensland, and because he played very aggressively. While fishing off the coast of the city of Jupiter in Florida, he managed to hook an 80-pound blacktip shark, which was then immediately attacked and eaten by a hammerhead shark 10 times as big. Norman and his friends eventually wrestled the hammerhead alongside the boat, swam next to it for a bit, then released it.

In other apposite news of the year:

▶ Gillette recalled 87,000 disposable Venus razors because, thanks to a manufacturing error, they posed a cutting hazard.

▶ A Disney café was closed because someone spotted a mouse. The café – located in Birmingham, inside the world's biggest Primark – serves mouse-shaped pancakes and has pictures of Mickey everywhere, but when a customer saw an actual mouse in there, the café was (temporarily) shut down.

▶ There was a lunar eclipse in the UK on the anniversary of the Moon landings.

▶ Five guys were arrested at Five Guys. The men got into a fist-fight inside a Florida branch of the burger restaurant.

▶ The *Spirit of Britain* abandoned the UK and fled to the Continent. It was a P&O ferry, and the firm changed the country of registration to Cyprus to avoid getting caught up in any UK/EU disruption caused by ▨▨▨▨.

▶ A rapper who wrote songs about credit-card fraud was charged with credit-card fraud. Twenty-five-year-old Selfmade Kash, real name Jonathan Woods, has written songs including 'In Swipe I Trust', in which he describes making a killing from credit cards. Prosecutors said, 'Woods claimed to be sophisticated at credit-card fraud when, in fact, he is not.'

ARKS ▶

The owners of the world's largest replica of Noah's Ark sued for rain damage.

Ken Ham's Ark Encounter is a fundamentalist Catholic theme park in Kentucky whose centrepiece is a full-sized replica of Noah's Ark. It's probably the largest wooden structure in the world.

In 2017 and 2018, Kentucky suffered from extremely heavy rains, which, while not quite heavy enough to cover the entire planet with 15 cubits of water (as happens in the Old Testament), were enough to cause landslides at the park. Ham's company demanded $1 million from its insurers and claim that they have so far refused to pay out. The case continues, with barely an olive branch in sight.

ARMAGEDDON

If Bruce Willis managed to blow up an Earth-threatening asteroid, it would simply re-form and hit the planet anyway.

That was the conclusion of a group of scientists at Johns Hopkins University who built a computer simulation of asteroid collisions to study what happens when the space-rocks break apart. They found that asteroids are stronger than we thought, and that existing technology is not capable of flinging the pieces far enough apart, or causing enough damage to the asteroids' cores, to stop their gravity from bringing them back together.

One way and another, the world's scientists had a pretty bad year fighting theoretical apocalypse scenarios. Around the same time as the Johns Hopkins calculations were being made, some of the world's greatest minds gathered at the International Academy of Astronautics' Planetary Defense Conference and similarly failed miserably to save the Earth from a fictional head-on asteroid impact.

The simulation, which was created by a NASA engineer, began with an alert that a 200-metre-wide asteroid had been detected and had a 1 per cent chance of striking the planet in 2027. The team challenged to deal with it decided to build six 'kinetic impactors' – probes designed to hit the asteroid to change its trajectory. The probes managed to deflect the main body, but caused a fragment to break off, which then headed for the eastern US. So despite having eight fictional years to devise a plan to save the world, the team was unable to stop New York from being flattened. The European Space Agency tweeted along with the simulation, although every tweet had to be accompanied by the hashtag #FICTIONAL-EVENT so that people didn't freak out.

The threat of an asteroid strike isn't entirely theoretical. In July, a 100-metre meteor with the deceptively unthreatening name of '2019 OK'* came within 45,000 kilometres of the Earth, and it was discovered only a day before it skimmed past the planet. Had it hit the Earth, it would have exploded with the power of a large nuclear bomb. Scientists who subsequently tried to work out why they had missed it until the last minute realised that it had actually been captured twice by telescopes, but nobody had recognised what it was. And '2019 OK' isn't alone. There are an estimated 30,000 asteroids of between 100 and 300 metres out there, but we have only spotted 16 per cent of them. So if an asteroid is heading our way, it's unlikely Bruce Willis will have time to do anything about it.

*The 2019 in the asteroid name '2019 OK' comes from the year it was discovered. The O is the designated letter for the half-month of 16–31 July when it was spotted. And the K is because K is the 11th letter of the alphabet – and the asteroid was the 11th such discovery in that period.

AUSSIE ELECTION

A pre-election poll revealed that Australia's most trusted politician is the prime minister of New Zealand.

On the day of the election, a poster appeared outside one polling station in the same colours and font as the official signage, but in Mandarin. Translated into English it read: 'Correct way to vote. On the green voting card, put preference 1 next to the Liberal Party. The other boxes can be numbered from smallest to highest.' The fine print revealed that the sign had been paid for by the Liberal Party.

When he called the election, Australia's Liberal prime minister Scott Morrison asked the electorate, 'Who do you trust to deliver that strong economy which your essential services rely on?' The answer, according to the polls, was increasingly 'Nobody'. The controversies that plagued the election didn't help: Liberal candidates were forced to step down over claims of Islamophobia and homophobia. The opposition Labor Party had to drop candidates for alleged sexism and anti-Semitism. And the government was caught up in a scandal that centred on a claim that it had improperly spent $80 million to purchase water from farms. Nicknames about scandals tend to end with -gate. This scandal was about water: so the Aussie press, somewhat lacking originality, dubbed it 'Watergate', which also made the scandal nearly impossible to google.

Despite the failings of the main parties, voters didn't flock to smaller parties such as the 'Great Australian Party', the 'Love Australia or Leave Party', the unnecessarily shouty 'Climate Action! Immigration Action! Accountable Politicians!' party or the party with probably the world's most contrived acronym: the 'Help End Marijuana Prohibition (HEMP) Party'. This was perhaps because some of the candidates from these parties didn't show much more integrity than the front-runners. One activist from the United Australia Party was fined for exposing himself at a polling station, while a candidate for the anti-immigrant 'One Nation' party shared a Facebook post of a naked woman Photoshopped to look like a centaur, with the caption: 'MMMM!!! Interesting thoughts' (he managed to avoid deselection).

All of which meant that although Scott Morrison managed to hold on to power, when it came to naming a politician they trusted, many Australians looked to the country on the other side of the Tasman Sea. New Zealand's prime minister Jacinda Ardern has been gaining plaudits around the world, thanks especially to her response to the terrorist attack in Christchurch, when she refused to mention the name of the attacker. Her personal integrity has been similarly unimpeachable. When a schoolchild wrote to her, asking that the government do some research into psychics and dragons and including NZ$5 by way of a sweetener, Ardern returned the bribe.

AUSTRALIANS

For a manager accused of farting on his staff, *see* **Bosses**; for the former prime minister who could sink a yard of ale in 11 seconds, *see* **Lager-filled**; for the man who accidentally won the lottery twice, *see* **Lucky**; for the boy who went from being called 'Egg Boy' to being called 'Egg Boy', *see* **Milkshaking**; for a father who wasn't arrested for murdering a spider, *see* **Pesky Pests**; for the politician who agreed with himself that he was great, *see* **Sockpuppets**; for the detective who arrested a suspect on live TV, *see* **Unusual Suspects**; and for the politician who received a really crap book, *see* **You've Got Mail**.

AVENGERS

The Avengers assembled against their biggest enemy: spoilers.

Avengers: Endgame is the last of a 10-year run of films for comic-book franchise Marvel and has become the highest-grossing film of all time. When it was released,

Google searches for 'how to avoid spoilers' reached a record high as fans desperately sought ways to avoid accidentally finding out what happens in the film.

In fact, in recent years Marvel actors themselves have been the main culprits when it comes to spoilers. Tom Holland, who plays Spiderman, has a reputation for repeatedly giving away details of films he's in. He once talked about the plot of a film at a screening, not realising that it hadn't yet been shown to assembled fans. And Mark Ruffalo, who plays the Hulk, once accidentally live-streamed the first 10 minutes of a Marvel film from his seat at the premiere.

The makers of *Avengers: Endgame* tried to ensure details of their film wouldn't emerge too early by giving members of the cast fake scripts that included fake scenes and fake plot twists. They did, however, break cover to pooh-pooh a sizeable online campaign to introduce a plot twist that would have involved one of the heroes, Ant-Man (who can miniaturise himself), making his way into the arch-villain Thanos's bottom, then rapidly expanding back to full size and tearing Thanos apart in the process. Explaining their decision, co-writer Christopher Markus pointed out that 'If Ant-Man expanded, he would be simply crushed against the immovable walls of Thanos's mighty rectum.'

IN WHICH WE LEARN . . .

*How 15 beers saved a life, what came instead
of a size 16 bikini, how 17 geese terrorised
a village, which Jeff Bezos photos are 18+,
where Donald Trump took 20 steps,
and where 21 Savage was really born.*

BABY SHARK

♫ *Clearing parks, do do do do do do*

Officials in the Florida resort of West Palm Beach played the popular song 'Baby Shark' (popular with children, that is; not necessarily with parents) at night, to deter homeless people from sleeping in one of the city's parks. It was played on a loop with another catchy but irritating song, 'Raining Tacos' (written, according to its creator Parry Gripp, for 'children and people who like tacos a lot').

♫ *Restarting hearts, do do do do do do*

The 'Baby Shark' song is being used for more noble reasons in the world of medicine, where it's seen as a perfect thing to hum while you're performing lifesaving chest compressions. The song has a tempo of 115 beats per minute, which is just about the perfect speed to perform CPR. It's an especially useful reference point when teaching first aid to children.

♫ *Eating larks, do do do do do do*

Scientists from Chicago's Field Museum have found that baby tiger sharks living in the Gulf of Mexico sometimes eat small birds that might normally be found in your back garden. When migrating, the songbirds often get exhausted – especially when flying through storms – and when they stop to rest on the ocean surface, they are unable to defend themselves against the sharks.

♫ *Glows in the dark, do do do do do do*

A new species of tiny shark has been discovered that can fire glowing clouds into the water. *Mollisquama mississippiensis* is less than 6 inches in length, and has two tiny pockets at the front of its body that send out plumes of luminous fluid, which confuse potential predators or prey.

BEES, COUNTING

Scientists have discovered that a bee sees its 1, 2, 3s.

It's long been known that bees can distinguish between different amounts and can understand the concept of zero (see *The Book of the Year 2018*). Now they have excelled themselves by showing that they can associate quantities with symbols – that is, they can work out that the symbols '2' and '3' refer to groups of two or three things.

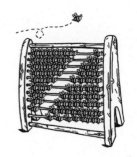

Scientists from RMIT University in Melbourne demonstrated this in June by placing a bee in a maze with just two possible routes, one marked by a picture of two stars and the other by an image of three stars. The insect learned that every time it chose the corridor with two stars it would get a sweet treat, but crucially when the scientists used abstract symbols rather than a specific number of objects, the bees still passed the test. This showed conclusively that bees can join the exclusive list of animals – which includes pigeons, parrots, primates and humans over 12 months of age – that can tell the difference between '2 bees' and 'not 2 bees'.

BEES, SPELLING

America's biggest spelling test was abandoned because the judges ran out of difficult words.

The Scripps National Spelling Bee is one of America's oldest competitions. It has been testing American teenagers on their spelling ability for a full 94 years, which makes it 42 years older than the Super Bowl and 93 years older than the Fortnite World Cup. This year eight competitors battled for several hours, until almost midnight, spelling word after word correctly before organisers decided that enough was enough and allowed them all to share first place.

Never in the competition's history have more than three players shared the prize. The announcer, Jacques Bailly, said, 'We're throwing the dictionary at you, and, so far, you are showing the dictionary who's boss.' The official Merriam-Webster dictionary Twitter account agreed, tweeting, 'The Dictionary concedes and adds that it is SO PROUD.'

See if you can spell as well as a 13-year-old with the fiendishly difficult spelling test below.

Auslaut _____

Palama _____

Cernuous _____

Odylic _____

Erysipelas _____

Aiguillette _____

(Answers on page 358)

BEZOS, JEFF ▶

The head of Amazon sued a man called Pecker for blackmailing him over his pecker.

When Jeff and MacKenzie Bezos divorced this year, she instantly became the world's third-richest woman. She then pledged to give at least half of her money to charity (Jeff has given away less than 2 per cent of his fortune).

When tabloid newspaper the *National Enquirer* got hold of, and then published, intimate text messages sent by Amazon boss Jeff Bezos to a woman who was not his wife, a tangled story began to emerge of sex, lies, compromising photos and general skulduggery. The world's wealthiest man strongly suspected that the reason the *Enquirer* had run the story was because it was owned by media firm AMI, whose political influence and links to Saudi Arabia happened to form part of an investigation by Bezos's paper, the *Washington Post*.

Bezos hired security chief Gavin de Becker to investigate AMI's CEO, David Pecker. He then wrote an explosive blog post alleging that AMI had threatened to publish various intimate pictures they had obtained of him, including a 'scantily-clad body shot' and what they called a 'below the belt selfie – otherwise colloquially know as a "d*ck pic"' unless Bezos issued a public statement saying that AMI's motivation for writing about him wasn't political. (Pecker's lawyer denied the blackmail allegations.)

The *Enquirer* went rather quiet, and a few days later it was reported that AMI was trying to sell off the magazine due to the embarrassment.

BIG BROTHER

Big Billboard is watching you.

The Sunday Times identified more than 50 billboards across the UK that are fitted with cameras and facial-detection software. They can identify the age, gender and mood of passers-by and then show an advert best suited to the individual walking past. The founders of one of the companies that designs technology for these billboards say they were inspired by the dystopian sci-fi film *Minority Report*.

On French streets, Big Brother was listening as well as watching: the powers-that-be in the town of Saint-Etienne installed 50 microphones in public places that would automatically alert police to suspicious sounds, such as shouting or breaking glass. The US, meanwhile, went one better: the Pentagon developed a laser-based system that can identify people from a distance simply by monitoring their heartbeat (astonishingly enough, your heartbeat is as distinctive as your fingerprints).

Even schoolchildren weren't beyond the reach of the surveillance state. This year Guangdong Guangya High School in China announced it was buying bracelets for children that will not only measure their weight, heart rate, sleep schedule and how far they have walked each day, but will also record how often they put up their hands in class.

BIGFOOT

A man who asked the FBI to find out if Bigfoot exists got his answer 42 years later. (It doesn't.)

In the 1970s Peter Byrne, the director of the Bigfoot Information Center and Exhibition in Oregon, provided the FBI with fifteen hairs that he said might have come from a Bigfoot and asked them to run an analysis. Surprisingly, the FBI said it would do so, 'in the interest of research and scientific inquiry'. It duly inspected the hairs under the microscope and came to the conclusion that the samples were not actually from the legendary monster, but belonged to a member of the deer family.

The FBI attempted to tell Mr Byrne the news, but he claims he never received the letter because he was out of the country, in Nepal, searching for the Yeti. So when the relevant papers were declassified this year, it was the first he'd heard of the result – or so he says. Benjamin Radford, deputy editor of *Skeptical Inquirer* magazine is not so sure. 'Obviously I can't speak for Peter Byrne,' Radford told the History Channel, 'but if you're going to make a big enough deal about this unknown specimen to give it to the FBI, then you're not going to want to publicise the fact that it turned out to be deer.' The truth – about the letter *and* the sasquatch – remains out there.

BIKINIS

A woman ordered a size 16 bikini but the shop sent her two size 8s instead.

Twenty-nine-year-old Katrina Harradine ordered the swimwear online, along with other summer clothes, while stocking up for a holiday in St Lucia. When the package arrived, she discovered that rather than sending her one pair of bikini bottoms in the correct size, the retailer Boohoo had dispatched two pairs in half of that size. Katrina assumed it was 'a maths joke'.

Over in China, bikinis fell foul of the fashion police – or, at least, the so-called 'Beijing bikini' did. The term refers to the practice among men of rolling up one's T-shirt in hot weather to uncover a bare stomach. There's even a phrase for the people who do this: *bang ye*, meaning 'exposing grandfathers'. Authorities in Jinan banned the practice, calling it 'uncivilised behaviour' and claiming it was damaging the city's image.

BLACKOUT

12,000 people in Japan were delayed by a single slug.

Twenty-six trains had to be cancelled and others delayed because of a power failure on the island of Kyushu. The culprit was initially thought to be a glitch in the system, but further investigation revealed that it wasn't a bug – it was a slug. They found the gastropod's fried remains in an electrical power device near the track. It had squeezed into a gap and short-circuited the system, annihilating itself in the process.

Slugs weren't the only creatures causing havoc on the grid. In Perth, Australia, sparks literally flew when a pair of horny kookaburras chose to copulate on top

BIRDS, ANGRY

1 Residents on the isle of Jersey faced a feral chicken outbreak. Because there are no natural predators – such as foxes – on the island, pet chickens that had been abandoned were able to breed rapidly, forming gangs of up to 100 birds, which then took to stalking Jersey's mean streets, causing traffic chaos and chasing joggers.

2 The Norfolk village of Costessey was terrorised by a pheasant called Phil, who was so violent defending his territory that villagers had to start carrying vinegar spray and umbrellas for self-defence. The RSPCA advised people to 'stay out of the pheasant's way'. It also said it might have to intervene – but only if anyone threatened the pheasant.

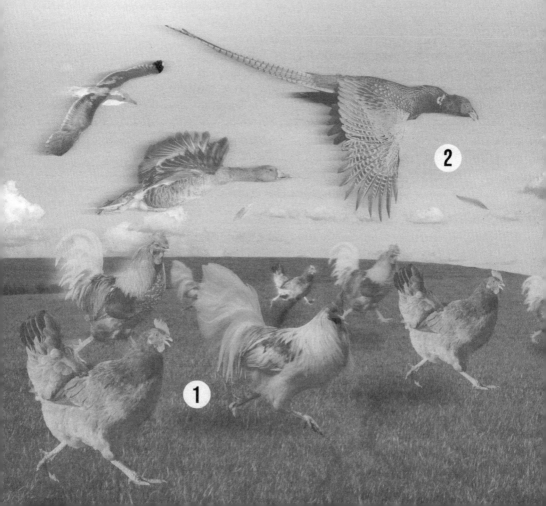

3 An elderly couple from Lancashire were trapped in their house for six days by angry herring gulls that attacked them whenever they tried to leave (they even required hospital treatment at one point for injuries they sustained). Roy and Brenda Pickard's options were limited, as the birds are a protected species. The only way for them to leave their home without being assaulted was by putting up a gazebo to provide them with cover.

4 Three rogue geese terrorised the village of Upavon, in Wiltshire. They formed a breakaway faction from a flock of 17 domestic geese and set up camp in a local square. Residents said they were 'living in fear' as the birds attacked cars, bit locals and chased children off the school bus. The geese had previously been tagged, but unfortunately they were too violent for anyone to get up close and find out what the tags said.

of an electricity pole. They got too close to the power line and, in what one witness reported as 'two big blue flashes', were electrocuted, switching off the lights in 1,000 homes in the process.

South America faced a far more serious blackout on Father's Day when a hydroelectric dam failed, plunging almost the entirety of Argentina and Uruguay, as well as parts of Paraguay, into darkness. It's estimated that 50 million people were left without power. The outage posed a particular challenge in Argentina, where local elections were taking place. Many provinces had to delay their votes, while in other areas people had to resort to candlelight or the torches on their smart-phones to see which box to cross on the ballot paper. Argentina's president, Mauricio Macri, had been contro-versially hiking electricity bills during his tenure to improve the quality of the service, but finally agreed to a price-freeze in April. As if to prove his point, the complete power failure began in an Argentinian power station only a month afterwards. He'll be hoping that this kind of foresight helps to keep him, as well as his country, in power.

BLESS YOU!

The Russian Orthodox Church stopped blessing Weapons of Mass Destruction.

Orthodox priests have been blessing rockets, tanks and intercontinental ballistic missiles for years, as well as assault rifles, fighter jets and nuclear submarines. But this year a Church commission announced that the practice of blessing actual nuclear warheads was inappropriate and should probably stop. Some traditionalists still insisted that the practice was fine.

In other blessing news:

▶ A new Christian prayer book suggested a prayer to use before going online. The prayer asks that 'through our journeys through the Internet we will direct our hands and eyes only to that which is pleasing to God'. There are also now prayers for computer systems, factories, shops, farms, fire engines, vans and warships.

▶ The Vatican launched a new website where you can submit a request online for a blessing. Previously you either had to turn up at the Vatican's Office of Papal Charities or send in your request by letter or fax. Despite the bow to modernity, you still receive a blessing written on parchment.

▶ In Vancouver, the Canadian Memorial United Church organised 'drive-thru' blessings on Ash Wednesday. All you had to do was to pull up outside the church and honk your car horn. A minister would then appear.

▶ And finally, the year's biggest planned mass-blessing was conceived by the Catholic Bishop of Buenaventura, Colombia, who wanted to dump holy water from a helicopter across the city to exorcise its demons and hopefully get the crime rate down. In the event, he couldn't secure a helicopter, so he drove round in a fire truck, drenching people with holy water instead.

BLOWN AWAY

Hurricanes make lizards 10 times clingier.

In 2016, a team of scientists travelled to Dominica to study the grip strength of two types of local lizard. They recently returned there, more than a year after Hurricane Maria had struck the island, to find that the latest generation of these same species of lizard can now grip onto surfaces and perches 10 times more powerfully than their predecessors. In what may be an example of extremely rapid evolution, researchers speculated that the lizards able to hold on tighter were more likely to escape being blown away by the hurricane, and so lived to pass on their clingy genes to the next generation.

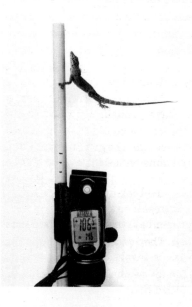

Name:
Jair Messias Bolsonaro

Nickname:
Trump of the Tropics

Representative in the US:
His son, Eduardo

Reason for that:
Because Eduardo is friends with Trump's sons

Reason for being in the news:
Bolsonaro became president of Brazil on New Year's Day, to the sound of his fans chanting, 'WhatsApp! Facebook!', celebrating the false rumours that spread across these platforms, which many believe helped put him in power. He has four sons, three of whom have government roles, and one eight-year-old daughter, who doesn't. He made his son Eduardo ambassador to the US, even though Eduardo has no diplomatic experience, partly on the grounds that 'He's friends with Donald Trump's children.' The minimum age for ambassadors is 35, and the appointment was announced the day after Eduardo's 35th birthday.

Another of Bolsonaro's sons, Carlos, is responsible for managing the president's social media accounts. When, for three days in April, Bolsonaro stayed unusually quiet on Twitter, the Brazilian magazine 'Época' reported it was because he'd had an argument with Carlos. In revenge, they wrote, Carlos had locked him out of his own account and gone on holiday. Both men denied the story.

Since Bolsonaro took office the rate of Amazon deforestation has doubled. The president denied this fact and challenged EU leaders to fly representatives over the Amazon and point out any deforestation to him. They didn't have to. The head of Brazil's space agency, which monitors levels of deforestation by satellite, produced visual evidence to challenge Bolsonaro's denial. Bolsonaro promptly fired him.

BOMBS ▶

The Allies blew up part of a German city, 75 years after the Second World War ended.

Donald Trump asked national security officials if they could deploy nuclear bombs inside hurricanes to destroy them before they hit the United States. Scientists pointed out that the most likely outcome of that plan would be that hurricanes would continue to hit the country, but this time they would be radioactive.

A building boom in Germany has resulted in Second World War bombs being unearthed with surprising regularity. They can usually be moved from populated areas, or safely detonated *in situ*, but the one found in the Bavarian city of Regensburg could not be dealt with in either way, and so everyone within a 1-mile radius was evacuated and a robot brought in to carry out a controlled explosion. The blast shattered nearby windows and could be heard for miles around. Second World War munitions are still a big problem across Western Europe. In May 2019 alone, Allied explosives were found in Cologne, Berlin, Hamburg, Stuttgart, Augsburg, Dortmund, Essen, Münster, Halle, Rheinberg, Bochum, Potsdam, Freiburg im Breisgau, Xanten, Erfurt and Gelsenkirchen.

The Dutch, meanwhile, were warned not to lie on top of bombs after a man in the Netherlands did precisely that. He had found an unexploded Second World War device in his garden, heard it hissing and, in an act of incredible self-sacrificing heroism, decided to try and use his body to cushion any potential explosion. The closest bomb-disposal team was 93 miles away, meaning that he lay in the cold for three hours before they arrived to safely remove the object (but not before giving him a blanket).

And in Hong Kong a grenade was found in a crisp factory in the middle of some potatoes that had been imported from France. Apparently it looked just like a potato. Kudos to the *Telegraph*, which ran with the headline 'Bomb de Terre'.

(NON-) BOMBS

A Kansas man caused a bomb scare with his bum.

The loo-seeker in question was visiting the Home Depot in Wichita, Kansas, when he was suddenly caught short. After declaring that he was going to 'blow up' the bathroom, he then made the mistake of doubling down on his questionable metaphor by yelling to other customers from inside his bathroom stall, 'You all need to get out of here, because I'm fixing to blow it up.' Although the Wichita Home Depot seems an unlikely terrorist target, someone nevertheless called the police.

A rather more calculated false alarm was raised in January by a 23-year-old French student who didn't want his parents to come and visit him at university. The hoax-bomb phone call that he made to the authorities came too late to cause the cancellation of his parents' flight, but it did mean that their plane had to be turned around in mid-air and sent back home; 159 people were delayed for several hours.

In London, officers were called to inspect a suspected unexploded bomb on the banks of the River Thames and found that it was in fact a giant Christmas bauble. Other devices found this year, and which turned out not to be bombs, included a flare found in a canal under the M5, a 'very old piece of corroded metal' found in Norfolk, and a suspected bomb in Finchampstead, which turned out to be a rock.

BOOKS

For how the *Then It Fell Apart* book tour fell apart, *see* **Dick, Moby's**; for how to get high while doing a spell in prison, *see* **Harry Potter and the . . .** ; for being sentenced to write sentences, *see* **Judges**; for ordering 100,000 copies of your own book, *see* **Mayor, Having a**; for the hunch-back's comeback, *see* **Notre-Dame**; and for an unpoopular present, *see* **You've Got Mail**.

BOOS

The English National Opera encouraged audiences to boo their productions.

Booing the bad guys on stage may more usually be associated with pantomimes, but English National Opera decided to condone the practice in the hope that it would endear young people to opera. Mezzo-soprano Patricia Bardon, who fell victim to particularly vicious booing at a show in Glasgow, said that she didn't take it personally. 'If there is a trend,' she explained, 'it just means that maybe the audiences are more relaxed. It's great they feel they can express themselves without any comments or people telling them to shush.'

BOOZE

Doctors in Vietnam saved a man's life by pumping 15 cans of beer into his body.

The man in question was in danger of dying from alcohol poisoning. Overindulgence in dodgy bootleg booze had caused his bloodstream to absorb high levels of methanol, a form of alcohol that the liver turns into potentially fatal formic acid. Since beer contains ethanol, which the liver always processes before methanol, doctors took the decision to pump 15 tins of the stuff into him over the course of a day. That bought them enough time to flush the dangerous alcohol out of his system through dialysis.

In other booze news:

▶ A new kind of alcohol has been invented that makes you feel drunk, but doesn't give you a hangover. The inventor, former chief UK government drugs adviser David Nutt, claims his 'alcosynth' will be commercially available in five years.

▶ The American rock band Guns N' Roses sued a brewery for making a beer called Guns 'n' Rosé. They said it had caused 'irreparable damage' to their brand.

▶ A British man posted his severed toe to a Canadian bar to be used in their famous Sourtoe Cocktail, so that next time he visits the bar he can put his own foot in his mouth. Former Royal Marine Nick Griffiths, who lost three toes to frostbite last year, posted the biggest of them to the Downtown Hotel in Dawson City, which has been serving cocktails containing severed human toes since 1973.

▶ A Pennsylvania police department was overwhelmed with offers of help after they asked for volunteers who would be 'willing to drink hard liquor to the point of inebriation'. The aim was to get locals drunk so that officers could practise conducting sobriety tests. They eventually had to post another message saying: 'THANK YOU FOR ALL YOUR INTEREST IN HELPING US OUT! WE HAVE HAD AN OVER-WHELMING RESPONSE FOR THIS AND AT THIS POINT WE HAVE ENOUGH VOLUNTEERS FOR THIS TRAINING!'

BOSSES ▶

The founder of Alibaba said employees should have sex 858 times every one thousand and one nights.

Jack Ma, who set up the online shopping behemoth and is now China's richest person, said that to achieve a good work–life balance, his staff should be having sex six times a week. Which, in Arabian Nights terms, works out to just 143 celibate sleeps per 1,001 nights. Ma clearly believes in burning the candle at both ends, since he also advocated employees working 12-hour days for six days a week.*

Ma doesn't envisage this being necessary for ever. Later in the year, he said that if artificial intelligence makes the world much more efficient, in the future we might only have to work 12 hours a week.

British businesses took a contrasting approach. Lingerie retailer Lara Intimates was one of many companies to switch this year to a four-day working week. Meanwhile the Labour Party commissioned a report into the social and economic impact of taking Fridays off work, while the Scottish Parliament debated the suggestion, both in response to the report that people in the UK work longer hours than other Europeans, but are among the least productive.

Notoriously overworked NHS employees were given some respite when bosses in certain trusts offered staff free Pilates, massage, Zumba and comedy sketch classes. It was an attempt to improve workplace well-being, in light of the revelation that more than half of all NHS employees said they were thinking about quitting their job.

One employee who could have done with some stress relief was the Australian worker who claimed that his manager had continually farted on him. David Hingst said his boss at the engineering firm where he worked had caused him severe stress by opening sesame directly onto him, in a windowless room, five or six times a day. The courts concluded it wasn't a deliberate attempt to harass Hingst.

BOYS ▶

For schoolboys, *see* **Judges**; for Egg Boy, *see* **Milkshaking**; for bellboys, *see* **On the Blink**; for teenage boys, *see* **Scientists Have Discovered**; for Heckboy, *see* **Signs**; and for Vengaboys, *see* **Vengaboys**.

BRAS ▶

Scientists used bras to give turtles a boost.

This very particular kind of support was offered in North Carolina, where an animal rescue group asked people to send in their old bras to help fix turtles' shells. The process involved gluing bra clasps to broken shells so that they act like hooks, and then weaving string or thread around them to pull the shell back together. The solution has the added advantage that the shells cannot be undone by most men.

Bras were less welcome in Kansas City, where it emerged that their underwires had been setting off prison metal detectors. Female attorneys were told that in future they would either have to remove their bras altogether before meeting their clients or submit them for scanning. The attorneys argued this was discriminatory, and protested on the steps of the county courthouse, yelling, 'We need support.'

For ▮▮▮▮, see **Apposite**; for ▮▮▮▮, see **Conservative Leadership Contest**; for ▮▮▮▮▮, see **Johnson, Boris**; for ▮▮▮▮, see **Milkshaking**; for ▮▮▮▮, see **Olives**; for ▮▮▮▮, see **Our Survey Said**; for ▮▮▮▮, see **Queen, The**; for ▮▮▮▮, see **Sausages**; for ▮▮▮▮, see **Stockpiling**; for ▮▮▮▮, see **Von Der Leyen, Ursula**; and for ▮▮▮▮, see **X-Word**.

BRITS ABROAD

American parents worried that Peppa Pig was turning their children British.

It was dubbed 'The Peppa Effect'. Parents took to social media to complain that not only were their children speaking with an English accent, but they were also using British words such as 'petrol' and 'lorry' instead of 'gas' and 'truck'. Perhaps a little more worryingly, they were punctuating their sentences with oinks.

Parents shouldn't worry, though. Linguists have pointed out that there's a difference between saying a few words in a different dialect or accent and actually acquiring that accent. The effect is likely to wear off, they say, when the children go to school and start interacting with other kids.

Peppa wasn't the only Brit to influence American culture this year. Rapper 21 Savage, the Grammy-nominated MC whose most popular video this year has had more than 150 million views on YouTube (which is *A Lot*), may be famous for evoking his childhood on the tough streets of Atlanta in his lyrics, but, it turns out, he was actually born in London and is British. This came to light when he criticised the US immigration service on national television while trying to sort out a visa that had expired when he was 13. He was arrested two days later while out driving with his cousin, a fellow rapper called Young Nudy. As a result of his experience with immigration control, Mr Savage later donated $25,000 to a charity for migrants.

BROMANCE

Donald Trump took 20 small steps for a man and un-giant leap for mankind.

When he met Kim Jong-un in June, Trump walked 20 steps into North Korea and 20 steps back, making him the first sitting president to (technically) visit the hermit kingdom. He claimed it had all been very spur-of-the-moment – the spontaneous result of Kim's positive response to a tweet Trump had sent just a few days earlier: 'If Chairman Kim of North Korea sees this, I would meet him at the Border/DMZ just to shake his hand and say Hello(?)!' North Korean expert Andrei Lankov of Kookmin University was not so sure. It was 'inconceivable', he argued, 'that the leaders of two powerful nations had arranged a meeting at such short notice'; their get-together must, he went on, have been prearranged. If Trump's version of events is true, it's probably as well that Kim hadn't seen an earlier Trump tweet from 2014 in which he said: 'Crazy Dennis Rodman is saying I wanted to go to North Korea with

Trump's bromance with President Macron of France fell apart this year: the tree they planted together in 2018 in the White House garden died, and during the D-Day commemorations their representatives spent two days arguing over the height of the lectern they would speak at, because one that fitted the 6' 3" Trump would make Macron look tiny.

BUCKET LIST

BY ANDREW HUNTER MURRAY

Many people have a 'bucket list' –
a list of amazing experiences to
have before they die. Thinking of
once-in-a-lifetime adventures can
be intimidating, but as the
official Book of the Year killjoy,
I'm here to say: don't worry about
it. If you don't have a gruelling adventure tick-list, you are missing
nothing but a lot of queuing and faff and hassle. You should just stay at
home with a cup of tea and a nice sausage (for more of my views on
this, see **Sausages**). It's far more important to have a list of tiresome
experiences to avoid. So here is the official Book of the Year List of
Things You Absolutely Shouldn't Do Before You Die:

DON'T go on the trip of a lifetime. Your big idea has almost certainly
been done. For example: this year an Iranian athlete set off on a round-
the-world journey on the back of a camel. A Royal Marine who lost a leg
beat the world record for rowing the Atlantic, 36 days faster than any
able-bodied person has managed it. And for the first time a blind sailor
traversed the Pacific (Mitsuhiro Iwamoto had a sighted navigator
offering guidance, but did all the sailing himself). These heroes have
had all the adventures already – and, frankly, they sound exhausting
anyway. Even if you do try to copy them, you'll probably come a
cropper. Best left alone.

DON'T see the Wonders of the World. These sites have seen a massive
spike in tourist numbers in recent years, thanks to rising incomes in
countries like China and falling air-travel costs. The Netherlands is so
sick of it all that the Dutch tourist board officially changed its mission
statement from 'destination promotion' to 'destination management' –

it won't be advertising for new visitors. In the same vein, the Czech tourist board is actively trying to funnel people away from Prague.

Over-tourism is a planetary plague. Mount Everest suffered huge queues of climbers trying to get to the summit. Scientists complained that people were endangering the statues on Easter Island by taking selfies of themselves picking the giant heads' noses. And when a climbing ban was introduced at Uluru in Australia, because the rock is so sacred to Australian Aborigines, hundreds of people raced to clamber all over it before the deadline, despite knowing it's extremely offensive. My advice: STAY HOME. Nobody will be offended, less queueing, and you don't have to stick your hand up a giant rock's nose. Job done.

DON'T live in your dream home. This can lead to disaster – as it did for the couple who had to flee the death penalty after they tried to live in a 'seahome' off the coast of Thailand. Chad Elwartowski and Supranee Thepdet had set up home in an octagonal platform on top of a pillar about 12 nautical miles offshore. They hoped to develop an alternative community there, with an underwater resort and restaurants. Unfortunately it was deemed a violation of Thai sovereignty and they had to go on the run. Even if the worst that happens to you is an embarrassing Grand Designs overspend, it's not worth the kerfuffle.

DON'T go to space. The British public actually agrees on this. When asked if they would want to go to the Moon (if guaranteed a safe return), 43 per cent said they would, but 48 per cent said they wouldn't. Of the people who said they couldn't be bothered, 23 per cent said they were 'just not interested'. Another 11 per cent worried there wouldn't be anything to do when they got there, which is fair enough. Once you've tried jumping around in slow-motion, you can basically pack up and get back in the spacecraft.

If you haven't done any of these things, great news: you've already completed your To Don't List. Congratulations!

him. Never discussed, no interest, last place on Earth I want to go to.'

The venue for the meeting was the Freedom House, also known as the Inter-Korean House of Freedom, which stands in the Demilitarised Zone (DMZ) between North and South Korea. The press wanted full access to the historic 53-minute meeting between two of the world's most high-profile leaders. Kim's bodyguards, however, had other ideas, and the result was a shoving match between the Korean guard, the US Secret Service, the press and White House press secretary Stephanie Grisham, who sustained bruises during the fracas. Tensions ran high throughout the meeting, and beyond. The very day after Trump met Kim, South Korean fighter jets were scrambled to the DMZ for what turned out to be a flock of birds that had shown up on their radars.

BUCKETS ▶

For a bucket of Becquerels, *see* **Radioactive**; and for a bucket of bananas, *see* **Robots**.

IN WHICH WE LEARN . . .

Why Britain got a bee in its bonnet,
which Aussies wore the wrong thongs,
how you can get Japan in a can, and
who got into trouble for Grylling a frog.

CANADIANS

For the man who donated his toe to a cocktail bar, *see* **Booze**; for the man who cracked a joke about cracking a safe, *see* **Crackers**; for the rapper who was ruining everyone's chances of winning, *see* **Drake Curse**; for the hotelier whose inn was caught out, *see* **Smuggling**; and for the driver who was given a ticket for not taking care of his other ticket, *see* **Unusual Suspects**.

CAPITAL PUNISHMENT

The British government issued a death sentence to a single bee.

According to scientists from São Paulo and Sussex, some stingless queen bees face death by execution if they mate with more than one male. Mating with two males makes a queen more prone to give birth to sterile males. Since these offspring are useless to the colony, the workers respond by executing the queen.

The insect in question had apparently hitched a ride in the luggage of a family returning from a holiday in Turkey. It then took up residence for a while in their conservatory, where it made houses out of rose petals. The fear was that it might be an *Osmia avosetta* – a species of mason bee that, according to the British Beekeepers Association, could have a 'devastating effect' on British bees by spreading disease or giving birth to offspring that might outcompete them. The UK's National Bee Unit announced that it would hunt the insect down and murder it in (literal) cold blood.

The decision did not go down well in Turkey: 'Don't kill the "Turkish bee",' ran a headline in *Hürriyet*, a popular Istanbul newspaper. But as luck would have it, before the British bee-killers could get to their prey, the immigrant insect managed to escape and the country was put on red alert to report any unusual bees to their local beekeeping association.

A few days later David Notton, chief bee curator at the Natural History Museum, announced that the bee was probably not Turkish after all. He had been studying the nests built in the conservatory and had come to the conclusion that they were simply much too messy to belong to *Osmia avosetta*. His view was that the fugitive insect was a patchwork leaf-cutter bee, *Megachile centuncularis*, which is native to Britain.

CARDI B

For a potty mouth, *see* **Festivals**; for a Petty mistake, *see* **Oops**; and for a panty malfunction, *see* **Show Must Go On, The**.

CELEBRITY TITTLE-TATTLE

Led Zeppelin guitarist Jimmy Page told his neighbours to turn the music down.

Page has been locked in a long-running property dispute with his next-door neighbour, who happens to be pop star Robbie Williams, about whether Williams' planned basement swimming pool in his west London mansion will damage Page's mansion. But that's not the only thing he's unhappy about. In a letter to the local council, Page complained that Williams was 'blasting Black Sabbath music' very loud, along with Deep Purple and Pink Floyd, even though he was fully aware of how much the noise upset Page. The letter also alleged that Williams had been dressing up in a long wig and fake beer-belly, in imitation of Page's Led Zeppelin bandmate Robert Plant. Williams' representatives denied the whole thing.

In other celebrity news . . . Mel B announced she was launching a range of sex toys, which would be 'upmarket', but would also feature 'a splash of leopard print'; Ariana Grande cancelled a gig due to a sudden allergic reaction to tomatoes; Iran deported Joss Stone, as it was concerned that she might start singing; Franz Ferdinand's drummer dropped out of their tour after a piece of art fell off a hotel wall and landed on his finger; Justin Bieber (25) challenged Tom Cruise (56) to a cage fight, then chickened out, claiming that Cruise would 'whoop his ass'; Nicholas Cage got married in Vegas; Nicholas Cage got divorced four days later; Tom Hanks was refused booze at a music festival because he didn't have ID; Russell Brand revealed that his second date with his wife was a trip to a marriage counsellor; Gwyneth Paltrow was sued for $3 million over a claim that she had injured someone in a hit-and-run skiing accident; actor Luke Perry was buried in a suit made of mushrooms, to help him decompose; Alex James of Blur had his bacteria turned into a block of Cheshire cheese (he is joined by Heston Blumenthal, who is a block of comté; Professor Green, who appears in the form of mozzarella; and Madness singer Suggs, who is a block of cheddar); Bear Grylls faced a fine of 5,000 lev (£2,500) for killing and eating a frog in Bulgaria; and Chelsea foot-baller Danny Drinkwater, who should have Drunkwater, was found guilty of Drinkdriving.

CHANGE UK ▶

See **Change UK – The Independent Group**.

CHANGE UK – THE INDEPENDENT GROUP ▶

See **Continuity Change UK**.

CHRYSANTHEMUM THRONE ▶

A Japanese company celebrated the new era of 'Beautiful Harmony' by selling commemorative toilet paper.

Never mind the Iron Throne. This year there was a changeover on one of the most important real-life thrones on the planet – Japan's Chrysanthemum Throne (for practical reasons, unlike the one in *Game of Thrones*, it's not actually made of the thing it's named after). After ruling for 30 years, Emperor Akihito abdicated, and his son Naruhito took over.

Naruhito's accession marked the beginning of a new official era in Japan, which therefore needed a new official name. The cabinet (which had been rehearsing the process annually for the past 30 years) therefore met in absolute secrecy, even having to hand over phones and smart watches before entering the room where the decision was to be made. The name they finally announced was Reiwa (令和), which roughly translates into English as 'beautiful harmony' and which was inspired by an eighth-century poem. Some Western commentators pointed out that 'Rei' means 'order' or 'command', as well as 'beautiful' or 'good', giving 'Reiwa' a somewhat authoritarian feel.

Soon the new word was everywhere: 70 sumo wrestlers were photographed spelling out the two characters with their bodies; a flock of sheep performed a ritual that spelled out the letters every day for an entire month; and a sea lion in a Japanese aquarium managed to learn how to write the era's name with a paintbrush within 20 minutes of the announcement being made.

The new era didn't just usher in a new name; it also meant that the entire calendar had to be reset to Year

One. Japan's Ministry of Economy, Trade and Industry advised companies who couldn't get their paperwork done in time to correct documents with rubber stamps. Unfortunately, firms making rubber stamps ran out of supplies within a few days because so many people were ordering them. Meanwhile, there was certainly no shortage of more gimmicky items available to commemorate the occasion, as wily marketing companies spotted their opportunity. Despite the intense secrecy behind the name's selection, it took just three minutes for one sake-firm in Hiroshima to sell cups inscribed with 'Reiwa'. Other commemorative products on offer included crisps sprinkled with powdered gold leaf; a £700 wagyu beefburger big enough for eight people; and toilet paper embossed with the new era name. Some entrepreneurs even took to selling 'the air of an outgoing era' – literally cans of the atmosphere from the time before Emperor Akihito abdicated. They cost nearly £7.50 each.

CIVILISATION, COLLAPSE OF

After centuries of doomsday predictions, the end might now actually be nigh.

At the UN Climate Action Summit of 2019, delegates were told that global emissions are at record levels and show no sign of tapering off; that the last four years were the hottest on record; that temperatures in the Arctic are up 3°C since 1990; that sea levels are rising, coral reefs are dying and human health is already being seriously affected. And as if that's not bad enough, scientists discovered that human-caused climate change has also resulted in the following:

Octopuses are going blind; reindeer are starving; the Acropolis is being eroded; trees are growing faster and dying younger; walruses are falling off cliffs; the oceans are changing colour; spring is starting sooner in the UK; more baby sea turtles are being born female; flesh-eating bacteria are becoming more common; dengue fever has come to Europe; wine will contain more pesticides; wasps are getting smaller, but super-nests of wasps are becoming more numerous; one-fifth of life in the sea will die; the Matterhorn is cracking; children now have lower IQs; humans are developing more heart defects; some types of cloud are disappearing; air turbulence will get three times worse; vegan ice cream is running out; great tits are eating other birds' brains; and . . . according to an Australian think tank called Breakthrough, there will be an entire collapse of human civilisation before 2050.

The first Icelandic glacier to be killed by climate change got a plaque to warn future generations. Okjökull (or just 'Ok', for short) lost its glacier status in 2014 and was adorned with the message: 'This monument is to acknowledge that we know what is happening and what needs to be done. Only you know if we did it.'

CLAMPING DOWN ▶

TfL unwittingly banned its own advert.

In a bid to encourage healthy eating, London's transport authority introduced new rules to govern what food can be advertised on public transport. Unfortunately, among the first campaigns to fall foul of the regulations was a Wimbledon poster commissioned by Transport for London itself, which featured a drawing of strawberries and cream. A suggestion by one employee that perhaps they could just edit out the cream was rejected, and so the quintessential Wimbledon treat was deemed 'junk food' and the ad was duly banned. But when it emerged that, under the new healthy-eating regulations, posters featuring KFC would be permitted, but ads for Farmdrop, an organic produce delivery company, would not, it became apparent that the guidelines weren't working as well as they might. They were rewritten.

In other banning news:

▶ A Muslim cleric issued a fatwa against *Who Wants to Be a Millionaire?* in Iran, and the Iranian government banned the show, on the grounds that it endangers the country's culture of hard work and productivity.

▶ The mayor of the Italian town of Sesto Fiorentino banned all broad-bean growing within a 300-metre radius of the house of a child who is allergic to them.

▶ San Francisco banned e-cigarettes, while permitting traditional cigarettes – which are 95 per cent more harmful – and cannabis to remain on sale.

▶ Sumo wrestlers in Japan were banned from growing beards, on the grounds that they're 'indecent'. Officials say the sumo ring is sacred and that facial hair is so unsightly it will ruin the atmosphere.

- Gender stereotypes were banned from UK adverts, which will now no longer be allowed to show, for instance, a woman failing to park a car or a man failing to change a nappy.

- Bruno Mars's songs 'Versace on the Floor' and 'That's What I Like' were deemed too sexual for the 48 million residents of Java, Indonesia, and so were banned from local airwaves between 3 a.m. and 10 p.m. No word on whether his collaboration with Ed Sheeran and Chris Stapleton, 'BLOW' (which opens with the lyric 'I'm comin', baby'), has made the list.

- And Australian prime minister Scott Morrison banned people from wearing thongs (the sandals, not the underwear) or beach shorts at citizenship ceremonies, deeming them inappropriate. He added that new citizens were welcome to don them 'for the barbecue afterwards'. A local mayor, Shane Van Styn, called the ban 'un-Australian' and told Morrison to 'bugger off'.

CLUBMOSS

Conservationists saved 3,000 highly endangered plants by running over them in a tractor.

Clubmoss is not actually a moss and it is almost never discussed in nightclubs. Green in colour and growing to only 3 inches in height, it belongs to one of the most ancient groups of land plants on the planet. It's also very rare. In the UK its habitat has shrunk to a few sites in Dorset and Hampshire and its numbers have fallen by 85 per cent in the last 85 years.

The plants grow best on disturbed, wet ground – the sort of terrain created by grazing animals or tracks. So the conservation charity Plantlife decided the best way to encourage them to grow was to drive up and down on

——— ▼ ———

A new study has found that clubmoss pollen has sponge-like qualities that allow it to remove pollutants from water and so could be used to clean the pharmaceutical-filled wastewater generated by hospitals.

The Belgian village of Adinkerke hosted the inaugural European Gull Screeching Championship, which unsurprisingly required competitors to screech like a gull. The competition is an attempt to redeem the reputation of the birds, which have been stealing food, pooing on things and tearing open bin bags. Some competitors even wore seagull costumes and flapped their wings while cawing. The winners were Reggy Laatsch and Bregje Iding.

The inaugural Male Slapping Championship, also known as the Siberian Power Show, was held in Krasnoyarsk in Siberia. The rules of the competition were refreshingly simple: two men took turns slapping each other until one of them gave up or passed out. A prize of 30,000 roubles (about £350) went to Vasily Kamotsky, a 28-year-old, 26-stone farmer nicknamed 'the Dumpling'.

The Finnish town of Joensuu held the world's first Heavy Metal Knitting Championship, which is exactly as you'd expect it to be. The application process required bands to submit a one-minute video of themselves knitting along to the song 'Fight or Die' by the band Maniac Abductor. The winners were 'Giga Body Metal' from Japan, who included two sumo wrestlers among their band members. They beat off the likes of Bulgakov Satan, Bunny Bandit and 9" Needles.

The winner of the Asturias international women's squash tournament made an official complaint when she was given a vibrator as a prize. Those in second and third places got an electronic foot-file and some hair-removal wax.

them in a 5-ton tractor, at a secret location near Bournemouth. This was done, and soon the 3,000 incredibly rare plants that had been crushed by the tractor had blossomed to 12,000. The managers of the project announced that their plan is to 'strategically mess up' more heaths to restore them to their former glory.

CONFINEMENT, SOLITARY ▶

A man called Rich got rich by shutting himself in the bathroom.

US poker player Rich Alati accepted a $100,000 bet that he couldn't stay put, shut alone in a soundproofed bathroom, in pitch darkness, for 30 days. Meals arrived at irregular times so he couldn't keep track of time. He was not allowed a TV, radio or phone, although he was allowed a yoga mat and massage ball, plus some lavender essential oils and a sugar-and-salt scrub. Rory Young, the fellow poker player who'd challenged him to the bet, was able to watch Rich's progress via a video feed linked to the bathroom. He found that it soon 'became a bit boring', and then panicked when Rich seemed to be finding the challenge surprisingly easy. Young pleaded with him, over a loudspeaker, to come out early for less money. Rich agreed to negotiate, and eventually accepted $62,400 for a 20-day stay.

CONSERVATION ▶

For shell-f assembly, *see* **Bras**; for an in-tractor-ble problem, *see* **Clubmoss**; for coral reef-fitting, *see* **Glue**; and for sex-ophones, *see* **Sax Appeal**.

CONSPIRACY THEORIES ▶

A school was forced to close its doors because it was paranoid it would be infiltrated by conspiracy theorists.

The Twitter meme '5 Jobs I've Had' was just meant to be a bit of fun. People shared selected highlights of their employment history, and this sometimes gave an interesting insight into the tweeter's background. However, when former FBI director James Comey took part, he triggered a conspiracy theory that resulted in a high-school fundraiser being cancelled.

Even for a conspiracy theory, it was a bit far-fetched. Someone who was clearly more interested in acronyms than common sense looked at 'Jobs **I've Had**' and came up with the word 'jihad'. They then took the initial letters from Comey's employment record: **G**rocery clerk, **V**ocalist, **C**hemist, **S**choolteacher & **F**BI Agent and searched for somewhere those initials might apply. That somewhere turned out to be the Grass Valley Charter School Foundation (GVCSF), and so, convinced that Comey must be issuing a coded warning, they raised the alarm.

Even though the authorities said there was 'zero foundation' to the threat, the school's fundraiser had to be cancelled, not least because there was a concern that hundreds of believers of the conspiracy theory might turn up and try to guard the place.

▼

Nevada's Area 51 has long been a favourite of conspiracy theorists, with many believing that the US government is hiding evidence of alien life there. So when Californian Matty Roberts set up a joke Facebook event entitled 'Storm Area 51, They Can't Stop All of Us', millions of people signed up. Some counties in the region, worried that they wouldn't be able to cope with the huge crowds they expected to congregate, duly declared a state of emergency.

1 MICHAEL GOVE

Before being voted out, Michael Gove, the former Lord Chancellor and Secretary of State for Justice, helped a drug user stay out of prison by confessing that he had taken cocaine 20 years ago, when he worked as a journalist. The presiding judge in the case said the offender should 'suffer no more for dabbling in cocaine than should a former Lord Chancellor'. So at least Gove did some good.

2 JEREMY HUNT

After one leadership debate, Hunt tweeted: 'Every older person should die with dignity and respect. We should be the party who sorts it out.' This sounded alarmingly like a message in support of euthanasia, but it didn't stop Hunt making the final two in the contest. Nor did the fact that he said he'd never broken the law – only to admit five hours later that he'd actually broken his own government's anti-money-laundering laws in 2018. Psychologists say broadcasters often call him 'Jeremy C***' because he's associated with other 'C-' words: he's a Conservative and was Culture Secretary. Not that Hunt himself helped matters. He joked that his campaign slogan was nearly 'Hunty McHuntface'.

3 SAJID JAVID

Javid compared himself to Homer Simpson and claimed he loved Nando's. He tried to push his working-class background by releasing a video in which he claimed to have grown up on 'the most dangerous street in Britain', and said that he had been 'told I couldn't do maths at school because boys like me didn't do maths'. Despite that, he limped home from the campaign in fourth place, before coming back as the head mathematician of the country: the new Chancellor of the Exchequer.

4 BORIS JOHNSON [NOT PICTURED]

see Johnson, Boris

5 DOMINIC RAAB

Raab has a black belt in karate and his office walls boast two posters, one of Muhammad Ali and another of Mother Teresa. Last year, the *Daily Mirror* revealed that he has the same chicken Caesar sandwich for his lunch every single day (an allegation he denied, though he did say he was scared of eating meatball sandwiches in case the sauce dripped on his tie). After the leadership contest he was given the role of Foreign Secretary, but it's uncertain how much respect he'll get in the international community. European sources claimed that Raab was so bad at negotiating, when he was ▓▓▓▓ Secretary, that he was nicknamed 'The Turnip' in Brussels. This was (also) a pun on the Dutch for turnip, which is *raap*.

6 RORY STEWART

Rory Stewart, whose name is technically 'Roderick' because the vicar at his christening flatly refused to call a child 'Rory', was the unexpected star of the campaign. A former diplomat, he briefly tutored Princes William and Harry; once spent a month walking across Afghanistan; and his life story was nearly turned into a film starring Brad Pitt (the film-makers presumably realised that becoming a Tory MP was not a feel-good ending). He felt compelled to deny the rumour that he had been an MI6 agent, but also pointed out that's just what he would say if he *had* been an MI6 agent. He also kick-started a drugs debate by announcing that he'd smoked opium at an Iranian wedding – although he said he'd only done so out of politeness.

CONTINUITY CHANGE UK

See **The Independent Group for Change.**

COUNTRIES VS COMPANIES

For the retailer taking on the rainforest, *see* **Amazon vs Amazon**; and for the retailer taking on Reykjavik, *see* **Iceland vs Iceland.**

CRACKERS

A combination safe that had stumped experts for 40 years was opened by a passing tourist on his first attempt.

The safe in question can be found at the Vermilion Heritage Museum in Alberta, Canada, and it was certainly good at its job. In the decades since the safe was closed, and the combination lost, the owners had tried everything to open it – blacksmiths, calling the manufacturer, brute force . . . you name it.

Then Stephen Mills visited the museum. He had no experience in safe-cracking, and no technique in mind. He simply turned the dial round a couple of times and, to his own and everyone else's astonishment, the door creaked open. 'I did a particular combination, which is three on the right, two on the left, and one on the right, tried the handle . . . and it opened!' said Mr Mills. 'It was a 100 per cent guess. I was fully amazed. I stepped back a little bit and thought, "I'm buying a lottery ticket tonight!"'

The chance of him guessing the correct sequence was something like 200,000/1, and so, of course, this astonishing feat made international news. The rest of the story was not quite so mind-blowing, though. According to CNN, 'The contents of the safe proved a little disappointing.'

It's hard to disagree. The safe turned out to house part of a restaurant order pad, a packet of cigarettes and a receipt for a mushroom burger.

IN WHICH WE LEARN . . .

How the Duke of Edinburgh encountered a pair of Queens, how the ISS bust its flush, how card dealers deal with drug dealers, who ducked the Drake curse, and who dicked the Donald.

DICK, MOBY

We don't know where Moby-Dick has been . . .

One of the whales that inspired *Moby-Dick* has gone
(partially) missing. Burton Constable Hall in East Yorkshire has had a sperm whale's skeleton on display since
the 1830s. Herman Melville heard about it, visited and
wrote about it in his novel. However, over the following
century or so many of the whale's bones disappeared,
including 11 vertebrae and most of the left flipper (the
fact that the skeleton sat in an open field and was used as
a child's playground for a number of years didn't help).
So, in an attempt to get the 58-foot whale back together,
the museum announced that anyone who happens to
have a bit of the skeleton in their possession can bring
it back without fear of punishment. 'It might have been
natural for people to take a bone home for "safe-keeping",'
the museum's curator announced diplomatically, adding
that the museum would still like them returned.

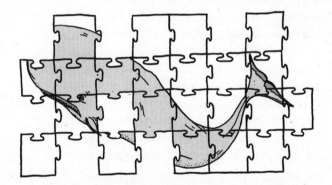

And in another act of whale restitution, a 77-year-old
Italian artist called Vittorio Fabris finally completed
a year-long mission to sail across the Atlantic, which
he saw as an act of apology to whales for the damage
humankind has done them. He first set off in 2018, but
that attempt ended in failure: having left Venice for

Nantucket on an old whaler's route, his boat struck mysterious objects, his steering system fell apart and he ran into the hurricane season. This year's effort was ultimately more successful, although it, too, involved its fair share of setbacks. Fabris's boat was again buffeted by terrible storms, and then – 1,500 feet short of Nantucket harbour – hit something underwater and capsized. It had to be tugged to a nearby harbour, 30 miles in the wrong direction, and Fabris ran up a bill of $7,000 in the process. Stranded in a nearby town, and not speaking English, it took a kindly soul and Kickstarter campaign to help him pay off his debts and go home.

DICK, MOBY'S ▶

. . . But we do know where Moby's dick has been.

Moby is related to *Moby-Dick*'s author Herman Melville. He has admitted, however, that he has never actually managed to finish the book.

The musician Moby offered us two seminal releases this year. The first was an album, *Long Ambients 2*, which was released exclusively on an app called 'Calm'. The album consists of six tracks, each around 37 minutes long, and is designed specifically to help you get a perfect night's sleep. The second release was his autobiography *Then It Fell Apart*, which contains disputed claims about Moby's alleged relationship with the actress Natalie Portman. In the controversy that ensued, his planned UK book tour fell apart. But not before many had already read a passage from the book that might give us nightmares for the rest of our lives.

Moby related the relevant anecdote on the talk show *Real Time with Bill Maher*:

'There was one night, it was about 2001, and I was out at a party and I was very drunk. [. . .] I was with some friends and they were telling me about this game they used to play in college called Knob Touch. [. . .] Knob

Touch is where you take your flaccid penis out of your pants [. . .] and you walk around a room and you brush your flaccid penis up against people indiscriminately – it's not sexual [. . .] And my girlfriend at the time dared me to Knob Touch Donald Trump.'

One can only hope he washed it thoroughly afterwards.

DICKRUN CLAIRES

Two Claires fought over who invented the 'dickrun'.

At the start of the year, *Vice* magazine ran a profile of Claire Pisano, whose hobby is to run routes in the shape of penises, record them on her route-tracker and post the finished creations on Instagram under the name @dick_run_claire.

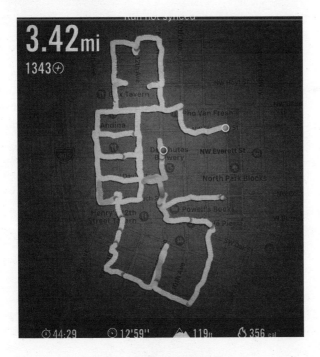

DICTIONARY

AMLOVER (n.) a supporter of new Mexican leader Andrés Manuel López Obrador, who himself goes by the nickname 'AMLO' *see* **Obrador, López**

CRAPSULE (n.) human excrement that has been turned into a pill for the purpose of faecal transplants, *see* **Poo**

FAUXRARRI (n.) a fake Ferrari. Authorities in Brazil attempted to shut down a factory where a father-and-son team was discovered to be making fake Ferraris (nicknamed Fauxrarris) and Lamborghinis (Shamborghinis), then selling them on social media for under £60,000 each – far, far less than the genuine items would cost you. Despite the bust, the company continues to operate, arguing that because the vehicles do not '100 per cent' match industrial designs, they are not illegal copies.

IGELSEX (n.) this word trended in Germany in the summer. It literally translates as 'Hedgehog Sex' and hit the news thanks to a number of people who called the emergency services to investigate noises that sounded like animals in distress but were actually horny hogs.

KIMONO (n.) ~~a long loose robe traditionally worn in Japan~~ a new line of undergarments released by Kim Kardashian. When the brand was announced, many accused her of cultural appropriation. The anger intensified when it was later learned that she had attempted to trademark the word 'Kimono', too. Kardashian has since said she will rename the brand. She then moved on to announce her new cosmetics line, which includes products called 'Kilauea' and 'Pele's Curse' – two terms considered by Hawaiians to be sacred.

MARROT (n.) a meaty carrot, *see* **Vegans**

PLOONET (n.) an orphaned moon that has escaped the orbit of its planetary parent, making it neither a planet nor a moon. The newly coined word, proposed in a scientific paper currently under peer review, follows in the wake of 'moonmoon' (suggested by another group of scientists, but not yet accepted by the research community) – which is a moon that orbits another moon.

RICKYLEAKS (n.) the intentional disclosure of secret messages slagging off pop star Ricky Martin. Protests erupted in Puerto Rico when messages between senior politicians were leaked that showed them to be misogynistic, homophobic and insulting towards those who died in last year's hurricane. One set of texts in particular focused directly on insulting Ricky Martin, which led to a secondary protest that used the hashtag #RickyLeaks.

TWIZPIPE (v., vulgar slang) a fictional curse word, made up for an experiment that sought to establish whether using fake swear words increases pain tolerance as much as real ones. Another word invented for the experiment was 'fouch'. Volunteers were invited to test the new words, along with traditional swear words, while their hands were submerged in an iced water bath. The results showed that the new words didn't work as well as the good old-fashioned ones.

It turns out she's not the only Claire who dickruns. Pisano says she fell into it by accident when she got lost in 2015 and inadvertently traced out a penis on her run-tracker app. But Claire Wyckoff (Instagram profile: @og_dick_run_claire) says *she* came up with it in 2014 when she began 'pioneering it as an art form', and claims Pisano follows her feed and steals her runs. The two of them also post remarkably similar vagina-shaped routes on their feeds.

The last we heard, Wyckoff had challenged Pisano to 'a dick run-off – a dickathlon'.

DINING, FINE

Preston's best restaurant is officially Nando's.

For an awards ceremony designed to celebrate local businesses, the people of Preston were asked to vote on the city's best establishments; 200 were nominated, but after the 68,000 votes had been counted, it was a local branch of the Nando's chicken chain that came out on top as the city's best restaurant. Mark O'Rourke, whose restaurant 'We Don't Give A Fork' was runner-up, said, 'It just makes Preston look bad. Not that it doesn't anyway. It's not a crown jewel of the north-west.'

At the same event, the Best Customer Service prize went to Greggs, while Pub of the Year was awarded to a local branch of Wetherspoon's.

Fine dining took a hit in America, too, when, owing to problems with its suppliers, Mexican chain Taco Bell ran out of tortillas. With about half its menu unavailable to customers, the chain encouraged patrons to 'try any of our other delicious menu items' in an attempt to make the most of the so-called 'Tortillapocalypse'.

DIY ISS

International Space Station crew had to deal with a leaky loo.

Ten litres of waste water flooded into the cabin of the ISS when astronauts accidentally twisted off an important bit of metal while trying to fit a new pair of stalls to create a bit more privacy. Their attempts to mop up the spillage with a bunch of towels were frustrated by the fact that the water floated rather than flowed around the cabin. As if that wasn't bad enough, mould was thriving both on the inside and the outside of the space station – and it's very resilient. In fact, as a team of scientists discovered, some moulds can cope with radiation doses of 500–1,000 grays – 200 times more than would kill a human being. This means that they may end up being the only Earth life-form that survives a journey to another planet.

Baking in space is incredibly difficult – everything floats, so the dough inside the oven has to be held in a special pouch.

Not only have the astronauts had to cope with mould and leaky toilets, but they are also scheduled to have the truly awful experience of very, very nearly – but not quite – being allowed to eat biscuits. A company called Zero G Kitchen is planning to send an oven that will enable them to bake cookies in space for the first time ever.* Unfortunately, once the experiment is over, all five of the planned bakes will have to be sent back to Earth for testing.

DOOMSDAY

For Poppypalooza, *see* **Apoppylypse**; for the Tortillapocalypse, *see* **Dining, Fine**; for Swarmageddon, *see* **Earthquakes**, and for Wormageddon, *see* **Pesky Pests**.

DOPES

The sports of bridge, pétanque and nonagenarian cycling were hit by doping scandals.

The sport of pétanque has been so dogged by its players' bad behaviour that the French press has coined the word 'bouliganism'. Still, it came as a surprise when the Netherlands team accused some of their Belgian opponents of using cocaine as a performance-enhancing drug in international matches. 'They go to the toilet and do not throw a wrong ball when they come back,' said one Dutch player. Another added, 'We were far ahead and had played flawlessly. Then they went to the bathroom for ten minutes and came back with huge eyes. Everything went well for them.' The leading Belgian bowler, Stefaan Kausse, strongly denied that the Belgian team were taking cocaine, but did acknowledge that doping went on in the world of pétanque.

The world of bridge was also struck by an unlikely doping scandal, when world champion Geir Helgemo was ordered to hand back his medals after he was found to have been using banned testosterone supplements. It's unclear why anyone would want to take testosterone to help their card-playing: a recent Dutch study shows that it doesn't help at all.

Cycling is no stranger to doping controversy, of course, but it was quite a surprise when 90-year-old Carl Grove tested positive for anabolic steroids. Grove claimed that the offending substance had come from some tainted meat he had eaten, but while the US anti-doping agency accepted his explanation he was still forced to hand back the gold medal he had won in the 90- to 94-year-old 'individual pursuit' category. Grove was actually the only participant in that event, which raises two questions: first, what did he have to gain by taking drugs; and second, who the hell was he pursuing?

Scientists have discovered that spinach really does make you big and strong, because it contains the steroid ecdysterone. They've recommended that the chemical be added to the WADA banned substances list in its capsule form – although you could get the same effect by eating 4 kilos of spinach a day.

63

DOUBLE TROUBLE ▶

For one week, Moldova had two governments.

In February, Vlad Luca Filat, son of the country's former prime minister, was ordered to pay back nearly £500,000 of public money that it was claimed had been used to fund his lavish lifestyle. His father is currently in prison, having been found guilty of stealing 12.5 per cent of the country's entire GDP.

In the Eastern European country's February elections, neither of the two main parties won enough seats to form a majority, so the third-placed Democratic Party of Moldova (DPM) governed while they reached an agreement. But by the time this had happened, the DPM was reluctant to quit power. Their argument relied on a quibble over deadlines: the law stated that any coalition had to be agreed within three months of the 9 March election result. The coalition interpreted this to mean 9 June, so it reached its agreement on 8 June. But the courts – and the DPM – interpreted 'three months' as being 90 days, so they claimed that the new government had missed the deadline by a day.

The DPM refused to vacate the government buildings and continued to hold cabinet meetings. For seven days, therefore, Moldova had two governments ruling in parallel, sometimes making contradictory decisions. At one point, for instance, the coalition voted to dismiss the heads of the police, while the DPM instructed them to continue their work.

People took to the streets of the capital city to protest, but there were suggestions they had been paid to do so. One TV station asked a group of them which of the two governments they supported, and they appeared not to know.

The DPM eventually gave up and relinquished power, but not before declaring that it believed the new government to be ruling illegally. They had previously tried to persuade America to take their side by promising to move Moldova's embassy in Israel to Jerusalem, hoping that would impress President Trump. However, the party's chairman, Vlad Plahotniuc, was so internationally disliked that he achieved the incredible feat of uniting America, Russia and the EU in demanding that he step down.

DRAKE CURSE

Multiple sportspeople fell fowl of the Drake Curse.

In April, Arsenal striker Pierre-Emerick Aubameyang posted an image on social media of him posing with Canadian rapper Drake. Three days later, Arsenal suffered a shock defeat against Everton. A week later, Paris Saint-Germain defender Layvin Kurzawa posed with Drake, only for his team subsequently to suffer a crushing defeat, 5–1, to rivals Lille. These were the latest pieces of evidence pointing to a 'Drake Curse' – an online theory that any sportsperson meeting the artist is destined to suffer an embarrassing defeat.

Boxer Anthony Joshua made light of the superstition, posting a picture with Drake before his bout with Andy Ruiz Jr – the seemingly hopelessly out-of-shape Mexican heavyweight – captioning the image with 'bout to break the curse'. Joshua ended up being beaten by Ruiz in one of the biggest shocks in boxing history. Italian football team A.S. Roma banned any of its players from taking photos with Drake, and Toronto Maple Leafs ice-hockey fans begged him to stop attending matches.

The curse was finally broken in June, when Drake's beloved basketball team, the Toronto Raptors, beat the odds to become the first-ever Canadian NBA champions. Interviewed after the final game, Drake commented, 'They said I was a curse, now they cursing each other out.'

In June, Drake achieved his 35th top 10 hit in the Billboard charts, breaking a record previously held by the Beatles. Last year, he beat the Fab 4 by having seven singles in the top 10 at the same time. To celebrate his success, he got a tattoo of himself waving goodbye to the Beatles as they walked across Abbey Road.

DRUGS ▶

The earliest known pot was found in a pot.

Robert Spengler of Germany's Max Planck Institute for the Science of Human History said his team had scanned a 2,500-year-old wooden bowl for evidence of hemp seeds and found 'a solid, unequivocal data point for actual use of this plant as a drug'. The seeds had apparently been burned, and there were large traces of cannabis's psychoactive compound, THC, present. The fact that the pot was found beside a burial site suggests that it might have been used in a ceremony 'to communicate with nature, or spirits, or deceased people'. Although the previous contender for the most ancient cannabis vessel turned out to be a ceramic cheese-strainer, archaeologists are convinced this one is the real deal.

In other drug news:

▶ A grandfather in Cheshire gave a cake left over from his grandson's 18th birthday party to Warrington Hospital as a gift for treating him, unaware that it was full of cannabis. One hospital staff member said, on condition of anonymity, that three or four nurses ate it and ended up 'off their faces'. The police were called in, and the rest of the cake was destroyed.

▶ A repairman in California who used his finger to dislodge 'a crust or a crystalline residue' from a broken 1960s synthesiser felt 'a weird, tingling sensation' after 45 minutes, then ended up tripping for a full nine hours on what turned out to be LSD. Once he had recovered, Eliot Curtis resumed the work of restoration wearing gloves.

▶ One of the largest drug busts in Australian history was made when a car containing 273 kilos of meth (worth AU$200 million) crashed into a parked police car.

▶ And back to early pot-taking: scientists discovered that cannabis evolved atop the Tibetan plateau, 3,000 metres above sea level. This means that in order to get high, any ancient humans would first have needed to get high.

DUKE OF HAZARDS ▶

Prince Philip crashed his car on a road named after his wife, and was then treated in a hospital also named after his wife.

The Duke of Edinburgh, who was driving near the royal family's Sandringham residence, pulled out too quickly onto a stretch of road called Queen Elizabeth Way, causing an oncoming car to crash into him and knock his Land Rover onto its side. The two women in the car that he hit sustained minor injuries and, to add insult to these, were treated at a hospital called the Queen Elizabeth. The 97-year-old prince was unharmed, but the next day also attended the nearby Queen Elizabeth

Hospital just in case. Norfolk Police said they had offered Philip 'suitable words of advice', although it's unclear how much good they did, given that he was seen driving without a seatbelt in another Land Rover just two days after the crash.

Three small pieces of plastic debris from the crash were put up for sale on eBay and attracted 139 bids. The highest was a (possibly not entirely serious) £65,000. The seller suggested that the plastic might have the Duke's DNA on it and should therefore appeal to cloning enthusiasts. However, eBay took down the listing, on the grounds that no item can be sold on the site 'that seeks to profit from human suffering'.

In response to all the brouhaha, Philip eventually gave up his driver's licence. However, he was still able to drive his horse and carriage, and kept doing so even after his 98th birthday. Arguably, he had got off lightly – the Crown Prosecution Service eventually decided 'It would not be in the public interest to prosecute.' Had they decided otherwise, Philip could have made legal history: the fine for careless driving is based on how much the offender earns, and if your spouse earns a lot more than you do, their income can be taken into account, too.

IN WHICH WE LEARN . . .

Why California was shaken but not stirred, who won a mandate from a man-cave, which politician campaigned with a wink and a smiley, who was expelled due to excrement, why Extinction Rebellion got sticky, and why British pilots XL in the cockpit.

EARTHQUAKES ▶

While looking for 'the big one', Californian scientists found 1.8 million little ones.

Seismologists discovered that a series of quakes that hit Yellowstone National Park over the last few years were actually aftershocks from an earthquake that occurred 60 years ago.

The team at the California Institute of Technology discovered that the state experiences hundreds of thousands of tiny earthquakes every year. These rumbles may only be the equivalent of a truck driving over a rough road, or a crowd stomping its feet, but their discovery could revolutionise how we predict larger quakes. Previously, scientists have focused on major events when mapping historical quakes, and because they are few and far between, they can appear quite random. But once all the tiny quakes are added in, patterns start to emerge, and it may make it easier to notice when a bigger one is on the way.

So when California was hit by two huge earthquakes in July – the largest in two decades – they didn't come as a complete surprise, because they followed a period known as 'Swarmageddon' when seismologists had detected more than 1,000 small earthquakes.

While specialists' computers continue to crunch huge amounts of data, the rest of us may want to resort to a more low-tech way of studying earthquakes by looking for PBRs – Precariously Balanced Rocks. PBRs are old-looking piles of stones that appear as if they could collapse at a moment's notice. If they haven't collapsed, then that is a good sign you're in an area that hasn't had a big earthquake for some time. It may not be as impressive as a computer system looking at 1.8 million minuscule earthquakes over a 10-year timeframe. But at least it's something.

ECUADORIAN EMBASSY

Julian Assange no longer resides in this article. For more details, *see* **Evicted**.

EJECTOR SEATS

The RAF's new jets were fitted with extra-powerful ejector seats for its extra-large pilots.

Britain's previous Tornado jets could only eject pilots whose 'nude mass' was 214 pounds (15 stone) or lower, although it wasn't explained why they were likely to be nude in the cockpit. In 2002, in response to concerns that pilots were getting larger, the seats were redesigned to accommodate up to 237 pounds (16.9 stone). Now, the ejector seats have been made even more powerful and can take pilots with an 'unclothed weight' – naked pilots again – of up to 245 pounds (17.5 stone). At the same time, the ejector seats have to be finessed to cope with lighter pilots, especially now that more women are joining the Royal Air Force. In the past, being underweight has been a serious drawback; in 2016, US pilots weighing less than 136 pounds (9.7 stone) were briefly banned from flying in case the ejector seat broke their necks.

It seems unlikely that even these new improved ejector seats will work for long. Because of what defence sources diplomatically describe as the 'increasingly diverse physical profile' of modern pilots, aircrew are continuing to get heavier. Either the planes will have to be modified yet again, or future F-35 pilots are going to have to lose a bit of excess baggage.

Perhaps the most iconic object with an ejector seat – James Bond's car from *Goldfinger* – was put up for auction this year. Complete with revolving number

——— ▼ ———

In March a 64-year-old civilian passenger on a flight was accidentally ejected from a fighter jet mid-flight. (He was fine.)

71

FUNGUS

MONDAY TIMETABLE

09:00 REGISTRATION	**09:30 RELIGIOUS EDUCATION**	**M O R N I N G**
A farmer enrolled 15 sheep in a French primary school to get pupil numbers up and thus prevent a class having to close. Those registered included Baa-bete, Dolly and Shaun. 	The Italian Ministry of Education offered exorcism classes for teachers. Designed to combat what some Catholics see as an epidemic of possessions in the country (a Sicilian priest recently claimed that 500,000 Italians a year are being possessed by the devil), they take the form of a 40-hour crash course in 'Exorcism and Prayer of Liberation'.	
12:00 BUSINESS STUDIES	**12:30 LUNCH**	**A F T E R N O O N**
An investigation revealed that more than 1,000 schools in the UK have to source their classroom supplies, such as pencils, notebooks and glue sticks, by raising money on crowdfunding sites.	School dinners in Madagascar are having dried crickets sprinkled onto them to tackle malnutrition. Crickets are about 60 per cent protein, represent a good source of vitamins and minerals and, according to the pupils, are really quite tasty.	

11:00 CHEMISTRY	**11:30 PHYSICS**
A professor in Japan taught his students how to make ecstasy. Tatsunori Iwamura, a professor at Matsuyama University, said he was trying to 'further their knowledge' of pharmaceuticals. 	A 12-year-old boy became the youngest person ever to build a working nuclear-fusion reactor. The Open Source Fusor Research Consortium verified that Jackson Oswalt successfully achieved fusion in his bedroom, which his parents had let him convert into a nuclear lab. Jackson said that his reactor 'takes in more energy than it produces, which is why I'm not a billionaire'.
14:30 SEX EDUCATION	**15:00 CLASS DISMISSED**
A newly built school in Scotland installed frosted windows in one of its stairwells, so that pupils won't see the 74-year-old man sunbathing in the nude on the other side of it. Antoni Bogulak, who has been a naturist for 40 years, insisted on the windows being installed so that he could keep sunbathing without causing offence.	An Ofsted investigation found around 500 suspected illegal schools operating in England. One of the clues that tips off visiting Ofsted inspectors is the sight of children scarpering out of the back door as a member of staff tries to stall for time.

B R E A K T I M E

B R E A K T I M E

plates, an oil sprayer and more, it's one of just four of the special Aston Martin DB5s in existence. The maximum load on Bond's ejector seat is unknown, although he is at least more likely to be naked in the car.

EMOJIS

A Nigerian political party released its manifesto in emojis.

More than 500 languages are spoken in Nigeria, but when opposition leader Atiku Abubakar wanted to talk to the country's youth, he decided to put out his key pledges in what he thought was their preferred way of communicating: emojis. Not that it helped his campaign much: he lost out to the incumbent Muhammadu Buhari by nearly four million votes 😨. No independent observers saw evidence of fraud, but Abubakar described the result as a 'throwback to the jackboot era of military dictatorship'. He made that statement in English, not emoji.

Given just how ambiguous emojis can be, Abubakar's effort seems all the more impressive. Here is a genuine pledge from his manifesto. See if you can work out what it means (answer on page 358):

If you found that difficult, then pity American judges, who are increasingly having to deal with emojis during trials (50 cases alone in the first half of 2019, compared with 53 in the whole of 2018). The problem is that one emoji can be interpreted in so many different ways: a face with sunglasses, for example, can denote a sunny day, or feeling cool or can simply mean 'deal with it'. An aubergine emoji may be a suggestive depiction of the male sex organ or just that you fancy moussaka for dinner, and this led to an advertising dispute in New Zealand in June. The complainant said that his daughter had asked him what the symbol meant, after seeing it in an ad, and that, 'upon looking it up', he had discovered that 'the eggplant emoji also refers to a man's penis'. The advertising standards authority responded with the moussaka defence: 'consumers who were familiar with the eggplant emoji were unlikely to take serious offence to its use in this context,' they said, 'while those who did not know the meaning would not understand the reference'.

ERROR 404

Somalia blocked all social-media sites to stop exam cheats, even though only 2 per cent of the population has access to the Internet.

The education secretary postponed nationwide tests following reports that the exam papers were being shared on social media, and imposed a five-day social-media blackout when they were rescheduled. The ban

—— ◆ ——

Amid independence protests in Kashmir, India completely cut off the contested region's Internet and phone services. The blackout was so comprehensive that some locals weren't even aware that in the meantime India had rewritten its constitution to revoke Kashmiri autonomy. The people of Kashmir are used to such disruption: last year India cut off the state's Internet 134 times.

must have had limited effect, since only 1.9 per cent of Somalis have regular Internet access, and even then the average speed is 0.6 megabytes per second, compared to the UK average of 46.2.

Only about 21 per cent of people living in Africa can get online, but that doesn't stop governments restricting Internet usage when they think it poses a threat. Ethiopia did so, like Somalia, in order to prevent exam cheats. Sudan barred access to social media during its election, while DR Congo, Benin, Mauritania and Algeria cut off the Internet entirely for theirs. Their defence was that they wanted to prevent the spread of rumours and hate-speech that might lead to chaos. Perhaps inspired by their example, Vladimir Putin signed a law that allows him to cut off Russia's Internet from the rest of the world's. In effect, he's seeking to create an internal network for the whole of the country.

Governments aren't always to blame for Internet blackouts. In January a British man was sentenced to 32 months in jail for committing a cyber-attack that brought down the whole of Liberia's Internet (it's the first time a single hacker has managed to take an entire nation offline). His defence was that he'd only intended to hack a few networks there, but that the bot he built had got out of hand.

ESPORTS

There was an international tournament for virtual farming.

Organisers said they were expecting large crowds around the world to watch competitors vie for prizes totalling 250,000 euros as they stacked virtual bales of hay, raised virtual crops and dealt with virtual pest outbreaks in the game *Farming Simulator 19*. On its release in 2018, *FS19* (as fans call it) sold one million copies in its first 10 days, despite (or perhaps because of) one review that described gameplay as 'labour intensive and utterly monotonous'.

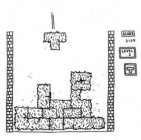

Virtual farming remains niche, even in gaming circles, but eSports are very much mainstream, particularly online war games. More people watched players battle in the *League of Legends* World Championship than saw the Major League Baseball World Series. And for the first time British universities have more eSports teams than real-life ones. There are now, for example, 662 university football teams, as opposed to 685 eSports squads.

There is big money to be made in eSports. This year's *Fortnite* World Cup had a prize pool of $30,000,000 and its final took place in a packed-out Arthur Ashe Stadium, the largest tennis stadium in the world. But it's a surprisingly gruelling profession. Many eSports players suffer from 'gamer's thumb', a complaint in which one's thumb becomes locked in place, due to extended periods holding a controller. And worse still, while most elite athletes can play well into their thirties, if you're a gamer you can be past it while you're still in your twenties. Your hand–eye coordination begins to deteriorate after the age of 25, and new players who have been shooting demons since they were old enough to hold a controller are queuing up to take your place. Once you're in your thirties, it's GAME OVER.

ETERNAL EMPLOYMENT

Sweden's public art body plans to hire someone to do absolutely nothing for the next 120 years.

A competition to supply public artwork for Gothenburg's new train station, Korsvägen, was won by artists Simon Goldin and Jakob Senneby for their idea: 'Eternal Employment'. This involves using the prize money of

£500,000 to hire someone to do whatever they like. The successful candidate will have to check in and check out of their work at the station each day, but while there can decide whether to sit in a room visible to the public, sit in a private room or clock in and then immediately leave for the day. The only thing they're not allowed to do is take another job. In return they will receive 21,600 Swedish kronor (£1,900 a month), increasing by 3.2 per cent a year for the next 120 years. As Goldin and Senneby put it: 'The position holds no duties or responsibilities . . . Whatever the employee chooses to do constitutes the work.' The job also comes with a pension, and a holiday in case doing nothing gets too tiring. If the employee quits, they'll be replaced. No qualifications are required.

The idea was inspired by Thomas Piketty's book *Capital in the 21st Century*, in which the French economist points out that the return you can earn on capital grows faster than the average increase in wages. By investing the prize money, the artists will be able to pay a salary for more than a century. If you're interested in the job, the hiring process starts in 2025, so you can sit tight and do nothing until then – which should be good practice.

EUROVISION

The Eurovision Song Contest brought (extremely temporary) peace to the Middle East.

In the two weeks leading up to this year's competition, which was hosted by Israel in Tel Aviv, the Israeli military was engaged in a fierce rocket and air-strike exchange with Hamas and Islamic Jihad, the organisations controlling the neighbouring Palestinian territory of Gaza. Desperate to avoid any front-line explosions that might interrupt the pop bonanza, Israel's government negotiated a short truce with its enemies. They agreed, for example, to allow millions of dollars in aid sent by Qatar to pass into Gaza. The period of goodwill was short-lived: one Israeli politician wrote that his country must evict Hamas from Gaza 'right after our holidays and Eurovision'.

In the end, organisers couldn't avoid conflict affecting the contest completely, as Ukraine declined to take part, thanks to tensions with Russia. This isn't the first time this sort of thing has happened. Last year Israel's embassy complained to the Netherlands after the national broadcaster had made fun of the Israeli winner; in 2008 Greece censored Ireland's lyrics to stop them mentioning the country of Macedonia; and in 2006 they censored Finland for being 'satanic'; but Finland censored Israel a year later for mentioning nuclear weapons. When Israel won in 1978, broadcasters in nearby Jordan told viewers that Belgium had won instead; Turkey pulled out in 1976 because Greece was taking part; but that was a response to the fact that Greece had pulled out in 1975 because Turkey was taking part. And in 1973, Portugal actually arrested the writer of its own song because they thought it wasn't fascist enough.

Britain has, by and large, managed to keep out of all the political drama, but it had another dismal year in Tel Aviv, scoring just 16 points (to put that in context, the Netherlands came first, with 498 points). Belarus, Europe's last dictatorship, came second from bottom, with twice as many points as the UK. There was brief hope when the judges announced that the scores had been miscalculated. They duly adjusted Britain's . . . downwards . . . to 11 points.

A YouGov poll of 1,693 people found that 52 per cent of Britons wanted to leave the Eurovision Song Contest and 48 per cent wanted to remain; 19 per cent of people who watch said they only do so to make fun of it, which was more than in every other country surveyed except Norway.

EVICTED

A look at the rooms inside the Ecuadorian embassy in London that, until his eviction on 5 April, Julian Assange called home for nearly seven years:

1 HIS SKATEBOARD

According to embassy staff, Assange liked to skateboard around the embassy's hallways – an activity that annoyed them greatly as it was 'ruining the floorboards'. Assange's staff denied he'd ever used a skateboard – during office hours.

2 A TREADMILL

A gift from director Ken Loach in December 2012, Assange claimed he ran three to five miles a day on it. If so, by the time he was evicted, Assange must have run roughly the equivalent of the distance from the Ecuadorian embassy in London to the British embassy in Ecuador and back.

3 A COPY OF VIRGINIA WOOLF'S *A ROOM OF ONE'S OWN*

Other apt items on Assange's bookshelf included a book about Guantánamo, a Spanish dictionary (so he could communicate with embassy staff) and a movie called *This is How You'll Make Your Bed in Prison*.

4 HIS FAECES, SMEARED ON A WALL

According to Ecuador's president Lenín Moreno, one of the key reasons for expelling Assange was that he smeared his own excrement on the embassy walls – something Assange's lawyers deny.

5 A VERY EXPENSIVE SHOWER

When Assange's shower broke, the embassy called in a plumber from Valencia because they were worried that if they used a British one, UK intelligence might use them as a way of infiltrating the embassy. As a result the shower cost over 4,000 euros.

6 A SUN LAMP

Assange invested in an ultraviolet lamp to boost his Vitamin D levels. He first used it two days before an appearance in front of the world's media, and things didn't go well. A member of Assange's staff told him: 'Julian, your face on one side is beetroot, and your neck as well.' In an attempt to balance things out, he tanned the other half of his face, but his eyes started burning, blisters formed, and his skin started to fall off. Eventually a friend's wife spent an hour and a half covering him in makeup, 'to ensure I didn't look like a Chernobyl victim'.

7 ABSOLUTELY NO HAIR BLEACHING PRODUCTS

Journalists reported that they received an email from WikiLeaks staff listing 140 statements not to make about Assange. They included: 'It is false and defamatory to suggest that Julian Assange does not use cutlery'; 'It is false and defamatory to suggest Julian Assange lives in a cupboard or under the stairs'; and 'It is false and defamatory to suggest that Julian Assange bleaches his hair.'

EVERY VOTE COUNTS ▶

In a country of 1.3 billion people, a polling station was set up in the middle of the jungle for a single person.

The Indian Electoral Commission ruled that, in the period after the vote when exit polls are banned, it was also against the law to predict election results using tarot cards or astrologers.

In preparation for the Indian election, five officials travelled 70 kilometres into the jungle to install the polling station. It was for a priest called Darshandas, who looks after a remote forest temple in a wildlife sanctuary in Gujarat. He still had to walk for half an hour to vote because for some reason, after travelling so far, the officials decided to place the voting booth 1 kilometre from where he lived.

Prime minister Narendra Modi's party won the election in the world's biggest democracy: 900 million people are registered to vote, and an impressive 600 million actually went to the polls. Modi was photographed meditating in a cave, in an attempt to appeal to his more ascetic followers, but was roundly mocked when it turned out the 'cave' was man-made, supplied full breakfast, lunch and dinner to its occupants and came with its own electricity, phone line and a bell for summoning a servant.

In his own constituency of Varanasi, Modi faced some opposition from the living dead. The Mritak Sangh organisation is a charity that assists people in the country who are alive but have been declared dead, either fraudulently or by mistake (for more surprisingly active dead people, *see* **In Memoriam**). This is quite a major problem in India and, to draw attention to it, Mritak Sangh announced that it would field officially deceased candidates in the election, including in the PM's own back yard.

EXTINCTION REBELLION ▶

A woman glued her breasts to the road to protest
against climate change.

Many participants in Extinction Rebellion, the worldwide campaign against climate change and mass
extinction, made good use of superglue. This particular
woman lay face-down and stuck her torso to the ground
outside the headquarters of investment company
Goldman Sachs in London. When the police arrived to
peel her off, they had to surround her with a screen to
protect her modesty. Her brothers and sisters in arms
(but not clothes) stripped off in the House of Commons
and glued their bottoms to the glass of the viewing
gallery during a parliamentary debate. The MPs adapted
by incorporating references to 'the bottom line' and 'the
naked truth' in their speeches.

While all this was going on, other protesters glued themselves to train windows and roofs across the city. Some
stuck themselves to a lorry on Waterloo Bridge for more
than a day. And in Hollywood two people glued themselves to the top of the globe outside Universal Studios.
Four rebels in North London fixed themselves to Jeremy
Corbyn's home, although they admitted they felt 'absolutely terrible' about upsetting his wife, and had flowers
and Easter eggs delivered to the house to apologise for
the inconvenience.

To unglue protesters, police resorted to a 'fluid
debonding agent', but refused to say exactly what it was.
One chemist speculated that it might be nail-varnish
remover, which makes superglue easier to loosen, but
he also said 'easier' is very much a relative term. Frustrated police complained that protesters were clearly
having a great time – the team-bonding evidenced
by the fact that they 'just cheer whenever they get
arrested'.

———— ▼ ————

Thanks to a reduction
in traffic levels while
the Extinction Rebellion
protest was in full sway,
pollution on Oxford
Street fell by up to
45 per cent.

IN WHICH WE LEARN . . .

*How casinos spot cash cows,
who earned a pony selling horse droppings,
why the whole of America was brass
monkeys, and what's making cicadas cic.*

FACIAL RECOGNITION

An MEP discovered his kids were unlocking his laptop by using a leaflet with his face on it.

Matt Carthy, a Northern Irish MEP, only realised his children were hacking into his laptop after noticing how quickly the battery kept running down. He wrote that he wasn't sure whether he should be proud about his children's cunning or 'concerned about the sneakiness'.

Not that facial-recognition technology always works. In London the police revealed that trials of a new system had recorded a 96 per cent 'false positive' rate (mis-identifying non-criminals as crooks). And in New York police had to abandon attempts to track down a beer thief via CCTV footage of him because the images were too blurry. Interestingly, though, when they fed high-def images of actor Woody Harrelson into the system, having been informed that the thief resembled him, they were successful: matches were produced, and an arrest eventually made. (Harrelson remains at large.)

For Taylor Swift, facial recognition has become a key weapon in her fight against her many stalkers. Fans at her gigs are snapped as they arrive and the photos are then transferred to a command post and cross-referenced with any known Swift stalkers.

In China, things have gone even further. Police officers now routinely wear sunglasses with facial-recognition systems embedded in them, so they can check whether passers-by are wanted by the police. And casinos in Macau have started pairing up data algorithms and facial recognition to work out which gamblers are likely to make big bets, and therefore if it's worth offering them perks to encourage them to keep playing. They can make these calls whether or not the players wear their poker face.

Facial-recognition technology is now being used to help combat the illegal trade in chimpanzees. Scientists have created an algorithm that searches for photographs of trafficked animals on social media.

FALL OF THE BERLIN WALL

It's 30 years since the Berlin Wall, erected in the 1960s to stop people from East Berlin escaping to the West, came down . . .

Some people successfully crossed the border by flashing their membership cards for a gentleman's club in Munich. The cards so closely resembled diplomatic passports that they could fool the authorities.

Over the course of 14 years, three brothers successfully escaped from East Germany to the West. In 1975, the eldest, Ingo Bethke, managed it by floating on an inflatable mattress across the River Elbe. In 1983, the youngest, Holger, fired a steel cable over the Berlin Wall and onto a rooftop on the other side, then pulled himself along it. And in 1989, both brothers flew back into East Berlin in ultra-light planes, picked up the middle brother Egbert, and flew back out again.

Four tonnes of Berlin Wall are currently sitting in storage in Christchurch, New Zealand, because councillors are divided on where to display it.

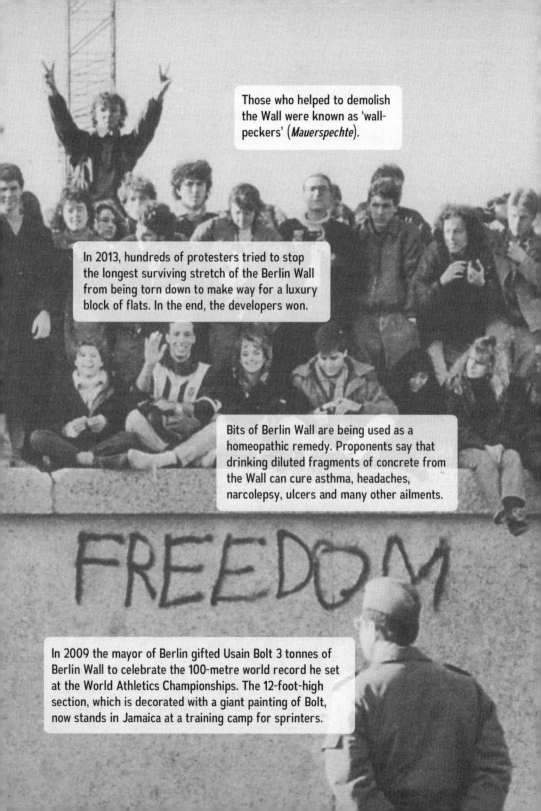

Those who helped to demolish the Wall were known as 'wall-peckers' (*Mauerspechte*).

In 2013, hundreds of protesters tried to stop the longest surviving stretch of the Berlin Wall from being torn down to make way for a luxury block of flats. In the end, the developers won.

Bits of Berlin Wall are being used as a homeopathic remedy. Proponents say that drinking diluted fragments of concrete from the Wall can cure asthma, headaches, narcolepsy, ulcers and many other ailments.

FREEDOM

In 2009 the mayor of Berlin gifted Usain Bolt 3 tonnes of Berlin Wall to celebrate the 100-metre world record he set at the World Athletics Championships. The 12-foot-high section, which is decorated with a giant painting of Bolt, now stands in Jamaica at a training camp for sprinters.

FARMERS ▶

For a ploughman's punch, *see* **Competitions**; for woolly thinking, *see* **Education**; for data harvesting, *see* **eSports**; for aggro-culture, *see* **Olives**; for a wave of watermelons, *see* **Surplus, Fruit**; and for crop stars, *see* **YouTube**.

FESTIVALS ▶

A festival of snow was cancelled because there was too much snow.

The organisers of Montreal's Festival of Snow told punters that it was 'Much more than snow!' – but in the end, adverse weather meant it wasn't even that. A whole day's events, such as dog-sledding and 'snow archery', had to be cancelled because it was too snowy.

In other festival news:

▶ Prague's witch-burning festival was saved by rain. The festival – which involves burning lots of effigies of witches – had previously been in doubt because of a ban on fires imposed due to a local drought. The deputy mayor of Prague, Petr Hlubuček, said, 'Burning witches is a popular tradition, especially among children, and it is of course always sad when they are disappointed.'

▶ Gwyneth Paltrow's company, Goop, charged people up to £4,500 to attend the brand's two-day, three-night festival (marketed as a 'summit'), 'In Goop Health'. The cost of admission covered 'far-infrared gemstone therapy' and the crystal-based sound-healing baths, but attendees had to fork out an extra £100 if they wanted to visit the workshop on 'how to dissolve negativity'. Unsurprisingly, a few people felt they'd been ripped off, and one person disillusioned by the event said: 'I was a huge fan of Gwyneth; now I feel like I have lost my faith in God.'

▶ Haringey Council in London told performers at the Wireless music festival that they should avoid swearing. This made things tricky for one of the biggest stars attending, Cardi B, whose songs include 'Got Me F***ed Up', 'Stripper Hoe' and 'Leave That Bitch Alone'.

▶ And organisers of the Gothenburg Film Festival announced they had created 'the world's most claustrophobic cinema' and that brave attendees could watch the movie *Aniara* from inside a custom-made, locked sarcophagus.

FIRST AID ▶

For a beat to restart your heart, *see* **Baby Shark**; for a beer to sober you up, *see* **Booze**; and for someone on the road to recovery, *see* **Holes, Pot**.

FLYING FIASCOS ▶

A British Airways flight to Düsseldorf accidentally flew to Edinburgh.

Passengers aboard the departure from London City Airport initially thought the pilot was joking when he announced that they were about to land in Edinburgh, but it turned out there had been a mix-up with the paperwork and the crew were working from the previous day's flight plan. According to the BBC, BA 'declined to say how many passengers were affected by the mistake', but we know that when the pilot asked people to raise their hands if they'd been expecting to land in Düsseldorf, every single hand on board went up, so we can safely assume all the passengers were affected.

Other flying fiascos included:

▶ A naked man tried to board a flight in Moscow, claiming that wearing clothes impaired his aero-dynamics and that he flew with greater agility when undressed.

▶ The Mexican environment minister felt compelled to quit after admitting that she'd asked for a flight to be delayed so she wouldn't miss it. Josefa González-Blanco phoned a friend at Aeromexico, who held up the plane by 38 minutes so that she could get on board.

▶ Passengers on a KLM flight and an easyJet flight from Amsterdam were delayed when their planes reversed into each other and got lodged together while still on the runway.

▶ A woman flying from Manchester to Islamabad mistook the emergency exit for a toilet door and opened it before take-off, launching the emergency slide and causing the plane to be delayed on the tarmac for eight hours.

FOR SALE ▶

Denmark's government said it was interested in buying the USA.

This counter-statement came soon after Donald Trump announced that he was keen on buying the Danish-run territory of Greenland. 'As we have stated, Greenland is not for sale,' a spokesperson for the Danish government said, 'We have noted, however, that during the Trump regime pretty much everything in the United States, including its government, has most definitely been for sale. Denmark would be interested in purchasing the United States in its entirety, with the exception of its government.'

Trump's interest in buying the world's largest island is not without precedent. The USA bought parts of New Mexico and Arizona from Mexico for $10 million in 1853, and Alaska from Russia for a similar price 14 years later. Greenland, though, has historically been beyond America's reach. In 1946, US President Harry Truman was given short shrift when he tried to buy it from Denmark for $100 million (today, the *Financial Times* has valued the island at approximately $1.1 trillion). And, in any case, now may not be the best time to buy. Trump's offer came in August, at a time when the country was 217 billion tons lighter than the month before – thanks to massive amounts of ice melting into the sea.*

By the middle of the summer, more than half of the surface of the largest ice sheet in Greenland had turned to slush.

Other items for sale this year included:

▶ *Some grass*: Labelled as 'Holy Grass', the blades were pulled from the ground close to where Kanye West and gospel choir Sunday Service performed a concert at Coachella.

▶ *Horseshit*: Bottles of manure from 1997 Kentucky Derby winner Silver Charm were sold for $200. The money went towards a thoroughbred retirement facility where Silver Charm now lives.

▶ *A bottle of real Mount Everest air*: The air was one of the 200,000 items available on the 'Amazon for millionaires' website HushHush.com. Others included a Boeing jet ($58 million) and a diamond-encrusted Rubik's Cube ($2 million). Millionaires could also advertise for things they wanted to buy – one looked to hire a 'game maker' to design a real-life 'Battle Royale' arena where people could hunt one another;

91

while another wanted to buy a mountain in the UK, to carve his family's faces into.

▶ *Bury FC*: Bury was bought in 2018 for just £1 and appears to have since fallen in value, as it was unable to find a new owner in time to prevent it from being kicked out of the English Football League in August. The club had been members of the football league for 134 years, were the first team to score 1,000 goals in all of the top four divisions, and still hold the record for the biggest ever win in the FA Cup final.

FOR YOUR EYES ONLY ▶

The Trump administration intensified its cyber-attacks on Russia, without Trump knowing about it.

The Pentagon told *The New York Times* it was scaling up its use of cyber-tools against Russia in retaliation for Putin's hacking operations in the US, but that they hadn't kept the president entirely informed of the details, in case he cancelled the operation or leaked it to the Russians. (He has form: in 2017 Trump leaked highly classified intelligence about an Islamic State plot to the Russian foreign minister.) Trump immediately denied that America was intensifying cyber-attacks on Russia, and tweeted that it was 'a virtual act of treason' that the newspaper had published the story.

On the other side of the Atlantic, Boris Johnson was similarly frozen out when he was foreign secretary. Government sources claimed Theresa May had withheld certain confidential information from him because she and the intelligence community worried that he wouldn't be able to keep it secret. She also altered the rankings of cabinet posts so that the home secretary, not the foreign secretary, would chair meetings of the Cobra emergency committee and the National Security Council in her

▼

Mumsnet reported itself to the authorities for a data glitch that switched users' accounts if they logged in at precisely the same moment as someone else did. A total of 46 mums found themselves accidentally signed in as each other.

absence, on the grounds that 'she just didn't want him taking charge in a crisis'. Which worked out well.

Leaking was endemic in British government circles. One cabinet secretary's secret plan to prevent leaks from ministerial meetings was leaked. And top-secret files from Britain's Porton Down chemical weapons research centre were found dumped in a public bin. They were discovered by a member of the public, who naturally alerted the most trustworthy organisation out there, the *Daily Star*.

FOURTH OF JULY

Donald Trump claimed that American patriots captured airports in 1775 – an impressive feat, given that the first airport wouldn't be built for another 134 years.

The claim was made in a speech the president delivered during an ostentatious Independence Day parade that featured fighter jets, helicopters and tanks. Trump had promised 'brand-new Sherman tanks' as well, which would have been tricky, because the US military hasn't used Sherman tanks since the 1950s. That minor gaffe was, however, dwarfed by his claim of 18th-century airports.

'On June of 1775, the Continental Congress created a unified army out of the revolutionary forces encamped around Boston and New York, and named after the great George Washington, Commander-in-Chief,' Trump announced to the crowds in pouring rain. 'Our Army manned the air, it rammed the ramparts. It took over the airports. It did everything it had to do. And at Fort McHenry, under the rockets' red glare, it had nothing but victory.' It's perhaps worth pointing out that not only were there obviously no airports in 1775 (the first was built in 1909), there was no Fort McHenry, either. It was actually built some years later, in 1798, and in the US national anthem 'the rockets' red glare' is a reference to its defence during the War of 1812.

Trump blamed his gaffes on the terrible weather, which had caused his teleprompter to fail, but then rather undermined that excuse by saying, 'I knew the speech very well, so I was able to do it without a tele-prompter.' He no doubt drew inspiration from George Washington, who also experienced teleprompter prob-lems in iconic speeches, and even suffered a complete Internet blackout during his 1790 State of the Union Address.

FREEZING

Hell froze over.

The town of Hell, Michigan froze this year as a result of a cold snap that broke meteorological records, brought down electrical grids and kept North Americans house-bound. The phenomenon responsible for this was the 'Polar Vortex', a colossal blast of Arctic air that normally spins at 150 mph, 30 miles above the Arctic, but that on this occasion spread across North America, causing temperatures to drop as low as −48ºC.

It was so cold that eggs that were cracked on the ground froze in a few minutes. Jeans froze stiff and could be stood upright. Some people discovered ice had formed inside their microwaves. In Chicago, railway tracks had to be set on fire to keep the trains running – effectively turning the railway network into a giant barbecue – and police warned that citizens were being mugged at gunpoint for their warm coats. Firefighters in Wisconsin found that when they blasted water at a fire, it fell back on them as ice pellets, and their eyes started freezing shut. Theatres suffered, too: the Chicago show *Disney on Ice* was cancelled due to the cold.

The National Weather Service warned Iowans not to talk if they went outside, and to avoid taking deep breaths, as the air was so cold it could irritate the lungs or trigger asthma attacks. Some people reported spontaneous nosebleeds when they set foot outdoors. Cities in the Midwest opened 'warming shelters'. Even so, at least 21 people perished in the cold.

In response to all this, President Trump tweeted: 'What the hell is going on with Global Waming [*sic*]? Please come back fast, we need you!' His plea is at odds with 97 per cent of the world's climate scientists, who say – regardless of short-term cold snaps – that, thanks to the actions of humans, the world is warming quicker than ever (*see* **Civilisation, Collapse of**).

FUNGI, NOT SUCH A

By James Harkin

It won't come as news to listeners of the podcast that I find all mushrooms, toadstools, yeasts (except brewer's yeast), and slime moulds absolutely disgusting.

They are often parasites on dead things. They reproduce using spores. And – let me be clear on this – they're not a vegetable. They belong to a completely different branch of the tree of life, so stop putting mushrooms in my vegetable madras.

What's more, they're after us. Killer fungi are on the rampage. There's a super-fungus called Candida auris, for instance, that is currently spreading around the world. It's resistant to all current treatments and can kill you if your immune system is already struggling, especially if it spreads to your heart. The head of the fungal branch at the Center for Disease Control and Prevention (CDC) has called it 'the creature from the black lagoon'.

Animals are also in danger from this mushrooming threat. Batrachochytrium dendrobatidis, which was described this year as 'the most deadly pathogen known to science', is believed to have completely wiped out 90 species of frog and drastically cut populations of some 500 other amphibians. Horrifying stuff.

OK. They're not all bad. Like I said, Saccharomyces cerevisiae, or brewer's yeast, is a rare friend in the fungal kingdom. A study released this year found that we've been using it to make wine for more than 9,000 years. And researchers also found that its role in the history of ale is more interesting still. Ale yeast doesn't appear in the wild. It was

actually bred from two different yeasts, one that was used to make Asian sake, and the other to make European wine. It seems that at some stage, the two strains were traded and then bred together – ancient traders acting like matchmakers to help the fungi have sex.

Fungi and sex are obviously two words you don't particularly want to hear in the same sentence. A fact that is particularly true if you're a cicada. These poor insects can be turned into hypersexual zombies by the fungus known as Massospora cicadina; and before you say that this isn't the worst kind of zombie, it's worth considering that this fungus doesn't just make the cicada horny, it also causes the insect's genitals to explode. Far from killing the mood, the cicadas still want to have sex, even though their sexual organs are now scattered over the garden. A team from the University of Connecticut have just worked out that the fungus also makes cicadas bisexual. An infected male will start flicking his wings out just like a female so that other males also want to mate with him – it doubles the number of potential partners and helps the sneaky fungus to infect even more insects.

Fungi are evil bastards. Don't ever forget it. And make sure you know exactly which fungus you're ingesting when you next order a mushroom pizza – you never know when a new species will evolve that can make human genitals explode.

F***ING BAD LANGUAGE

Ukraine's health minister announced that swearing is good for you.

—— ◆ ——

US presidential candidate Beto O'Rourke harnessed the power of profanity, selling a campaign T-shirt all about gun violence. It just read, 'THIS IS F*CKED UP' six times over, with – in rather smaller letters – 'End gun violence now' and 'Beto for America' at the bottom.

Ulana Suprun was arguing against a new law that proposed fining public figures the equivalent of £39 if they were caught using inappropriate language. 'In a number of cases the use of swear words means that people are close to each other,' she wrote in a post on Facebook, 'and there is a good emotional contact between them.' The post got more than 20,000 'likes' and comments, including one from musician Yevhen Halahan, who wondered how anyone could possibly talk about life in Ukraine without swearing.

Over the border in Russia, a new law was passed, which banned people from showing disrespect to government officials. Within two days a man was given a fine for calling Putin a 'fantastical fuckhead'. And in Salford, a ban on swearing in the quayside area was overturned after five years, during which not a single person had been fined for swearing there. Comedian Mark Thomas, who campaigned for the ban to be overturned, tweeted: 'Whoo-fucking-hooo'.

In other f***ing news:

▶ The US Supreme Court ruled that clothing brand FUCT could be trademarked. This went against the wishes of the US government, which wanted it banned, on the grounds of its use of 'scandalous' and 'immoral' language. One Supreme Court Justice said she was disappointed by the ruling, as it was likely to cause a 'rush' of applications to register 'the most vulgar, profane or obscene words and images imaginable'.

▶ A former soldier called Kenny Kennard revealed that since changing his surname by deed poll to

'Fu-Kennard' he had been unable to get a passport, as the Home Office said his name 'may cause offence'.

▶ And during the European elections one voter in Leicester wrote the word 'wank' next to every box apart from the Green Party, beside which the voter wrote 'not wank'. The vote was counted for the Greens.

IN WHICH WE LEARN . . .

*How to become a tree-lionnaire,
how coke got woke, why Vladimir Putin
is such a runway success, who won a
game of drones, and which is the
only place you'll get points for
'upskirting' and 'manspreading'.*

GAME OF THRONES

Chinese television showed Game of Thrones *without the sex, violence and dragons.*

The season-eight premiere of *Game of Thrones* gave HBO its largest night of streaming activity ever, with more than 17 million viewers tuning in. But those numbers were dwarfed by the 55 million viewers who tuned in illegally. Many of the illegal downloaders were in China, where the show was available legally, but it was heavily censored. One Internet user remarked, 'They've cut about a quarter of all the fight scenes, then a quarter of the nude scenes. I guess that's okay if all you want to watch is a medieval European castle documentary.'

The filming was largely done in Dubrovnik, Croatia, where eight of the 18 walking tours available for tourists were *Game of Thrones*-based; and in Northern Ireland, where in 2018 one in six foreign tourists was inspired by the show to visit. Shooting was extremely secretive: so much so that parts of the show were filmed close to Belfast airport, a dedicated no-drone zone, so that drones couldn't spy on them. For other scenes, drone-killers were deployed, which intercept flying cameras and force them to land.

In the end, some details of the plot did get out, although superfans could at least take out 'Spoiler Cover' from Endsleigh Insurance, which would allow them to claim up to £100 if the show was ruined for them by social media. For those who had vindictive friends, that may have been very useful, given that you can now download an app called spoiled.io that allows you to send spoilers anonymously to a friend's phone by text message. The developers were apparently inspired by the story of a woman who took vengeance on a cheating ex-boyfriend by messaging him *Game of Thrones* spoilers each week.

A newly discovered species of bee fly in Australia has been named *Paramonovius nightking*, after the show's main villain, the Night King. The choice wasn't completely random: the insect thrives in winter, has spines that look (slightly) like the TV character's, and it can turn other insects into walking zombies by laying eggs inside them.

GENDER ▸

A Scottish museum made all its ships gender neutral.

In 2015, Sweden adopted a gender-neutral pronoun, *hen*, to go with the words for 'he' and 'she'. Psychological research this year found that the term is already helping raise gender awareness and could help make society more tolerant.

Ships have traditionally been referred to as 'she'. But this year the Scottish Maritime Museum said that from now on it would be calling all its ships 'it', partly in response to a vandal who scratched out the word 'she' on signs in the museum. People quickly took sides. Trade association British Marine said it would continue calling ships 'she', because they were 'part of the family'. The retired admiral Lord West said that there was no need for a change, and that 'A ship is like a mother, they preserve us from the dangers of the sea'. By contrast, Richard Meade, the current editor of the shipping journal *Lloyd's List*, said: 'Perhaps making them feminine was understandable in the days of wooden sailing ships that arguably had a personality, but I challenge anyone to look at a modern 400 metre-long container ship and identify a gender.' Lloyd's, incidentally, stopped referring to ships as 'she' back in 2002. The debate rages on.

This year, for the first time, the Collins Scrabble dictionary included a gender-neutral pronoun, 'ze' – a step forward not only for inclusivity, but also for people who are stuck with a letter-Z tile. The chair of the World English Language Scrabble® Players Association defended the use of modern words, saying that 'When we had "lolz" they turned their noses up at text speak, but now they are much happier to play those words.' Other new words that are now allowed in Scrabble include: genderqueer, cisgender, agender and transperson, as well as fatbergs, upskirting and manspreading.

Another big win for gender neutrality came courtesy of the Archbishop of Canterbury, Justin Welby. He argued that human language is completely inadequate to describe God, who is therefore not male or female and so, logically, must be gender-neutral.

GEOENGINEERING

A study found that climate change could be stopped, if we plant a trillion trees.

'Geoengineering' is the idea of tinkering with the Earth's natural systems to fight man-made climate change. Various schemes have been suggested: some designed to remove carbon dioxide from the atmosphere, others to regrow melting ice caps or reflect sunlight back into space. But perhaps the simplest proposed method is to plant trees. A new study by researchers at the Swiss Federal Institute of Technology has found that because trees are so effective at sucking carbon dioxide from the air and replacing it with oxygen, planting one trillion of them would cut carbon in the atmosphere by 25 per cent, taking us back to the levels of a century ago.

One trillion is an unbelievably enormous number: to plant that many trees would involve re-foresting an area the size of the USA. The researchers pointed out, however, that there are lots of places on the planet where trees could be grown without affecting existing human land use – they cited Russia, Canada, China, Australia and Brazil (the last somewhat ironically, given the current rate of deforestation there, *see* **Bolsonaro, Jair**). One country leading the way is Ethiopia, which broke the world record for tree-planting, managing 350 million in a single day. Even so, to get to one trillion, Ethiopia would need to repeat that feat every day for eight years.

An equally ambitious scheme came courtesy of the Potsdam Institute for Climate Impact Research. Scientists there suggested that water could be taken from the ocean, turned into artificial snow and fired over the Antarctic. The amount of sea water needed is equivalent in volume to 125 Mount Everests; the plan would require the power of 12,000 wind turbines; and it would take half

Mexican scientists are moving an entire forest 1,000 feet up a mountain to help save butterflies; the trees they rely on are suffering from climate change and need to grow at higher, colder altitudes. One thousand saplings have already been moved.

a century. But the Antarctic has lost an area of sea ice the size of Mexico between 2014 and 2017 alone, so this idea, or something like it, might soon become necessary.

GLUE ▶

Divers in Thailand are saving coral reefs by sticking them back together.

Scientists at Swansea University's Energy Safety Research Institute have developed a chemical that – when mixed with a common, normal glue – can capture one-fifth of its own weight in carbon dioxide.

Ever since the tiny Thai beach of Maya Bay featured in the Leonardo DiCaprio movie *The Beach* it has been ravaged by tourists, up to 5,000 of whom have been known to turn up in a single day. With the beach collapsing, and its coral reef suffering terribly from the pollution of so many boats, the government took the decision to close it off. Now scientists have started using superglue to attach pieces of sick or broken coral, taken from otherwise healthy reefs, back onto the rocks. And it's working. It takes a week for the coral to start gripping by itself, and when the glue dissolves the reef starts flourishing again.

Another miraculous glue that made the news was created by researchers at the University of Pennsylvania. It's so strong that just two squares the size of postage stamps can stick a 13-stone man to the ceiling. Even more excitingly, this new adhesive has conquered a problem that glue researchers have been stuck on for decades. Until now, glues could be either strong and irreversible, or weak and reversible. This one is strong *and* reversible. Scientists came up with the solution after studying snail mucus, a substance that enables snails to slip along, but which also dries as a strong adhesive. The new glue is so delicate that it can be applied to a butterfly's wing and then detached without causing tissue damage.

GOING GREEN ▶

*A Birmingham drug dealer started selling cocaine in
environmentally friendly pods.*

A drug user told the local paper he initially thought
his dealer was joking when he presented him with the
reusable container. But he was told they weren't using
plastic Ziploc bags or wraps any more, and that he
should bring his pod back if he wanted a refill. The man
said that when the dealer informed him this was better
for the environment, 'I told him I was not bothered
about the environment, and surely cocaine itself can't
be that be eco-friendly. But he reckoned he had a load
of hipster customers and they loved it.'

In other environmentally friendly news:

▶ A Canadian construction company built a house out
of 600,000 plastic bottles. JD Composites shredded
and melted down the containers, then shaped them
into a bungalow on the shores of Nova Scotia. It
hopes to sell it or rent it on Airbnb.

▶ Mayors in the town of Binalonan in the Philippines
banned gossip, on pain of being fined and forced
to clear up rubbish. If you claim someone's having
an affair, or spread rumours about their money or
property, you can be made to clean up the streets.

▶ And recycled credit cards are being used as feeders
to revive bees. They're produced by a designer who
makes them out of old plastic cards, putting indenta-
tions in them and filling them with sugar solution.
He came up with the idea when 'It struck me that
everyone who walks around a city will have walked
past an exhausted bee.'

GOODBYE ▶

This year the world said farewell to . . .

Entertainer **Doris Day** (97), who only found out how old she was two years before she died. A document uncovered on her 93rd birthday showed she was in fact 95. Day was best known for her role in the movie *Calamity Jane*, and for her hit song 'Que Sera, Sera', which was commissioned by director Alfred Hitchcock for the movie *The Man Who Knew Too Much*. Hitchcock's brief to the songwriters included, 'I don't know what kind of song I want' and 'it would be nice if the song had some foreign words in the title'. Despite its success, Day hated the song, and couldn't understand why it was included in a movie about a kidnapped boy.

*Racing driver **Niki Lauda** (70), the three-time Formula 1 World Drivers' Champion, who hated the design of the F1 trophies so much, he traded all of his for a lifetime of free car washes.*

Mathematician **Simon Norton** (66), who represented Britain at the International Mathematical Olympiads three times, scoring the top grade each time. Norton was a mathematical prodigy. After he sat the Eton entrance exam aged 10, his marking examiner simply wrote '!!' on the paper. He loved numbers so much that when he was five years old he changed his name to 5, and referred to his mum as 45.

Singer **Keith Flint** (49) who, as well as fronting the band Prodigy – whose hits included 'Breathe' and 'Firestarter' – ran a pub called The Leather Bottle, where he kept a swear jar on top of the fireplace. The rule was that any patron who made a 'firestarter' joke whenever Keith was adding wood to the fireplace had to put a pound in the jar.

Comedian Ian Cognito (60), who died while on stage. Cognito's usual act was so outrageous that the audience spent five minutes thinking that his death was part of the show.

Actor **Peter Mayhew** (74), the 7'2" actor best known for his iconic portrayal of Chewbacca in the *Star Wars* series. While Mayhew may have been the man inside the wookie suit, his wookie roar never made it to the screen. That was instead performed by some bears, a badger, a lion, a seal and a walrus. Despite the fact that Mayhew last appeared as Chewbacca in 2015's *The Force Awakens*, he continued to be credited in the subsequent films under the title 'Chewbacca consultant'.

Nancy Wigginton (93), the first woman to read the national news on BBC Television. When she got the job in 1960, BBC bosses thought women were 'too frivolous to be the bearers of grave news'. She was sacked after a few months because viewers reportedly didn't like a woman reading the news.

Sybil Hicks (81), whose first-person obituary made the news for including the line: 'I finally have the smoking hot body I have always wanted . . . having been cremated.'

Rip Torn (88), the Oscar-nominated and Emmy-winning movie and TV star who, near the end of life, was more often in the headlines for his eccentric personal life than for his work. In 2008, he was arrested for drink driving, then charged with resisting arrest, after being caught driving in the breakdown lane with a Christmas tree tied to his car roof. Then, in 2010, aged 80, he broke into a bank carrying a loaded handgun while drunk, and fell asleep. When police arrived to arrest him, he claimed he had been so drunk he had mistaken the bank for his home.

GOLF

Fore a water hazard, *see* **Apposite**; fore holy holes, *see* **Helter-Skelter**; fore losing your head cover, *see* **Sherlock Clones**; and fore an absolute lack of any kind of golfing etiquette whatsoever, *see* **Under Par**.

GPS

When Vladimir Putin travels, he goes disguised as an airport.

Whenever Vladimir Putin gets near a harbour, the Global Positioning Systems of the ships moored there go crazy. Suddenly it appears as though the ships are actually in a nearby airport.

The reason for this, according to a new report by American security group C4ADS, is that in order to throw would-be assassins off the scent, Putin probably travels with a 'GPS spoofer'. This is a system that deliberately broadcasts incorrect GPS signals; so if, say, you were using a satnav and drove past a spoofer, your car might suddenly think you're in Timbuktu. This trick also works on drones, and since commercial drones shut down automatically if they get too near commercial runways, Putin's spoofer specifically makes him appear as though he's in an airport. The system could ultimately prove to be something of a double-edged sword. If this sort of GPS spoofing suddenly happens in a certain area, it follows that Putin may well be nearby – so ironically, by creating a Putin-cloaking device, the Russian security services may have simultaneously created a pretty decent Putin-detector.

If that's the cleverest approach to GPS this year, the least impressive has to be North Cornwall MP Scott Mann's suggestion that Britain's knife-crime epidemic could be solved by putting a GPS tracker into the handle of 'every knife sold in the UK'. He said, 'If you're carrying it around you'd better have a bloody good explanation, obvious exemptions for fishing, etc.' Critics pointed out that this was a ridiculous proposal. It would make knives hugely expensive, would require an enormous monitoring operation, would need people to regularly charge up their entire knife drawers, would collapse all GPS systems due to the bandwidth required, and would simply lead to a black market in knives that *didn't* have GPS trackers in the base. Mann was told he was 'not the sharpest knife in the drawer'.

GROOVE, BUSTING A

Scientists concluded that cockatoos can choreograph.

Snowball the Eleonora cockatoo shot to Internet fame in 2008, thanks to his impressive ability to dance to a beat. He is, in fact, the only non-human known to be able to do so. Intrigued by his talent, one neuroscientist bet a colleague an expensive bottle of wine that he could demonstrate that the parrot really can hear and appreciate music in the same way humans do.

The subsequent study showed that not only is this the case, but also that Snowball invented the moves himself, rather than learning them from others. Although his owner dances with him sometimes, she acknowledges that her moves are limited to 'nodding her head and waving her arms'. Snowball's, however, are more advanced. In fact it would appear that he's taught himself 14 different, original dance steps.

The study author said his research persuaded him that rather than being something we learn, musical appreciation is something we're born with.

IN WHICH WE LEARN . . .

Who looked up to the world's best bosses, who should have been the leader of the lion pack, why the glory hole is working overtime, how a black hole made the Internet redundant, and what wizards used to do with their jobbies.

HAKUNA MATATA ▶

The Lion King *should have been* The Lion Queen.

In the time between Disney's 1994 version of *The Lion King* and the 2019 remake, the world's population of lions has halved.

This was the news that zoologist Craig Packer waited a quarter of a century to tell us. *National Geographic* got in touch with Packer, director of the Lion Research Center at the University of Minnesota, to get his perspective on *The Lion King* remake, released in July. Packer immediately Skyped the magazine from Kenya to say he'd been longing for this moment ever since the original Disney film came out. Lion societies, he announced, are matrilineal. The lionesses rule the pride and are its 'heart and soul', while the males come and go. It would have been Sarabi, the mother character, who handed over her dominion to the next in line, who would have been Simba's mate, Nala.

Packer also revealed that genetically superior males in a pride have darker manes, so in reality the film's villain, Scar, would probably have started out in charge. But anyway, he added, neither Scar nor Mufasa, nor Simba, would have ended up dominant because in the wild, rivalry would have weakened them all, enabling another group of more cooperative males to take their place.

The film may not have been accurate zoologically, but it did win praise for its visual realism. To achieve this, the creators made a full virtual-reality world and wore VR headsets during development, so they could plot the action from within that world. Every single moment was animated or computer-generated – bar one. For the opening shot, director Jon Favreau used a single, genuine photo that he took in Africa, to see if anyone would notice. (He then spoiled the trick by tweeting about it.)

A HANDBAG!?

A woman from Manchester wanted to pay an arm and a leg for a leg on her arm.

The woman, known only as Joan, needs to have the lower part of her leg amputated due to peripheral arterial disease. But when she read that amputated body parts are often simply dumped, she decided she wanted to recycle at least some of her limb by turning it into a handbag. 'I know it's a bit odd and gross and some might think I'm crazy,' she wrote to fashion firm Sewport, 'but it's my leg, and I can't bear the thought of it being left to rot somewhere. It's part of me and I want to keep it.' She said she was willing to spend £3,000 on it, but she has not, as yet, found a manufacturer willing to work with her.

In other handbag news:

▶ A tiny handbag just 2 inches long and known as the 'Jacquemus Mini Le Chiquito' made its debut during Paris Fashion Week. One fashion writer tweeted a list of things it could hold: 'loose floss, a spare acrylic nail or a singular lock of curled hair retrieved from the head of Jude Law circa 1999'.

▶ A handbag has been invented that can order an Uber. It syncs up with your phone and has a button that, when pressed, can not only find a taxi, but can also turn on the lights in your house or help you find your keys.

▶ The big award at the Independent Handbag Designer Awards, known as the 'Oscars for Handbags', went to a pair of designers from Suffolk who made bags from old seatbelts and used the proceeds to feed homeless people.

▶ And in a pre-emptive strike, the owners of the poo-shaped handbag brand 'Pooey Puitton' sued French

HARRY POTTER AND THE...

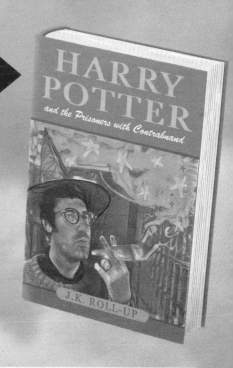

...PRISONERS WITH CONTRABAND

Police accused the inmates at Nottingham Prison of smoking a Harry Potter book after a copy of *The Goblet of Fire* tested positive for a psychoactive drug. Police suspect the substance was sprayed onto the pages of the book and smuggled into the prison where prisoners then tore up pages into strips and smoked them. By the time police got their hands on it, 400 pages of the 636-page book were missing.

...HALF-BURNED PRINTS

Father Rafał Jarosiewicz, a priest in northern Poland, led a public burning of 'evil' items that included Harry Potter books. He has since apologised for his actions saying that he had not intended to condemn specific authors. Other objects burned included a small Buddhist figure, an African mask, and some figures of elephants. As well as receiving much criticism for the burning, Jarosiewicz was also reported by an anti-smog group.

...ODOUR OF THE FAECES

Thanks to a tweet published by the official Harry Potter Twitter account on World Trivia Day, the world now knows that before they adopted 'Muggle' plumbing methods, wizards and witches who needed a poo relieved themselves where they stood, and made the evidence vanish when they were done.

fashion house Louis Vuitton. They assumed that once Louis Vuitton learned of their existence, it would sue them. The judge found no evidence that the more prestigious brand had any interest whatsoever in Pooey Puitton.

HELTER-SKELTER ▶

Norwich Cathedral installed a helter-skelter so that visitors could better admire the medieval roof.

The 55-foot slide was temporarily placed in the cathedral nave in August, the idea being that thrill-seeking architecture fans prepared to part with £2 could climb up it, admire the prospect from a viewing platform and then slide down. The Rev. Andy Bryant came up the idea on a visit to the Sistine Chapel in the Vatican, when he reflected that Norwich Cathedral's vault decorations were 'every bit as wonderful', but too high up to be fully appreciated. The cathedral features the world's largest collection of roof bosses – intricately carved, colourful

— ▼ —

The Bishop of Lynn read a sermon from halfway up the ride. He told the congregation that 'God is a tourist attraction' before sliding the rest of the way down, to huge cheers.

PRAWN TO BE WILD
Cocaine found in all shrimp tested in rural UK county

FLICKY LEAKS
WHEN SHOULD YOU PEE DURING LONG FILMS?

Head of Planned Parenthood Forced Out After Eight Months

US Treasury to Name-Shame Vietnam for Manipulating Its Dong

Cocaine in Spain puts Bolsonaro under strain

Aqua Park Suffolk goes into liquidation

GRAN WHO GAGGED ON 2-IN BONES SAVED AT LAST GASP

New Lion King no classic, but well worth seeing in the mane

GRANDMASTER FLUSH: CHESS PLAYER CHEATED IN TOILET

PASS THE DUCHY: Luxembourg's grand plan to legalise cannabis

figures that protrude from intersecting points in the ceiling. For those who can't make it to Norwich, you can also get a close-up guided tour of the more than 1,000 sculptures by downloading the cathedral's roof-boss app.

The helter-skelter inevitably provoked a number of complaints. One visitor from the Netherlands said that she was rather disappointed it was there, because it blocked her view of a stained-glass window that she'd particularly wanted to have a look at. But the dean insisted it was 'certainly not a gimmick'.*

*Another definitely-not-a-gimmick appeared at Rochester Cathedral, where a temporary nine-hole crazy-golf course was installed. Every single journalist quite rightly dubbed it a 'Fairway to Heaven'.

HOLES, BLACK ▶

The first-ever photo of a black hole had to be transported by plane because the file was too large to send as an email attachment.

The volume of data required to develop the famous photo was five Petabytes, which is equivalent to 5,000 years' worth of MP3 songs. In fact it turned out to be quicker to load it onto hard drives and have it flown to data analysts than to send it via the Internet – even though, thanks to the Antarctic winter affecting flight schedules, scientists had to wait half a year for the hard drives from the South Pole telescope to arrive.

The black hole in question is in the middle of Messier 87, a galaxy 55 million light years away. It's 38 billion kilometres across, 6.5 billion times bigger than the Sun and more than a thousand times bigger than our own galaxy's black hole – which at least makes it easier to photograph. Despite its unimaginable size, it's so far away that it looks as big to us as a single coin would do on the surface of the Moon – and if that didn't make it

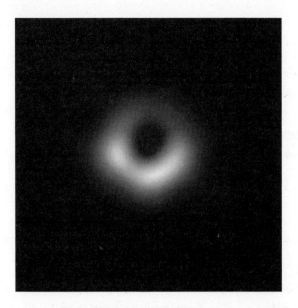

difficult enough to see, it's so dense that it sucks in all light. Photographing that, with Earth-based telescopes, was going to be tricky.

A single telescope wasn't going to cut it, so the 'telescope' used was the entire planet. The 'Event Horizon Telescope' is a network of eight observatories stretching all the way from Spain to Hawaii, Chile and Antarctica. By combining data from across the planet, the astronomers effectively made a telescope with an aperture as big as Earth. Each instrument had to be tethered to an atomic clock to perfectly synchronise the observations.

In the resulting image the black hole itself appears totally dark, which is only to be expected, as no light can escape from a black hole. Around the darkness one can see an 'accretion disc', which swirls around a black hole and feeds it. What looks like a faint glow to us is a ring of gas and dust particles that can reach temperatures of billions of degrees.

More than 200 scientists spent years working on the project, but they did, at least, get two photos for the price of one. Because of the intense gravity, warping light around a black hole, they were able to see what was behind the dead star as well as the front of it.*

HOLES, GLORY ▶

A duck was swallowed through a glory hole.

The 'Glory Hole' is the name given to a flood drain in the Lake Berryessa reservoir, 75 miles north of San Francisco. It's also sometimes known by another name that is frankly just as suggestive: the 'Morning Glory Spillway'. When it was installed, it was designed to be used just once every 50 years, but because climate change has led to more frequent, heavier rains, it has had to be used twice in the last two years alone.

Local wildlife is evidently still coming to terms with things. A spokeswoman for the hole, Brionna Ruff, said that a duck that was swallowed by the drain in March was probably dead: 'From what I understand, that water is going down really fast and when things come out the other side . . . I don't want to get really graphic,' she said. However, the water-resources manager for the lake, Rick Fowler, wasn't so sure; he said he saw the bird 'shoot out like a bullet', alive.

HOLES, POT ▶

A man in Nebraska had his life saved by a pothole.

The 59-year-old was in an ambulance being rushed to hospital with a life-threatening abnormal heartbeat when the vehicle hit the hole – jolting his heart back to a normal rhythm. The local authorities declined to name where the pothole was, supposedly to keep the patient's privacy secure (but maybe so that people didn't start taking their own medical problems to the magical, lifesaving hole-in-the-road).

Most people this year, though, were busy trying to make potholes disappear. In Oakland, California, despite pleas from the city authorities not to do so, two masked crusaders called the Pothole Vigilantes filled in more than 50. In Kansas, a local hero called Frank Sereno threw a 'birthday party' for a pothole on his street (it was actually only three months old, so did not remotely deserve a celebration), putting a slice of cake into it. An embarrassed council filled it in within days. Elsewhere, people resorted to the tried-and-tested method of drawing penises around potholes, following the method of Manchester's street crusader, Wanksy. The trend spread to Middlesbrough, Pembrokeshire, Essex and even as far as Alabama.

With luck, soon everyone will be able to lay down their spray cans. Researchers at the University of Leeds are developing a drone that will fly around at night spraying 3D-printed asphalt inside small cracks to stop them

——— ▼ ———

Children in Shropshire who got a chance to name the county's pothole-filling machines opted for Harry Pothole and Fill.I.Am.

121

getting any worse. If they're successful, the roads in and around Leeds will be both pothole-free and completely self-mending by 2035.

HONG KONG ▶

Hong Kong protesters stormed government buildings, emptied the fridges, then left money to pay for what they'd eaten.

——— ▼ ———

After being criticised for being too heavy-handed when dealing with protesters – for instance, using tear gas and rubber bullets – Hong Kong police swapped male policemen on the streets for female ones.

By some estimates, more than a quarter of Hong Kong's population demonstrated against the proposed introduction of a law to allow criminals to be extradited from Hong Kong to Taiwan, Macau and mainland China. Its critics feared it would be used to deport political activists, who would then face unfair trials in China. The protesters were incredibly persistent, repeatedly taking to the streets for more than four months, despite concessions from the region's chief executive, Carrie Lam. Initially the vast majority were non-violent: even when some of them broke the windows of the Legislative Council and fought their way in, they left payments for drinks they'd removed, and urged each other not to destroy documents.

The demonstrators communicated using hand signals, which they sketched and circulated via smartphone. These included signs for tools such as scissors, marker pens and umbrellas, which they'd pass among their number by forming human chains. They also sent each other messages with the Tinder and Pokémon Go apps. Some marched with Pikachu dolls, because the name of Hong Kong's secretary for security, John Lee Ka-chiu, sounds similar to 'Pikachu'.

They also repeatedly sang 'Do You Hear the People Sing?' from *Les Misérables*. In response, the Chinese government censored the song on the country's biggest streaming services, saying it was for 'copyright reasons', even though the rest of *Les Mis* remained freely available. In addition, people protested by singing the Christian hymn 'Hallelujah to the Lord', even if they weren't Christians, and by waving around the Union Jack, the symbol of their former British colonisers, even though they were absolutely not demanding a return to British rule.

Despite two million people marching against the extradition laws on a single day, that day's edition of the Chinese government-owned newspaper, *China Daily*, focused on a different angle. It led with the headline 'HK parents march against US meddling'. The story explained that 30 local dignitaries had protested at the US consulate against foreign meddling stirring up the youth against the extradition bill – but unaccountably forgot to mention the two million protesters.

Even the porn industry backed the rebels in Hong Kong, with two adult sites displaying messages telling visitors to stop masturbating and join the demonstrations.

HOT AS HELL

A pile of manure spontaneously combusted in Spain and started a 10,000-acre fire.

It was the worst fire Catalonia had seen in 20 years, and was one of the most spectacular results of the 'Hell' heatwave that struck Europe in the early summer and saw not just parts of Spain, but also France, Germany, Poland and Czechia experience the highest June temperatures in their histories. New speed limits were introduced to Germany's autobahns, due to fears the surfaces would otherwise crack up; horse-drawn carriages were banned in Vienna, due to fears for the animals' health; and France postponed its national exams because school halls were too hot.

As people struggled to cope, tempers flared, especially in France, where there was a conflict between nudist

123

swimmers and Muslim bathers who wanted to wear the full-body swimsuits known as 'burkinis'. A group calling themselves the 'Muslim Rosa Parks' had turned up at the public baths in Grenoble wearing their burkinis, only to be fined (the rules on swimming costumes are very strict in France). When they threatened to do so again, another group called 'Everyone Naked' responded by organising a nudist swimming event at the same time.

A row about swimwear also broke out in Germany, where, after they heard that a group of women had been ordered to put on bikini tops when sunbathing, the Green Party tabled a motion that women are as entitled as men to go topless. The Christian Social Union disagreed, announcing that bathers must wear 'swimwear that completely keeps their main sex organs covered', unless they happen to be in areas specifically designated for nudists. One man who conspicuously failed to take this advice was a resident in the small German town of Hemer, who attempted to cool down by taking off all his clothes and running through the freezer section of his local supermarket.

IN WHICH WE LEARN . . .

How to avoid the influencer virus,
which new party made people want to
CHUK up, who received an extremely
painful pool-shot, which politician
operates with surgical precision, and
which robot can make a cutting remark.

ICELAND VS ICELAND

Iceland won a lawsuit against Iceland over the word 'Iceland'.

Iceland and Iceland's relationship has seen happier times. In the 2016 European Championship, the supermarket decided to sponsor the country's football team. The two released joint-branded scarves, and the supermarket declared itself officially neutral when England were beaten by Iceland, tweeting as the final whistle went: 'Unexpected result in bagging area.'

'In 874, the country of Iceland was settled,' Hannah Jane Cohen wrote in the *Iceland Grapevine* magazine. 'Years later, in 1970,' she went on, 'some bullshit Brits created the supermarket Iceland Foods and trademarked the name Iceland in the entirety of Europe. First question: How drunk was the guy who allowed someone to trademark the name of a country?'

Despite being founded more than 1,000 years ago, the nation is arguably only 26 years older than the supermarket, as the modern-day Republic of Iceland was founded in 1944 after dissolving its union with Denmark. But Cohen's irritation is understandable, given how aggressively the frozen food company was protecting its trademark. First the supermarket targeted Icelandic companies that used the word 'Iceland'. Then it blocked the country's 'Inspired by Iceland' campaign. Iceland eventually decided that what Iceland was doing was not cool, and petitioned the EU.

In April, the European Union Intellectual Property Office finally found in favour of the country, allowing it to push its own 'Iceland' brand. That brand now includes luxury tap water, named after the Icelandic word for water from the tap, 'Kranavatn'. The intention is to dissuade tourists from buying water in plastic bottles. A pop-up bar offering nothing but Kranavatn fresh from the tap even appeared in Reykjavik Airport. Of course, the more you choose to drink Kranavatn instead of strong Icelandic liquor, the less likely you are to make silly trademark decisions.

IGUANA INVASION ▶

A Florida man accidentally shot a pool maintenance worker, thinking he was an iguana.

Iguanas are a big problem in Florida. They have spread to the region from Central America, and because they have no natural predators in the Sunshine State, they're taking it over. In 2007 there were just five reported sightings of iguanas in Florida. Last year there were 2,700. They have been swimming up people's toilet pipes, pooing in their swimming pools, and stealing lettuce from the gorillas at Miami Zoo. One home owner said iguanas are so numerous that he sometimes can't get through his front door – though that sounds unlikely.

Desperate times call for desperate measures. The Florida Fish and Wildlife Conservation Commission (FWC) issued a statement encouraging home owners to kill green iguanas on their own property. Poisoning, drowning and freezing were not allowed, but it is legal in Florida to use pellet guns or to decapitate them. All of which meant that a cottage industry in iguana-hunting popped up. This was bad news for one particular pool cleaner who was working on the same premises as an iguana-hunter. Neither knew the other was there, and the pool cleaner ended up being shot in the leg. Luckily it was just a flesh wound.

The FWC soon clarified its position. It suggested that rather than committing iguanacide, residents might

Name:
Ekrem İmamoğlu

Occupation
New Mayor of Istanbul

Campaigning Advice:
Avoid sarcasm

How did that work?
Really, really well. Genuinely.

Reason for being in the news:
İmamoğlu won Istanbul's mayoral election in March by 13,000 votes. Turkish President Erdoğan annulled the result and demanded a rerun, refusing to admit his party, the AKP, had been beaten. But this backfired spectacularly for Erdoğan: in the follow-up election on 23 June, İmamoğlu increased his majority sixty-fold, to 777,000.

The new mayor ran with the campaign slogan, 'Herşey çok güzel olacak', which translates as 'Everything will be fine'. He stole this phrase from a 14-year-old boy who ran alongside his campaign bus in March, calling out, 'Don't worry, brother Ekrem, don't worry, never give up! Everything will be fine.' Ekrem's campaign manager, Ates Ilyas Bassoy, said their whole strategy depended on two central rules: ignore Erdoğan, and love those who love Erdoğan. He wrote a booklet for the campaign on how to win votes with 'radical love' and avoid sarcasm and arrogance.

By the time the second election came around, İmamoğlu had whipped up so much support that even people outside Istanbul, apparently forgetting where they lived, tried to vote for him. For instance, one person in Diyarbakir, 1,300 kilometres from Istanbul, turned up at a local polling station hoping to cast a vote.

People cancelled their holidays to vote: airlines allowed them to reschedule their flights for free, and the holiday resort of Bodrum jokily put out the travel advice: 'Don't come to Bodrum on 23 June as heavy snowfall is expected and the beaches will be shut.' The average temperature in Bodrum at that time of year is 30°C.

want to 'humanely harass' the lizards by spraying them with water, or by 'creating an unwelcome atmosphere' by hanging CDs in trees so the iguanas will be scared off by the glint. 'Unfortunately, the message has been conveyed that we are asking the public to just go out there and shoot them up,' they announced. 'This is not what we are about; this is not the "wild west".'

IN MEMORIAM

Facebook stopped suggesting that users invite dead people to parties.

When someone dies, their friends' Facebook accounts often suggest they get in touch with the deceased. They may also be prompted to wish their dead friend a happy birthday or invite them to events. This can understand-ably be upsetting, and so Facebook pledged to deploy artificial intelligence to stop such messages being received. However, the company's chief operating officer wouldn't guarantee that some won't make their way through, so it might be as well to click the site's 'Delete After Death' button in Settings. If you do so, as soon as Facebook is informed of your death, all data about you will be automatically erased.

If a recent Oxford University study is to be believed, 'Delete After Death' might be no bad idea. This func-tion ensures that your data is completely erased from the site when you die and can't be sold or used by any private companies. At current registration levels there will be plenty of data for these companies to harvest; according to some estimates, if people's accounts aren't deleted post mortem, by the end of this century more than four billion Facebook 'users' will be very much inactive (i.e. deceased).

INDECISIVE POLITICIANS

By Anna Ptaszynski

All of us sometimes struggle to make and
stick to our decisions, whether it's choosing
food from a menu, selecting a pair of socks
to match our mood or deciding whether it's
a beer day, a wine day or an absinthe day.
And so we could all sympathise with the plight of the handful of Labour
and Conservative, pro-EU MPs who broke away from their respective
parties in February. Many critics claimed to be confused by their
attempts to a) form a new party and b) give it a name. In actual fact, it
was all perfectly comprehensible – so long as you quit your job,
abandoned your social life, and committed yourself to paying incredibly
close attention 24 hours a day to what was going on. But just in case you
didn't do that, here's the gist.

In February, seven MPs abandoned the Labour party and formed **The
Independent Group** (sometimes known as **TIG**). Soon afterwards
they were joined by three renegade Conservative MPs, and over the
next couple of months this new grouping started going by the name
Change UK. Wily journalists quickly shortened that to **CHUK**, largely
in order to make fun of its resemblance to the name of the group's
spokesperson, Chuka Umunna. When the MPs did officially register,
they did so as **Change UK – The Independent Group**, apparently
trying to have their (disappointingly dry) cake and eat it.

There followed a triumphant European election in which they failed to
win any new seats, despite fielding an array of candidates that included
former BBC newsreader Gavin Esler, former deputy Prime Minister of
Poland Jacek Rostowski, Boris Johnson's sister, and Sophie Ellis-Bextor's
dad. Six of their eleven MPs promptly abandoned ship, including leader

Heidi Allen and party namesake, Chuka. The rest ended up in a dispute with petitions website Change.org, who threatened legal action on the grounds of name-theft, and so the fivesome passed themselves off as **Continuity Change UK** for a couple of weeks, before asking to be renamed **The Independent Group for Change**. Umunna had meanwhile defected to the Lib Dems, presumably yearning for a place Where Everybody Knows Your Name, while Allen was busy launching **The Independents**, 'a new home for independent politicians', and simult-aneously setting up a new cross-party alliance, **Unite to Remain**, which included but was not limited to the remaining members of **The Independent Group for Change**.

While the nation watched, utterly gripped as this series of identity crises played out, I reflected on the profoundly uninspiring nature of every one of the above options. How hard can it be to come up with a party name that doesn't sound as though it was generated by an algorithm set to Middle Manager Mode? Other countries manage it. Take, for instance, the Polish Beer Lovers' Party. This formed in 1990 with the actually-quite-sensible aim of transforming Poland's vodka-drinking culture, which was leading to widespread alcoholism, into a more innocuous but still fun beer-drinking culture. Despite starting out as a prank, they got 16 seats in parliament, although tragically they split soon afterwards into two factions, Big Beer and Small Beer (I know which side I would have picked). Its frustrated leader made a speech proclaiming, 'Beer is neither big, nor small, it is just tasty.' Truly the Martin Luther King of beer-based politics.

Poland has long since abandoned the original beer lovers' noble aims. For many years, the party of government has been the Law and Justice party, Prawo i Sprawiedliwość, which is commonly known by its acronym – so after all that talk of good beer, Poland ended up with PiS.

But back to Britain, and what next for our fledgling party of Remainers in the UK Parliament, who have gone by almost twice as many names as they have MPs? Well, it's not entirely clear, but I suggest they start by talking it out over, or at least drowning their sorrows in, a pint of really good ale.

INCISIVE POLITICIANS

Bhutan's prime minister winds down by cutting people up.

'Some people play golf, some do archery, and I like to operate,' Dr Lotay Tshering told a reporter from the French news agency Agence France-Presse. 'I will continue doing this until I die.' The prime minister holds the title of 'honorary standby surgeon' at the Jigme Dorji Wangchuck National Referral Hospital and, because of the lack of qualified physicians in the country, is always on call if somebody needs emergency abdominal surgery. In fact at one stage Tshering was the only urological surgeon in the whole of Bhutan. Before going into politics he regularly appeared on television to give advice about health and answer medical queries from the public.

Bhutan values its healthcare professionals very highly. So much so, in fact, that in June it was announced that, along with teachers, they would be getting a huge pay rise that would make them the highest-paid civil servants in the country. There was no suggestion that this decision was related to the PM's part-time role as a urological surgeon, though it's hard not to suspect that he might have been taking the piss.

INFLUENCERS

One of the year's hottest new Instagram destinations was a toxic waste dump.

The lake just outside the Russian city of Novosibirsk is nicknamed the 'Siberian Maldives', due to its mesmerising turquoise hue. This year the Siberian Generating Company was forced to warn visitors that it's not a good idea to swim in it – it is an ash dump, and the beautiful colours come from toxic chemicals that can cause a severe allergic reaction. The energy firm's plea was pretty clear: 'WE VERY MUCH ASK THAT THOSE CHASING SELFIES NOT FALL INTO THE ASH DUMP.' Sadly, the warnings simply attracted more visitors, wanting a good background for wedding photos or scantily clad social-media posts.

The anti-influencer backlash continued around the world. One business owner in the Philippines was hailed a hero after announcing that visitors would not be able to pay for drinks at his bar, food in his restaurant or beds in his hotel with social-media 'influence' rather than actual money. The exhausted proprietor, Gianluca Casaccia, had received more than a hundred messages asking for freebies, and posted on Facebook that he wasn't interested in letting people stay, eat or drink for free. Perhaps irritatingly for him, his post was then shared more than 3,000 times and generated considerable publicity. (Exactly the same thing happened to an ice-cream-van man, Joe Nicchi, who put a sign in his van this year saying, 'Influencers pay double'.)

One breakout influencer of 2019 was Jose Simms, a wanted criminal suspect in Connecticut. He struck a deal with police that he would turn himself in, if they managed to get 15,000 'likes' for his 'Wanted' poster on Facebook. (He demanded 20,000 at first, but they haggled him down.) They achieved that number in less than 48 hours, but Simms still refused to hand himself over. The police should have been able to work out that might happen: he was wanted for seven counts of failure to appear in court. Simms criticised the police mugshot of him, saying it was 'trash'. The police told him, 'It's the only one we had . . . hopefully we will get a "good" one soon.' Within a month they got their chance, when Simms finally handed himself in.

Another row concerning social media and toxic waste came in the wake of the hit Sky TV show *Chernobyl*. Multiple media outlets reported that influencers had started taking scantily-clad selfies at the site. However, the *Atlantic* investigated and found almost nobody was actually doing it.

INTRODUCING THE BAND

Ladies and gentlemen, please give it up for . . . on the mandolin, a Frenchman in a barrel (*see* **Adventuring**); (not) on drums, the drummer for Franz Ferdinand (*see* **Celebrity Tittle-Tattle**); on violin, the Italian town of Cremona (*see* **Quiet**); on saxophone, the New Zealand Conservation Department (*see* **Sax Appeal**); on guitar, the president of Turkmenistan (*see* **Songs, Berdy**); and on vocals, the endangered nightingales of Britain (*see* **Songs, Birdie**).

INVENTIONS

Owners of the world's most technologically advanced trainers found they couldn't do up their own laces.

Nike launched trainers with inbuilt, phone-app-controlled motors that enabled users to adjust the tightness automatically. They cost about £300. Unfortunately, those with Android phones often reported that the app failed to connect, with the result that the self-tightening trainers didn't actually fit.

Other inventions of the year included:

▶ A sticker that keeps food fresh. It is coated with salt and beeswax, which sucks up ethylene, the ripening chemical that causes fruit to go off. The sticker currently works best on pears, mangos, avocados and apples and could save billions of pounds in food waste a year.

▶ A mattress that nudges you away from your partner if you start getting too near them in bed. Sadly, this one exists only in prototype form. Built by the Ford motor company, it is designed to stop bed-hogging, and employs a 'lane-keeping' technology similar to the kind used in cars, which nudges the steering wheel the right way if it spots that a car has drifted out of its lane.

▶ A pillow that cancels out the noise of snoring. Currently only a prototype, this works just like noise-cancelling headphones, 'reversing' the sound as the sleeper snores. It then plays that anti-noise through speakers on the pillow of the snorer's partner, so that the snores are cancelled out.

▶ A drone cannon, which was invented in South Africa and fires seeds into soil at up to 300 metres a second – faster than a passenger jet. It's so fast that it can theoretically plant 20,000 trees a day.

▶ And a 'Consent Condom', which requires four hands to open it and was designed to emphasise the importance of consensual sex. It instantly became controversial. Some people worked out how to open it by themselves. Others objected that it wasn't suitable for disabled people. And some argued that it completely misconstrued the idea of consent. The firm responsible, Tulipán, pointed out it was just a design and was never intended to be commercially available, although that would rather seem to defeat the object of the exercise.

IRONY MAN ▶

The world's most sarcastic robot is SO not annoying at all.

The idea behind Irony Man is that irony-proficient robots tend to come across as more natural and trust-worthy than their straight-talking counterparts. The 30-centimetre-tall prototype combines a deadpan facial expression with the ability to speak in opposites, and to add appropriately sarcastic emphasis. For instance, it will change the phrase 'I hate rain. I usually have a bad mood when it rains' to 'Super! I utterly love raining', with the 'utterly' exaggeratedly emphasised.

When a small sample of students met Irony Man, they did indeed find him more likeable than a standard robot. However, there are glitches that still need irony-ing out – not least the problem that, as the maker admits, 'The robot is not yet able to determine whether and when there is a good moment to employ irony.' In sensitive situations, Irony Man is currently liable to make an inappropriately facetious comment, and so cause irritation or offence.

IN WHICH WE LEARN . . .

Which journalist avoided cooked-up charges, how to deal with a habitual poacher, why some rubbish caused a simmering row, and why Boris got roasted at Glastonbury.

JOHNSON, BORIS ▶

More people shouted 'F*** Boris' at Glastonbury than voted for him to become prime minister in July.

▼

A YouGov survey revealed that the top five words used to describe Boris Johnson by those who said they liked him were 'charismatic', 'eccentric', 'flamboyant', 'different' and 'intelligent'. The top five words among those who didn't like him were 'untrustworthy', 'buffoon', 'idiot', 'liar' and 'clown'. When asked to place him in the most suitable Hogwarts house, 42% of respondents selected Slytherin – and this was the popular choice even among people who claimed to like him.

British rapper Stormzy became the first black solo British headliner at the Glastonbury Festival, and celebrated by getting 100,000 people to chant an obscenity about the former mayor of London as he performed his number-one single 'Vossi Bop'. It didn't affect the outcome of the leadership election. A month later Johnson was prime minister, thanks to the votes of fewer than 100,000 Conservative Party members.

During his leadership campaign, Johnson claimed that his main hobby outside work was painting wine boxes to look like London buses. Some people suggested this might be an amazing strategic move, which meant that anyone googling 'bus' would find details of this odd pastime rather than his association with the infamous Vote Leave bus, which claimed that £350 million a week could go to the NHS instead of to the EU. If that was the plan, then it didn't work for long – a few weeks later Johnson hit the headlines for throwing Sir Kim Darroch 'under the bus' after the diplomat called Donald Trump 'inept', 'insecure' and 'incompetent' and felt forced to resign.

Despite him now having the top job in the country, there are some things about Boris Johnson that we don't know. We're not sure, for example, how many children he has, and we don't know why he suddenly decided to call himself Boris when he was at Eton (Boris is actually his middle name; his real name is Alexander). We do know, however, that when he was five years old, a young Boris told his sister that when he grew up he wanted to be 'World King'.

Johnson is not especially trusted. When surveyed, only 13 per cent of people said they would buy a used car from him, though more than twice as many did say that he was best placed to deliver ▮▮▮▮. Their confidence may have been thanks to the crack team he assembled to do that, which included two men who had previously made their livings dressed as a chicken. Both special adviser Ross Kempsell and director of communications Lee Cain, who had worn the bird suits to mock politicians, were given the job of aiding a man who had been mocked by an entire music festival. It seems that, for Boris, there are stormzy times ahead.

JOURNALISM ▶

A Russian journalist whose first article was about someone being arrested on allegedly fabricated drug charges was arrested on allegedly fabricated drug charges.

Ivan Golunov hit headlines worldwide when he was charged with possessing and dealing in the illegal drug mephedrone. Coincidentally, the first piece of investigative journalism Golunov ever published, for a magazine called *Bolshoi Gorod* ten years ago, was the story of an artist detained in Siberia on false drug charges. Golunov's journalism always focused on investigating institutional corruption like this. This time round he was investigating the monopoly that government cronies allegedly have on the funeral industry, for which he'd already received a threat that read: 'There are enough vacant plots on these graveyards you keep writing about.' Two hours after he'd filed the report, he was in jail. Understandably, then, most commentators believed he'd been framed by the authorities and wrongfully arrested.

What propelled Golunov to international fame was the unprecedented response to his arrest. Although intimidation of journalists is relatively common in Russia, this case unexpectedly captured the public imagination. Hundreds of people queued for more than eight hours to take their turn mounting a single-person picket – the only sort of demonstration that's allowed without a permit. Eventually they threw caution to the winds and illegally protested en masse, leading to hundreds more arrests. Eight thousand fellow journalists signed a petition to express their solidarity with Golunov, while three of Russia's biggest-circulation newspapers, which are usually obedient to the state, ran exactly the same front page on 10 June, with the headline 'We are Ivan Golunov'. All copies of all three papers had sold out by lunchtime.

Following the outcry, the drug charges were abruptly dropped and officially blamed on incompetent police. Golunov was set free, to the amazement of many of his allies. Galina Timchenko, general director of *Meduza*, the publication to which Golunov contributed, said, 'Such miracles don't usually happen in Russia.'

JUDGES

A poacher in Missouri was made to watch Bambi *every month of his prison sentence.*

County judge Robert George sentenced deer-poacher David Berry to a year in prison. But he also believes in punishments that fit the crimes. So he stipulated that while incarcerated, the offender must undergo a monthly viewing of *Bambi*. (Although Berry was also found guilty of a firearms violation, he was not ordered to watch *John Wick* or *Scarface* while in prison.) Because the jail in which Berry was held has only one recreation room, the other prisoners had to be sent back to their cells during his monthly *Bambi*-fest. This, presumably, didn't make him very popular.

Michael Cicconetti of Ohio, who retired this year, is another judge who believes in appropriate sentences. In the last two years he's sentenced a schoolboy who stole a lifebuoy to work at a park handing out water-safety information; sent a woman who kept her dog in filthy conditions to spend eight hours in a disgusting landfill site; and ordered a man who pushed over a portable toilet to clean up animal manure at county fairs.

In other judging news:

▶ The Italian Supreme Court ruled it a crime to use your partner's Facebook account without their permission, even if they have previously given you their password. The ruling was made after a case that involved a suspicious Sicilian husband monitoring his wife's social-media use. The maximum penalty is five years in prison.

▶ After calling the Ayatollah Ali Khamenei a despot, an Iranian dissident was sentenced to read three books and rewrite them by hand, word-for-word.

▶ And a man in Salisbury excused himself from jury duty on the grounds that he was scheduled to be the judge in the case in question. His appeal to be excused was rejected at first, and he was told to apply to the resident judge if he still wanted exemption. He replied, 'I am the resident judge.'

JUNK ▶

The Philippines threatened to declare war on Canada if it didn't collect its bins.

In 2013 and 2014, Canada shipped 2,500 tons of rubbish to the Philippines for recycling. But Filipino inspectors found that it wasn't 100 per cent recyclable, which meant they couldn't deal with it and Canada would have to take it back. Having waited five years for them to do so, President Rodrigo Duterte lost his temper, first saying he'd sail the rubbish back to Canada himself and dump it there, then upping the ante by threatening war. This may have been rhetorical hyperbole, but the spat nevertheless got so out of hand that the Philippines recalled their Canadian ambassador and issued a travel ban on all Canadians.

Eventually Canada agreed to foot the bill for transporting the garbage back to its shores. The Philippines' secretary of foreign affairs waved it off gladly, tweeting 'Baaaaaaaa bye, as we say it.' The travel ban was lifted and the envoys returned. As for the six-year-old rubbish, it ended its days in a Vancouver waste-to-energy plant, where it was processed and turned into electricity to power surrounding homes.

China experienced a similar problem to the Philippines when British waste firm Biffa sent it a consignment of what it claimed was recyclable paper, but was in fact a mix of waste that included dirty nappies, sanitary towels, condoms and an umbrella. And in India a pile of rubbish dubbed the 'Mount Everest of Rubbish' grew so high that the Supreme Court ruled it should be fitted with aircraft warning lights. Currently more than 65 metres high, within a year the pile will be taller than the Taj Mahal.

JUNK FOOD

For a fracas in Five Guys, *see* **Apposite**; for KFC on TfL, *see* **Clamping Down**; for Nando No.1, see **Dining, Fine**; for shaking things up at Burger King, *see* **Milkshaking**; for pizzas in the palace, *see* **Queen, The**; and for McEmbassies, *see* **Tourists**.

IN WHICH WE LEARN . . .

What has happened to Franz Kafka's works, which Georgians are fighting to be king of The Castle, how Lorraine Kelly won The Trial, and which country's pop stars enjoy a Metamorphosis.

K-POP

The South Korean government complained that its pop stars were too good-looking.

'Are the singers on TV music shows twins?' the country's gender ministry asked. 'They seriously look identical. Most of them are skinny and have similar hairstyles and makeup with outfits exposing their bodies.' Moreover, it said, these identical-looking pop stars were promoting 'lookism' – an unhealthy obsession with one's looks. The ministry therefore issued a new set of guidelines on the number of K-pop stars who should be allowed to appear on TV shows. An immediate backlash followed, from a country that still remembers a military dictatorship that cracked down on long hair and short skirts in the 1980s, and the government quickly backed down.

The K-beauty industry, which promotes unnaturally pale skin and perfect pink 'heart-shaped' lips, is worth an annual $20 billion for the Korean economy. And the K-pop phenomenon is worth even more: the most popular band, BTS, generates $3.6 billion on its own. In April they became only the third group in 50 years to have three number-one albums on the US Billboard 200 chart in less than 12 months, the other two being The Beatles and The Monkees.

Despite their success, BTS announced in August that they planned to take an 'extended break' from recording. Other K-pop stars are given less choice in the matter. It's very common for some of them to disappear from the limelight in a matter of months. One star, Leeteuk, from the band Super Junior, even set up a support group called Milk Club for fallen idols. Unfortunately it is now defunct.

Some K-Pop bands aren't actually Korean. Z Boys and Z Girls market themselves as K-Pop and sing in Korean, but are from Taiwan, Indonesia, Vietnam, the Philippines, India, Japan and Thailand. Another band, EXP Edition, are all from America and go by the tagline 'Born in NY, made in Seoul'.

KILLING, MAKING A

By JAMES HARKIN

WARNING: the following article includes massive spoilers, in particular for anyone reading this book a year before it is published.

One of the most important things to consider when you write any book about current affairs is how it will affect the world if someone buys it, then travels back in time and uses the information it contains to change the future. It's a problem that plagued the authors of 'Grays Sports Almanac', and something that certainly keeps me awake at night. Do we want to ensure that the brittle fabric of space-time is kept safe, or do we want to cash in on that lucrative time-traveller market? In the end, I think the commercial aspect has to win out, and so for those of you who bought this book to make a quick buck, dust off the old DeLorean, because below is my gambling guide for 2019.

Before we get to the bets themselves, there are the moral and legal aspects to consider. Gamble Responsibly. When the Fun Stops, Stop! Gambling is generally a mug's game. The bookmaker almost always wins (though that maxim was slightly called into question this year when the 'Financial Times' did an investigation into illegal gambling and accidentally won £2,000 in the process). What's more, the difference between winning and losing often comes down to an unexpected quirk of fate. This year, for example, you could bet on whether the National Anthem at the Super Bowl would last more or less than 1 minute 50 seconds. In the event Gladys Knight finished the final words, 'home of the brave', on 1:49, much to the delight of people who voted on 'under'; however, she then repeated the words 'the brave', meaning that 'over' was the winner. Gamblers were not very happy. Well, half of them weren't.

Luckily for those who like a flutter, 2019 was full of upsets. Despite the popularity of Liverpool striker Mo Salah, which led to a fall of 18.9 per cent in hate crimes against Muslims in the city, it was his defensive team-mate Virgil van Dijk who won the Premier League Player of the Season. He was 125/1 at the start of the season. Harry and Meghan's first child was 100/1 to be named Archie, which was seen as only 10 times more likely than the rank outsider Rodney. (SPOILER ALERT: If you're not a time-traveller and still don't know the ending to 'Game of Thrones', look away now . . .) In 'Game of Thrones' the fact that the Iron Throne was destroyed by dragons meant that bookmakers paid out on both Bran being the eventual leader of Westeros, and the fact that 'nobody' would sit on the throne. And there was also a double payout in horse racing when a race at Sandown came down to a photo-finish and the photo was taken from the wrong place on the track. The resulting confusion forced bookmakers to pay people who had bet on either horse.

Anyway, enough chat. Fire up the flux capacitor, get to a bookmaker in 2018 and place £1 on an accumulator that all of the events below will happen:

Andy Ruiz Jr to beat Anthony Joshua	25/1
Archie to be royal baby name	100/1
Toronto Raptors to win NBA Championship	60/1
Virgil van Dijk to win Player of the Season	125/1
Olivia Colman to win Best Actress at the Oscars	11/2
Tiger Woods to win The Masters	14/1
Liberals to retain power in the Australian elections	4/1
Nobody to sit on the Iron Throne	11/8
Bran to rule Westeros	14/1
'One for Rosie' to win the 1.10 at Sandown on 8 March 2019	12/1
'Third Wind' to win the 1.10 at Sandown on 8 March 2019	9/1

This won't just make you a millionaire, or even a billionaire. The amount of physical money in the world is estimated to be around $36.8 trillion, so I've picked 10 events that, for a £1 stake, will win you every single penny on Earth.

KAFKAESQUE

Kafka's papers were stuck in a bureaucratic nightmare.

Franz Kafka, the king of satirising faceless bureaucracy, didn't publish much in his lifetime – just a few short stories and his famous novella *The Metamorphosis*. When he died, he gave his papers to his friend and biographer, Max Brod, with the orders that they be destroyed.

Recognising that the manuscripts were absolutely priceless, Brod ignored this request and went on to publish many of the stories. He kept the rest of the writer's papers in a suitcase. As befits a friend of Kafka, Brod's life was a little on the unusual side: he lived in a *ménage à trois* relationship with a woman called Esther Hoffe and her husband Otto. When Brod died, he bequeathed the papers to Esther, who guarded them jealously. She in turn passed them to her daughters on her death. And so the documents ended up in Israel with Eva Hoffe, who kept them in a switched-off refrigerator in her apartment along with 'between 40 and 100' cats.

Israel's National Library issued a lawsuit in 2008 to retrieve the papers. The suit bounced around various courtrooms for more than a decade – outliving Ms Hoffe, who died in 2018 – until this year Israel's supreme court finally ruled that they should be sent to Israel's National Library, where they will soon be made available to the public.

KELLY, LORRAINE

Lorraine Kelly argued that she appears on TV playing a character called Lorraine Kelly.

It was a strange legal argument, but an important one for Ms Kelly's tax status. The thing is that if you are self-employed you can start a limited company, which offers certain tax allowances. However, there are rules in place to stop people taking advantage.

In Lorraine Kelly's case, if she is 'just' a presenter, then she is a normal employee; but if, on the other hand, she's an actor playing a role, then she counts as self-employed. If she's a normal employee, she doesn't get the tax benefits. If she's self-employed, she does.

The courts ultimately agreed with her assessment that she's putting on an act. The judgement stated that 'We should make clear we do not doubt that Ms Kelly is an entertaining lady, but the point is that for the time Ms Kelly is contracted to perform live on air she is public "Lorraine Kelly".'

Real life and fiction were also blurred in the UK courts when comedian Steve Coogan escaped a lengthy driving ban by claiming that his alter ego, Alan Partridge, needed to drive for an upcoming television series, since driving 'defines his character'.

KILOGRAM

The kilogram stopped being a thing. Literally.

Whenever you measured an item's weight in kilograms in the past, you were indirectly comparing it to an actual lump of metal in Paris, or more specifically a piece of platinum-iridium alloy. This was the physical prototype kilogram. The problem was that, even though that object had been taken out of its vault only three times in its 130-year lifespan, it was somehow losing weight: since 1889 it had lost approximately the mass of an eyelash. True, that's not the sort of discrepancy that will ruin a cake, but it could cause problems for, say, medicines that have to be weighed out with extreme precision. There are multiple theories as to what was causing the apparent weight loss. Scientists speculated that maybe it was the copies that were getting heavier, not the prototype that was getting lighter; or maybe the original had been cleaned too vigorously and had lost a few atoms in the process.

One thing was clear, though: the problem had to be fixed. So, on 20 May the kilogram was liberated from its physical reference point. From now on, it's defined in reference to Planck's constant. A constant is a figure in mathematical or scientific equations that always stays the same. For instance, pi is the constant that's used to help work out the area of a circle, and it always stays the same. Planck's constant is fixed at 0.000 000 000 000 000 000 000 000 006 626 joule-seconds, or about one-billionth of a billionth of a billionth of 1. It is the same everywhere in the universe.

So now, instead of using normal weighing scales to get a really accurate measurement, you should employ a Kibble balance. This doesn't follow the traditional route of weighing something by comparing it to the mass of another physical object, but compares it to the amount of electromagnetic force needed to lift it up. Full-size Kibble balances are huge, require multiple advanced physicists to operate them, and are unafford-able for all but the unbelievably wealthy. But a Lego version was built to demonstrate to the public how they work, and this inspired scientists to build mini Kibble balances, which are about the size of a suitcase and sell for $50,000, so they can be bought by labs around the world. For the rest of us, conventional weighing scales will still do the trick.

KINGS AND QUEENS

Two Georgians fought over a crown that has been defunct since 1810.

The Georgian royal family was dispossessed when the country was absorbed into the Russian Empire in the early 19th century, but they lived on in exile and eventually split into two branches, both of which claim the non-existent throne. In 2009, this seemingly pointless feud was resolved when Davit Bagration-Mukhraneli married Ana Bagration-Gruzinsky and brought the two lines together: tragically, in 2013 the couple divorced and the fault lines reopened.

One of three men to claim the defunct throne of France, Henri d'Orléans, Count of Paris, died in January, 226 years to the day after his distant cousin Louis XVI was guillotined.

The two families found themselves in court, bick-ering over who has the right to speak on behalf of the defunct royal family and give away 'knighthoods'. The case, which continues, has involved both legal teams questioning the rivals' royal authenticity: at one stage historian Giorgi Otkhmezuri, an expert witness, was asked by a lawyer to 'recall in detail what happened in 1512'.

KNOCK-OFFS

For Fauxrarris, *see* **Dictionary**; for Pooey Puitton, *see* **A Handbag!?**; and for some paintings that didn't look quite Reich, *see* **Under the Hammer**.

KOONS, JEFF

The most expensive artwork by a living artist is a silver bunny that symbolises masturbation.

Jeff Koons's 'Rabbit', a stainless-steel sculpture of a bunny that looks a bit like a shiny balloon animal, went for $91.1 million – the most expensive artwork ever sold by a living artist. It was bought by US treasury secretary Steven Mnuchin's father (he's a dealer and was buying on behalf of someone else). Koons said that the artwork is a symbol of 'being a leader, an orator, the carrot to the mouth is a symbol of masturbation. I see Pop Art as feeding people a dialogue that they can participate in. Instead of the artist being lost in this masturbative act of the subjective, the artist lets the public get lost in the act of masturbation.'

KUMBH MELA ▶

220 million people went on holiday to the same place at the same time.

Over a 50-day period in spring, Prayagraj (normal population: around a million) hosted the largest gathering of human beings in history, the Kumbh Mela pilgrimage. The total number of attendants who come to spend holy days bathing in the Ganges is about the same as the entire human population of the Earth at the time of Jesus Christ.

Such an enormous event poses obvious administration problems: 185 miles of temporary roads had to be built, and 120,000 toilets were shipped in. And the Lost and Found office was sent into overdrive. The *Guardian* gave examples of announcements that were broadcast, including: 'It is Babu speaking, I have lost my wallet and brother. Please come here the moment you hear this.' And: 'Whoever has taken my trousers, that were drying on my car, at least return the car keys from the pocket. You can keep the trousers.'

IN WHICH WE LEARN . . .

Who can fight with light, what's slower than a mower, why the Swiss are never remiss, and who got lucky with a fortune cookie.

LAGERFELD, KARL ▶

The world said goodbye to one of fashion's greatest designers, mourned by the whole industry (and his cat).

Karl Lagerfeld died this year aged 85. Or possibly 83, or 81 – he lied a lot about his age. He was renowned for his sunglasses, ponytail, high collar and fingerless gloves, as well as his designs. One of his greatest creations was his own back-story: according to Lagerfeld, his father was a German condensed-milk magnate and his mother an accomplished violinist; he grew up on a 12,000-acre estate and, aged four, had his own valet, so that he could change his clothes several times a day. Most of this was untrue: his father was nothing more than a moderately successful businessman, his mother was a lingerie saleswoman, and he grew up in the suburbs. As a child in Germany after the war, he and his family had to live in a cowshed for a year when the British Army requisitioned the family home. Even his surname wasn't authentic: he dropped the last letter from his real name – Lagerfeldt – to make it more marketable.

Lagerfeld went on to head Chanel for three decades and became famous for putting on extraordinary shows. He once had 240 tons of snow imported from Sweden to France and sculpted into an iceberg by 35 artisans over the course of a month, just to provide a backdrop for a catwalk. Thanks to his distinctive look, he became an icon in his own right: when Mattel released a Karl Lagerfeld Barbie doll in 2014, priced at $200, it sold out within an hour.

When Lagerfeld died, an undisclosed amount of his £153 million fortune went to his cat, Choupette. Choupette was a huge feature of his life, and lived almost as extravagantly as Lagerfeld did. She had a modelling contract, through which she made £2.3 million,

---

▼

After Lagerfeld's death, a group of arachnologists named a spider after him. According to one of them, Danilo Harms, the spider's black eyes reminded them of Lagerfeld's sunglasses.

advertising German cars and Japanese cosmetics. She also had two maids, a partnership with the German stuffed-toy firm Steiff, an Instagram feed with more than 200,000 followers, and her own website where diary entries were written on her behalf. Despite all these accoutrements, Choupette still had a taste for the simple things in life: one of her main hobbies was playing with shopping bags. Having outlived her owner, Choupette attended Karl's cremation in a special Louis Vuitton bag designed especially for her.

LAGER-FILLED

The world also said goodbye to the Aussie prime minister who broke a world record for drinking beer.

Bob Hawke admitted that his ability to down a yard of ale in 11 seconds probably made him more popular with the Aussie electorate than anything else he ever did. He was at Oxford University at the time, and had come to dinner without his gown ('some bastard' had borrowed it, he alleged). The punishment for failing to be correctly dressed was 'sconcing' – downing 2½ pints of beer in less time than it took the 'Sconcemaster' – or having to pay for a round of drinks. Hawke was broke at the time, so he accepted the challenge, saying later that 'necessity became the mother of ingestion'.

This wasn't the only record he broke. Hawke went on to become the Labor Party's longest-serving leader and guided them to an unprecedented four election victories between 1983 and 1991. He was – for a politician – extremely well liked, achieving the highest-ever approval rating for an Australian leader. He took office when the country's then-PM, Malcolm Fraser, called an election, thinking he'd be running against Labor leader Bill Hayden. Unfortunately for Fraser, just 20 minutes after he called it, the much more popular Hawke ousted Hayden and took over the Labor Party, meaning that Fraser inadvertently found himself running against the beer-loving man-of-the-people instead, and lost spectacularly.

Hawke was a good cricketer at university, but his most famous cricketing moment came while he was PM, during a parliamentarians-vs-press match, when he was struck in the face by a ball. His glasses smashed, sending shards of glass into his eyes. He was rushed to hospital, but returned to the stands to watch the afternoon session, complete with eye patch.

Hawke had a sizeable ego. When he was just 15 years old, he told friends he'd end up being prime minister, and in his memoirs he claimed responsibility for ending apartheid. Mandela, he said, had told him after leaving prison, 'I'm here because of you', and had adopted his famous Truth and Reconciliation programme on the Australian premier's advice. Hawke's name does not appear in Mandela's memoirs.

▼

When Australians boycotted Frank Sinatra's music in 1971 for sexist comments he had made and refused to apologise for, Hawke had a drink and a chat with Frank, persuaded him to apologise and thus ended the boycott.

As well as having a penchant for drinking and partying, Hawke was a notorious womaniser. When he was a trade-union leader in 1971, he was named 'Victorian Father of the Year', which his own wife called an 'absurd' choice. They eventually divorced in 1995 and he married his biographer. Hawke admitted that at times he relied too heavily on alcohol, and though he managed to swear off it completely throughout his time in office, he embraced it again soon afterwards and would make a show of downing glasses of beer at cricket games, always to the delight of the crowds. Finally, in 2017, he officially lent his approval, and name, to a new beer – Hawke's Lager – which, according to the company that produces it, is 'built on the values of a national icon'.

LATIN LOVERS

Primum nuntium radiophonio latine in mundo fuit finita.

Nuntii Latini, a Finnish five-minute weekly news broadcast in Latin, was once the only regular Latin radio bulletin in the world. On 14 June it broadcast its last show. The bulletin had been running for 30 years, but found that owing to a new glut of Latin shows, it had lost its unique selling point, and so decided to close down.

As *Nuntii Latini* jumped off the bandwagon, the Vatican jumped onto it, announcing a new five-minute Latin podcast called *Hebdomada Papae, notitiae vaticanae latine redditae*, or 'The Pope's Week – Vatican news in Latin'. It's a risky undertaking. While programmes entirely in Latin are evidently becoming more and more popular, it seems unlikely that podcasts will ever catch on.

LAWNMOWERS

The world's fastest lawnmower went from 0 to 100 mph in just over six seconds.

At the Austrian Grand Prix, Honda won its first Formula 1 race for 13 years, but arguably an even greater feat was achieved by its Mean Mower V2, which broke the record for the fastest lawnmower in the world. As well as accelerating to 100 mph faster than a Ferrari Enzo, and having a better power-to-weight ratio than a Bugatti Chiron, it can reach speeds in excess of 150 mph. And it can cut grass. It was driven on the day by racing driver Jess Hawkins, who spends most of her time as a stunt driver on *Fast and Furious Live*.

Less fast, but probably more furious, was Andy Maxfield, who broke the world record for the furthest anyone has ever pushed a lawnmower. He managed 58 miles, though he ended up with severe dehydration and breathing problems and threw up black blood. He didn't even have the luxury of enjoying the view on his walk, as it consisted of circling Blackburn Rovers' football pitch 273 times. He did at least raise some money for the Alzheimer's Society.

Also taking it on the chin was David Rush from Idaho, who broke the record for balancing a running lawnmower on one's chin. He kept the mower there for 3 minutes and 52 seconds. Rush has more than 100 other records to his name, including putting 146 blueberries in his mouth, having 100 lit candles in his mouth at the same time, and identifying the most flavours of ice cream in one minute while blindfolded (12). Given that he trained for more than three years to break the lawnmower record, it feels mean not to mention what he's raising awareness of, so we'll say it: he was raising awareness of Science, Technology, Engineering and Mathematics (STEM) education.

A man from Burnley was sentenced to 14 days in prison after he stole a robotic lawnmower whose GPS led police to his home while he slept. The *Lancashire Telegraph* reported that the thief had been 'grassed up' by the mower.

LAUNCHES

The following were all scheduled for lift-off this year . . .

A pair of balls. Charity bosses sent a pair of prosthetic testicles into space to raise awareness of testicular cancer. The chief executive of the Robin Cancer Trust said, 'This delivered something we've never seen before – a balls-eye view of the UK'.

Artificial meteors. A firm in Tokyo, ALE Co. Ltd, launched a micro-satellite full of little balls (not that sort). They will be released in 2020 and as they hit the atmosphere will hopefully unleash the world's first artificial meteor shower.

152 dead people. Elon Musk's rocket, *Falcon Heavy*, held the ashes of 152 people who wanted to rest in space, including those of Bill Pogue, an astronaut who worked on board NASA's first space station. The special 'cosmic urns' will orbit the earth until they burn up like shooting stars.

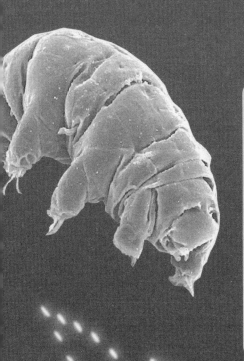

Eight-legged space pigs. An Israeli probe, Beresheet, crashed into the Moon – the first lunar crash since 1971. Designed to be a 'backup' of Earth, it carried human DNA samples, a 'lunar library' the size of a DVD holding almost all of Wikipedia, and thousands of live tardigrades. Tardigrades are tiny eight-legged animals, also known as 'moss piglets' or 'water bears', which are virtually indestructible. They can survive temperatures as low as -200°C and as high as 149°C, and they're also able to endure life without water or air, and at very high levels of radiation. The chances, then, are that these moss piglets are still alive on the Moon.

A big Pepsi advert. Pepsi's Russian branch abandoned an attempt to project adverts on the night sky using 200 satellites flying in formation. The plan was created by StartRocket, a firm which is planning to launch small satellites, but after a massive backlash from astronomers Pepsi quickly distanced themselves from it.

LIGHTSABERS

Lightsaber duelling is now an official competitive sport in France.

During a blackout in New York City, some residents took to directing traffic with toy lightsabers.

The French Fencing Federation officially recognised the lightsaber as a weapon of choice. It will now have the same status as the three traditional blades: the foil, epée and sabre. Explaining that this formed part of an initiative to reach out to youngsters, the Federation's secretary said, 'With young people today, it's a real public health issue. They don't do any sport and only exercise with their thumbs.'

Obviously, real lightsabers are hard to find – the ones that can cut your head off, anyway – so the swords used in the French leagues are made from tough plastic, lit from within by LED bulbs. But they do make the satisfying 'swoosh' noise, which is crucial. The organiser of a national tournament, Michel Ortiz, told the *Guardian* that 'most of all, we wanted it to produce something visual that looks like the movies'. This explains the rule that before you try to hit someone, the end of your lightsaber must start behind you, so that you end up making a big sweeping blow (much more filmic) rather than a quick pointy stab, which would be more efficient, but would look worse. May *Le Force* be with them all.

LIGHTSAVERS

A glow-in-the-dark cane caused a Titanic *family feud.*

The cane belonged to *Titanic* survivor Ella White, who had brought it aboard because she had an injured foot. It was very much a novelty item, being fitted with what was then state-of-the-art technology: a battery-powered electric light. Once the *Titanic* struck the iceberg, she adapted the gadget to the situation. According to

162

contemporary accounts, she waved it around from her lifeboat to attract rescue boats. *Titanic* expert Walter Lord said: 'Mrs J. Stuart White . . . appointed herself a sort of signalman . . . She had a cane with a built-in electric light, and during most of the night she waved it fiercely about, alternately helping and confusing everyone.'

Now, the auctioning of the cane has caused huge fights among those claiming to own it. The person who sold it, Brad Williams, argued that he inherited it from Ella's great-niece, but this was strongly denied by two brothers, John and Samuel Hoving, who insisted that the cane was given to their father, White's great-*nephew*, and that it disappeared from their family umbrella stand in the 1970s. It was sold for $62,500.

LIONS

For why the Lion King should be a lioness, *see* **Hakuna Matata**; for whom the lion sleeps with tonight, *see* **Pride**; and for the how the Lionesses became the Pride of England, *see* **World Cup, Football**.

LOST AND FOUND

The best place to lose your wallet is Switzerland.

Scientists conducted an experiment that involved handing in 17,000 'lost' wallets to officials in public places like banks, theatres or police stations, all over the world (the only continent they missed out was Antarctica). They then checked to see which ones were returned to their owners. What they found was that, almost universally, the more money a wallet contained, the more likely it was to be returned. Wallets with a

THE LONELIEST DUCK

Trevor, 'the world's loneliest duck', died at his home on the Pacific island of Niue. Nobody knows how he got there in 2018, though it's possible he was blown in from New Zealand by a storm. Because Niue has no rivers or lakes, Trevor had to live in a puddle which firefighters would often refill with their hoses. Locals discussed importing another duck to be his mate, but it was decided the puddle was only big enough for one. Before he died, Trevor made friends with a rooster, a chicken and a native weka bird, which all lived near the puddle.

THE LONELIEST SNAIL

George, 'the world's loneliest snail', was the last of a species of Hawaiian land snail called *Achatinella apexfulva*. Though referred to as a 'he', George was actually a hermaphrodite – he had both male and female parts. Unfortunately, George still needed a partner to reproduce and was unable to find one before his death, aged 14, on New Year's Day. One small part of him will live on, though – specifically a 2-millimetre snippet of his foot. Taken from him in 2017, this little clump of George's tissue is still alive in a deep freeze at the Frozen Zoo in San Diego.

THE LONELIEST BAT

The UK's last known greater mouse-eared bat lives alone in a tunnel in West Sussex for five months every year, during which time he stays almost completely motionless. He's been doing that for 17 years now, but nobody knows where he goes when he leaves the tunnel as nobody's ever seen him fly in or out. His story has been turned into a play, but rather than being five months of the actors motionlessly hanging upside down, the plot is instead about two bat spotters falling in love. The play, *Vespertilo* (which is also the genus of the bat), premiered in February in London, in a disused train tunnel.

THE LONELIEST FROG

Romeo, 'the world's loneliest frog', who was thought to be the last Sehuencas water frog, finally found a mate after a decade of solitude, thanks to scientists who located a female for him in a remote stream in Bolivia. Juliet, as she has inevitably been called, 'has beautiful eyes', according to one of the team who has probably been spending a bit too much time in the lab. At first the scientists worried she might not fancy Romeo, as he is shy, doesn't swim much and is 'a little overweight'. However, their first date went so well that they were moved to the same tank within days. Romantically, the moment they set up home together, Romeo started singing. Slightly less romantically he also attempted to mount her, but herpetologists reported that he needed 'more practice'.

large sum of money were returned 72 per cent of the time, compared with just 40 per cent for empty wallets. There were a few surprising results: for example, some wallets dropped at the Vatican and at anti-corruption bureaux never made it back. Switzerland came out top of the honesty stakes, with 76 per cent of wallets abandoned there making it back.

In other lost-and-found news:

▶ One of the five missing pieces of the ancient Lewis Chessmen set turned up in a Scottish family's drawer, having been missing for almost 200 years. The famous chessmen were originally found in the Outer Hebrides in 1831. The rediscovered piece sold for £735,000, having initially been bought by the family for a fiver in 1964.

▶ Papuan authorities started a hunt for nearly 300 cars, which the government had imported to drive world leaders to the Asia-Pacific Economic Cooperation forum the country hosted last year. Eventually the Maseratis and Bentleys – the most expensive cars – were tracked down, but 284 other vehicles remained mysteriously missing.

▶ Two large limestone reliefs, over 1000 years old and worth millions of pounds, had been missing since they were stolen from a Spanish church in 2004. This year they turned up in an English garden, after the thieves sold them as garden ornaments. The man who found them was Arthur Brand, an art detective nicknamed the 'Indiana Jones of the art world'.

▶ NASA thinks it has found the lunar lander from the Apollo 10 mission, 50 years after it went missing. Called 'Snoopy', it was used in a rehearsal for the Moon landing – the astronauts got into it, 50,000 feet above the Moon, then transferred back to their main command module (called 'Charlie Brown') and shot Snoopy off into space. Nick Howes from the Royal Astronomical Society, who has been looking for it since 2011, said, 'the approximate distance it travels in its orbit is 940 million kilometres. When you are looking for something four metres wide and the last reliable data you've got on it is 50 years ago, it's a bit tricky.' After eight years of hunting, he's 98 per cent sure they've found it – although it will be tough to verify: it won't be back in Earth's orbit for another 18 years.

LUCKY

An Australian man won AUD $46 million after accidentally buying two lottery tickets.

It was great news for the winner from Melbourne, whose two tickets had exactly the same, winning, numbers; but it was less good news for another player in Tasmania. The two men shared the AUD $70 million jackpot, but the Melbourne man's double-ticket meant that instead of a 50/50 split, the man from Tasmania only got one-third. Another interesting lottery split came a few months later in Colorado, where more than 2,000 people won a total of $7.8 million when a lottery that required players to pick four numbers came up with the incredibly popular combination 0-0-0-0.

One of the biggest individual wins of the year was in North Carolina, where a man won $344.6 million, with numbers that he found in a fortune cookie that he got at the end of a meal at a Vietnamese restaurant. He plans to use some of the money to visit Vietnam. Actually, lottery-winning numbers are often found in fortune cookies. In 2017, a mathematician called Walt Hickey looked at 1,050 groups of cookie-numbers and compared them to lottery numbers that had come up in the previous 20 years. He found that fortune-cookie-generated numbers turned a profit, while randomly generated numbers were likely to result in a large loss. But don't go out and buy a box of fortune cookies quite yet: his theory is that cookie companies simply used old successful numbers when printing their fortunes.

IN WHICH WE LEARN . . .

Where you'd find a village with no people, why the Arctic is wet wet wet, which fish needed some TLC, who was told 'no scrubs', and which milkshakes were brought to the attention of the boys from Scotland Yard.

MACABRE ▶

A funeral company said 2018 was a bad year for death – but 2019 should be a lot better.

Australia's largest private funeral company, InvoCare, told investors that its profits had been affected by 'soft market conditions, namely, a lower number of deaths', but added an assurance that the market was 'normalising'. Their logic is statistical – assuming that life expectancy and the overall population stay around the same, a lower-than-expected number of deaths one year probably means more deaths the next year.

Britain has the opposite problem. Because the provision of graveyards and crematoria has not kept in step with an increasing population, there is a burial crisis. One health expert has suggested that a solution might be to bury people along the sides of motorways and cycle paths. Former president of the Faculty of Public Health, John Ashton, argues that because people curate graveyards, this would also give us new green spaces and help the environment.

In other macabre news:

▶ The NHS warned that 'Dickensian' diseases are on the rise. Hospital visits for scarlet fever, malnutrition, whooping cough and gout have gone up by 3,000 per year since 2010 – a 52 per cent increase.

▶ A minivan driver in Nevada was stopped for driving in a lane reserved for vehicles with more than one occupant. It turned out that the man was an undertaker, his van was being used as a hearse, and he claimed that he was allowed to drive there because he had a corpse in the van.

- A woman from Long Island sued a cemetery after a sinkhole opened up and she was sucked into her parents' grave.

- And a theme park opened in Tennessee that features an attraction based on the death of Princess Diana. Visitors to National Enquirer Live can see an interactive map of the path her car took on the night of the crash, after which visitors are polled on whether they think Diana was murdered by the British royal family. The creator of the exhibit said it is 'definitely not in poor taste'.

MANTA RAYS

A swimmer and a giant ray had a manta-man conversation.

Jake Wilton was snorkelling just off the coast of Western Australia when he was approached by a manta ray, known to locals as Freckles because of her speckled belly. Once she was in front of him, she rolled over onto her back and unfurled the lobes at the front of her head, to reveal fishing hooks stuck in her eye. She waited while Wilton made multiple attempts to remove them: onlooker Monty Halls commented that it was like watching kids at the dentist, because Freckles kept jerking her head away at the last minute, then returning as if to request that he try again. As soon as Wilton had removed the fish hooks, Freckles swam off. The pair linked up again a couple of weeks later, when Wilton noticed Freckles swimming directly above him in the water for about 20 seconds. While acknowledging that we should try to avoid anthropomorphising animals too much, he did admit that he 'bawled his eyes out' with emotion immediately after the successful extraction.

MARATHONS ▶

A nurse who broke the record for the fastest marathon dressed as a nurse had her attempt rejected because she was dressed as a nurse.

——— ▼ ———

One of the most unusual marathons of the year was the first-ever 'Green 26.2 Mile', which took place in an abandoned prison in Shepton Mallet, Somerset. Runners had to go round the course 78 times.

NHS nurse Jessica Anderson completed the London Marathon in 3:08:22 while wearing her actual nursing uniform, a tunic and scrubs. However, Guinness World Records rules dictated that anyone entering that category must be wearing a 'blue or white dress, a white pinafore apron, and a traditional white nurse's cap'. After a social-media backlash, Guinness updated its rules to reflect what nurses actually wear and Anderson was awarded the record.

London Marathon organisers also faced complaints – from the slower runners at the back, who objected to having cleaners and marshals telling them to hurry up, clearing and sweeping up around them, and dismantling the course before they had a chance to finish. London Marathon apologised, offered them free

entry next year and says it has now amended its clean-up procedure.

Another runner with cause to complain was the ultra-marathon competitor Tom Fairbrother. Having won the 100-kilometre race by eight minutes, he was upset to learn that he'd been disqualified for taking a wrong turn and running an extra 1.6 kilometres.

MAYOR, HAVING A ▶

A mayor in Massachusetts was voted out of office, and then voted in, in the same vote.

Jasiel F. Correia II of Fall River has been charged with 13 criminal counts of wire fraud and filing false tax returns. He has denied the charges, but because of the scandal the council called a local referendum in which voters were asked two questions: first, whether Correia should be kicked out of office; and second, who should be the next mayor. There was good news and bad news for Correia. In the first count he was voted out by 7,829 votes to 4,911; but in the second he gained 35 per cent of the vote, which was enough to make him the public's choice as his own replacement.

Other local officials having a bit of a 'mare include:

▶ Virginio Merola, mayor of Bologna, who declared that spaghetti Bolognese does not exist. His point was that spaghetti is rarely sold in the city; and if it is, it is never sold with tomato-and-meat sauce. To build his case, he spent the year collecting photos of non-Bologna bolognese from around the world.

▶ Catherine Pugh, mayor of Baltimore, who resigned after she was exposed for having ordered more than 100,000 copies of her own self-published children's books for schools and hospitals.

- The Lord Mayor of Birmingham, Yvonne Mosquito, who turned up to officially open comedian Joe Lycett's new kitchen extension. Lycett's house now boasts a plaque commemorating the opening of the 'Mosquito Wing'.

- Bruno Dionis du Séjour, mayor of Gajac in France, who tried to have the mooing of cows recognised as a 'national heritage treasure' to stop lawsuits from city-dwellers who had moved to the countryside and then complained about the noise.

- And the mayor of Fair Haven, Vermont, whose first action after swearing-in was to defecate on the floor of the Town Hall; she's a three-year-old Nubian goat, called Lincoln.

MEASLES

Teenagers started getting vaccinated in secret.

Parents in the US, Australia and numerous European countries increasingly believe the long-debunked studies that link the measles vaccination to health problems like autism. As a result, many refuse to get their children immunised. But the children are now fighting back. Teenagers have started researching the science themselves, and many took to Reddit to ask the online community how to get inoculated behind their parents' backs. In Queensland, Australia and US states such as Washington, where it was legal, minors were able to get the jabs without parental consent.

Measles was eradicated in the US almost 20 years ago, but is now making a major comeback. Rates of the disease there are the highest they have been since 1992, and New York had to declare a state of emergency after reporting more than 1,000 cases in the first half of 2019. Cases of measles in Europe are also at their highest level in more than 20 years. Following a series of outbreaks, Italy banned children under the age of six who had not been vaccinated from attending kindergarten. The situation is even worse in the Philippines, where 33,000 people were diagnosed with the illness in an outbreak caused partly by a suspicion of vaccines. Vaccinators who visited villages there reported having doors slammed in their faces and local dogs set upon them.

MELTING ▶

Arctic ice is melting so fast, it keeps swallowing the equipment left to measure how fast it's melting.

Merritt Turetsky, a biologist researching the rate of permafrost thaw in the Canadian Arctic, lost cameras and temperature-measurement tools on dozens of study sites because the ice melted so quickly that lakes formed before she was able to retrieve her equipment. Even so, she was able to gather sufficient data to publish a report that, unsurprisingly, draws gloomy conclusions: as thawing permafrost exposes dead plants, animals and microbes once trapped within it, she argues, it will

———— ▼ ————

The ice in the Arctic was melting so quickly that, rather than being able to run across a firm surface, sled dogs had to wade through ankle-deep water, as shown in this photo taken by scientist Steffen Olsen.

release 50 per cent more greenhouse gases into the atmosphere than climate scientists previously believed.

News from the Bering Sea, which lies between Russia and North America, is similarly grim. It's usually frozen over until the end of May, but this year was completely free of ice by the end of March. This doesn't have a direct impact on water levels, because the ice was already in, and therefore displacing the water. But since sea water is darker than ice and thus absorbs more of the sun's energy, rather than reflecting it, the early thaw has a warming effect.

In the Russian Arctic, the thaw has revealed mammoth tusks that had been encased for as much as 30,000 years. This proved a boon to ivory prospectors, who have been seeking new raw material ever since a ban on elephant ivory was instituted in many countries last year. They're now flocking to Siberia, to take advantage of the newly revealed mammoth ivory.

Elsewhere in Russia, a woman in St Petersburg complained to her council in January that she couldn't get to her bus stop due to the piles of ice and snow that lay in the way. In April the council sent her a picture of a clear street and a note reading: 'problem solved'. Of course the fact that it was spring by then may have helped.

MILKSHAKING ▶

Burger King was accused of 'endorsing violence' by reminding people it sold milkshakes.

The fast-food joint tweeted: 'Dear people of Scotland. We're selling milkshakes all weekend. Have fun. Love BK #justsaying.' It was a reference to the fact that because left-wing activists had taken to throwing milkshakes at right-wing politicians, an Edinburgh branch of McDonald's had agreed not to sell milkshakes while a ▮▮▮▮▮▮ Party rally took place nearby. The tweet attracted criticism, with some arguing that Burger King was endorsing political violence. It quickly responded, 'We'd never endorse violence – or wasting our delicious milkshakes! So enjoy the weekend and please drink responsibly people.'

The milkshaking trend began with a drenching of far-right activist Stephen Yaxley-Lennon (who calls himself Tommy Robinson) in May. Within just six weeks, five guys had had the treatment, including Nigel Farage, who was hit by a Five Guys 'shake in Newcastle in June. A few days later a shaken Farage found himself trapped in a bus as milkshake-wielding hoodlums stood menacingly outside. The practice then spread to America, where there were rumours that people were mixing concrete into vegan milkshakes to give them extra impact. Nobody found any concrete evidence for this. One journalist who actually tried to add cement into a milkshake found that the resulting mixture looks, and acts, just like actual concrete. They concluded that it couldn't have been used, because it would be so difficult to wash off that evidence of any attacks would be obvious and easy to document.

While Brits and Americans favoured milk, Australians stuck with good old-fashioned egg-throwing. Seventeen-year-old Will Connolly became an Internet celebrity known as 'Egg Boy' after he smashed an egg on a far-right politician, Fraser Anning, who had blamed a right-wing terrorist attack on a mosque in Christchurch on Muslim immigration. The senator's response was to punch Connolly in the face, thereby gaining widespread sympathy – for Egg Boy. In later interviews, Connolly revealed that he had already been known as 'Egg Boy' before the event, as he used to bring hard-boiled eggs to school, and classmates complained of the smell. Supporters set up fundraising pages to cover his legal fees and to help him 'buy more eggs', but because he wasn't ultimately charged and because he'd probably had his fill of eggs, he chose to donate the AUD $100,000 raised to survivors of the Christchurch attack.

MIMICS

The 'Princess Leia of Ukrainian politics' suffered from an attack of the clones.

Former prime minister of Ukraine Yulia Volodymyrivna Tymoshenko, whose trademark braided hair has garnered comparisons between her and the *Star Wars* heroine, was one of the front-runners in the presidential election. But her campaign faced an unusual challenge when it emerged that the name next to hers on the ballot paper was that of one Yuriy Volodymyrovich Tymoshenko. Sceptics suggested

he was a shill candidate, chosen so that Ukrainians intending to vote for Yulia would be confused into voting for him. Yuriy denied the allegation, saying that he announced his candidacy 'two years ago, a long time before Yulia did. And I'm going to win!' He received just 0.62 per cent of the vote.

These so-called clones are becoming an ever-growing problem in Ukraine. In one district, four candidates called Guzdenko stood for election. Their first names were either Viktor or Vitaliy, and two of them even had the same middle name, Ivanovych. They were up against three Oleksandr Ferenets. And it's not just people's names that are being cloned: the new 'Servant of the People' party, whose candidate Volodymyr Zelensky won the election (*see* **Zelensky, Volodymyr**), was victorious despite finding itself up against candidates representing a mysterious 'Servant of the People Charity' party.

The week before people went to the polls in Ukraine, there was an election in Thailand that was similarly beset by mimics. One candidate, formerly known as Jiraroj Kiratisakvorakul, changed his name to 'Thaksin', after former prime minister Thaksin Shinawatra. He hoped it would make his name more memorable, but unfortunately nine other candidates did exactly the same thing. And five women changed their names to Yingluck, after Thaksin's sister, who also once served as prime minister. To our knowledge, nobody in the UK has yet changed their name to Alexander Boris de Pfeffel Johnson.

MISDIRECTION ▶

For directions to Rome, *see* **Aa**; and for directions to Å, *see* **When in Rom**.

MONTY PYTHON

It's 50 years since Graham Chapman, John Cleese, Eric Idle, Terry Gilliam, Terry Jones and Michael Palin debuted their sketch show Monty Python's Flying Circus *on BBC TV and changed the face of British comedy . . .*

Doune Castle, where *Monty Python and the Holy Grail* was partly filmed, rents coconut shells to its visitors.

In the first draft of their debut movie, *Monty Python and the Holy Grail*, the quest ended with the Holy Grail being discovered at Harrods department store, at the Holy Grail counter.

On its release, *Monty Python's Life of Brian* was widely accused of blasphemy. As a result, numerous UK councils banned it from their cinemas, including several councils that didn't even have cinemas. The ban remained in place in the Welsh town of Aberystwyth until 2008, when it was eventually lifted by the new mayor – Sue Jones-Davies, who played Brian's girlfriend in the film.

Game of Thrones linguist David Peterson translated quotes from Monty Python into Low Valyrian and included them in season four of the show. Lines used included the insults 'Your mother was a hamster and your father smelled of elderberries' and 'I fart in your general direction'.

The reunion performance, *Monty Python Live (Mostly)*, which aired in 2014, was investigated by Ofcom after viewers complained about the lack of swearing in it. The programme received 34 complaints from disgruntled fans about 'cuts' and 'censorship'.

Elvis Presley was a huge Monty Python fan, and would call his friends 'squire' in homage to the famous 'Nudge, nudge' sketch. According to his bodyguard, every time Elvis had a bad live show, he would tell everyone backstage, 'It's only a flesh wound.'

The show was named *Monty Python's Flying Circus* only after numerous other suggestions were rejected by the BBC. They included: *Owl Stretching Time*; *Bunn, Wackett, Buzzard, Stubble and Boot*; *The Toad Elevating Moment*; *A Horse, a Spoon and a Bucket*; and *The Algy Banging Hour*.

MOSQUITOES ▶

Burkina Faso has a village entirely for mosquitoes.

This is the 'MosquitoSphere', a decoy village that scientists from the US and Burkina Faso built to fight malaria. It wouldn't fool many humans: it mostly consists of a few huts, some small pools of stagnant water and several calves, brought along to act as bait for the bugs – all placed inside large domes of mesh netting. But according to research published this year, it's yielding some distinctly promising results.

One study involved milking venom from Australian funnel-web spiders, genetically splicing it into a special fungus, and spreading the fungus over cloth that was then hung up in the MosquitoSphere. Whereas mosquitoes outside the sphere continued to thrive, 99 per cent of those trapped inside died within a month.

And as researchers made this breakthrough in one of the most malaria-cursed places on the planet, a biotech firm in the US developed a mosquito guillotine. This separates the insect from its salivary glands, which contain the parasite that actually causes malaria. Previously scientists had to train for six hours a day, three days a week for two months to learn the skill. Now, it takes just six hours of training to operate a machine that can decapitate 30 mosquitoes at once.

According to researchers at the University of Malaysia in Sarawak, one way to deal with mosquitoes might be to play them dubstep music. Apparently yellow-fever-carrying mosquitoes that listened to music by the DJ Skrillex bit humans far less than normal, because they were 'entertained'. Skrillex was initially impressed by the study, but a few days later tweeted: 'No more mosquitoes man.'

MOTOR RACING ▶

Two Formula 1 teammates were told off for playing a game of real-life dodgems.

Kevin Magnussen and Romain Grosjean, who both drive for the Haas Formula 1 team, crashed into each other while jostling for sixth position at the Spanish Grand Prix. As a result they fell back to seventh and tenth place respectively, cost the team at least three points and were disciplined by their management for failing to work together. The seriousness of the situation was not lost on Grosjean: 'If you lose [by] three points at the end of the year,' he told reporters, 'you're going to eat your balls.'

Unfortunately they did exactly the same thing two months later at the British Grand Prix, this time hitting each other with such force that both cars had to be withdrawn from the race. The team manager said, 'We're a team, and everyone needs to work for the team, and not for himself. I want everybody to be steering in the same direction.' Perhaps Grosjean and Magnussen took that last piece of advice a little too literally.

——— ▼ ———

Vietnam, which is set to host a Grand Prix in 2020, announced that the new racetrack will incorporate a roundabout.

MOVIES ▶

For why there's no colon in *Avengers: Endgame*, *see* **Avengers**; for the Greatest Tory Never Told, *see* **Conservative Leadership Contest**; for watching a box-office smash in a box, *see* **Festivals**; for the pedant of Pride Rock, *see* **Hakuna Matata**; and for what the heck is going on with Hellboy, *see* **Signs**.

MUELLER REPORT
By Anna Ptaszynski

As a member of a book club, I know how hard
it can be to make that crucial selection. How
do you simultaneously satisfy the person
who's never read anything that doesn't have
a gold-embossed cover (thanks for purchasing
this, by the way), the one who can't bear to look
outside the Booker Prize shortlist, and the one who's only ever read 'Harry
Potter' – but at least they've done that a dozen times? Well, if you currently
find yourself in this quandary, let me present: the Mueller Report.

In April, author Robert Mueller published his 448-page investigation into
Russian interference in the 2016 US election. The response was
overwhelming. Twenty-four-hour-long public read-a-thons took place around
the US, attended by hundreds of fans. And an audio book went on sale on
Amazon – for the ominous price of $19.84.

So what's all the fuss about? Well, like any good book club selection the report
generates vigorous debate, yielding headlines as contradictory as 'Collusion
findings are devastating for Trump', 'Trump declares victory as Mueller
Report drops: no collusion', 'No co-ordination between Trump campaign and
Russia', and 'Trump campaign conspired with the Russians; Mueller proved
it'. One piece of writing, so many possible interpretations – and that's without
even mentioning the feminist, Marxist and postmodernist readings.

On the subject of postmodernism, Mueller is stylistically experimental in a
way that should please even the most highbrow book clubbers. Not satisfied
with a few blank pages, à la 'Tristram Shandy', he redacts a full 7 per cent of
the words in his piece. And the report breaks convention elsewhere, too.
Anyone who's ever read 'Infinite Jest' (don't do it to yourself) knows the
power of a well-placed footnote. Some of the juiciest details are hidden in the

footnotes here, like the fact that Trump's former policy adviser, George Papadopoulos, couldn't read his own handwriting, as Mueller discovered when he requested help in deciphering Papadopoulos's diary from Papadopoulos himself.

If it's entertaining characters you're after, Mueller's are positively Dickensian. There are stereotypical bad guys, like Trump ally Roger Stone, who has a tattoo of Richard Nixon on his back. And there's comic relief in Trump's bumbling lawyer, Michael Cohen. One moment we see him failing to contact Putin after mistyping an email address as .gof.ru instead of .gov.ru. The next, he's offered help by Russian government insider Dmitry Klokov, but ends up convinced he's talking to a World Champion weightlifter by the same name, after some faulty googling.

There are also some truly surreal touches, such as the revelation that the Russian Internet Research Agency (allegedly responsible for interference in the US election) paid people to dress up as Santa Claus in Trump masks and walk the streets of New York. And any reader who appreciates an unreliable narrator should enjoy the fact that Mueller inserts himself into the plot at the point when we learn that Trump objected to his appointment as Special Counsel on the grounds Mueller was once embroiled in a dispute with one of his golf courses. Mueller insists (another footnote) that, though he did resign his membership of a Trump golf club in 2011 and request a refund, that had been the end of the matter. Still, there's always the possibility the whole report was fabricated as revenge for some historical golf-related slight.

Not only is the report a great read, thanks to Mueller's televised testimony in June, it makes for fantastic viewing, too. Naturally, there's merchandise to accompany all this: you can buy a Robert Mueller action figure, featuring pockets 'to hold his strong moral compass' and an open hand 'ready for the smoking gun'.

The icing on the cake, from a book club point of view, is that while everyone sort of knows about the report, hardly anyone's actually bothered to read it. It's very much the 'Ulysses' of 21st-century literature. So nothing is going to impress people more than if, rather than just reciting a headline you saw about it, you're able to make a casual reference to footnote 112.

IN WHICH WE LEARN . . .

Who thought the name 'Michael Jackson' was Bad, who outraged Greece by showing their Vergina, who was hot under the dog collar, who sent America to Coventry, and who had an ice-creaming row in Blackburn.

NAME CHANGES

Swastika Acres finally changed its name.

The 55-home suburb of Denver, Colorado acquired its name back in 1908, when the swastika had rather more peaceful connotations. Attempts were made over the years to change it, but they failed because residents did not have the correct papers, and so while Swastika Acres did not appear on any street signs (thankfully), it did live on in title deeds. Thanks to a unanimous city council vote, however, the area has now become Old Cherry Hills.

In other name-change news:

▶ The Cook Islands government announced it will be changing the country's name in order to remove any association with Captain Cook, the first Westerner to chart the islands. A previous attempt to do so in 1994 was overwhelmingly rejected in a referendum. This time the government, fearing a further referendum might be divisive, made the decision unilaterally. It is looking for a new name that better reflects the Polynesian nature of the country and its population.

▶ A Spanish football team called Móstoles Balompié changed its name to Flat Earth FC, because their president is a supporter of the Flat Earth movement.

▶ The Christian Book Distributors, a Massachusetts company selling bibles and church supplies, changed its name to Christianbook, after getting too many enquiries about the other CBD – cannabidiol, a cannabis ingredient.

▶ A Swedish man called David Lind was refused the right to change his name to Tottenham. He was furious, especially after he learned there are already Swedes called Newcastle, Arsenal and Liverpool.

▶ And a Michael Jackson superfan from the West Midlands who changed his name to 'John Michael Jackson' by deed poll a few years ago successfully raised £120 from the public to change his name back. He suspected the name would cause him image problems in the wake of the release of the documentary *Leaving Neverland*, which exposed Jackson as an alleged paedophile. The man had previously changed his name to John Lennon.

NATIONAL ENQUIRER

For MAGAZINE IN NAKED PICTURE SHAME!, *see* **Bezos, Jeff**; and for SICK THEME PARK ACCUSED OF BAD TASTE!, *see* **Macabre**.

99 PROBLEMS

Mr Whippy accused Mr Creamy of whipping up an ice-cream feud.

The streets of Blackburn were terrorised this summer by two ice-cream-van drivers, Mr Whippy (aka Mohammed Mulla) and Mr Creamy (Jahangir Rashid), who spent the heatwave threatening and harassing each other. There is history between the two – Mr Creamy used to work for Mr Whippy, before going it alone in 2015 – but after years of simmering conflict, the relationship between Whippy and Creamy tipped over into full-blown screaming rows outside two mosques, which then escalated into ice-cream-van chases through the streets of the town. Mr Whippy said that Mr Creamy had 'harassed me repeatedly'. Creamy shot back, saying, 'I have not been harassing Mr Mulla. He has been harassing me. I did follow him on 21 June, but that was to try and resolve the matter.' Videos of the incident were posted on YouTube, which is how journalists got the scoop.

This isn't even the first such dispute to have traumatised the town – back in 2012 Mr Whippy had a fight with a third party, Mr Yummy, who smashed up Whippy's van with a spanner, for selling his ice creams 10p cheaper. Mr Whippy then rammed Mr Yummy's vehicle as he fled. The council said they were asking the vendors to 'cool it'.

It's been a bad year all round for ice-cream vans. In New York the authorities seized 46 trucks that had run up nearly $4.5 million in fines for traffic violations, in a sting officially named 'Operation Meltdown'. And ice-cream vans were banned from various parts of London because, since they need to keep their engines running all the time to keep the freezers going, they pump huge amounts of pollutants into the air. Camden council put up 'No ice-cream trading' signs, and one London politician said, 'No one wants to be the fun police or see people lose their businesses. But people don't want a side order of asthma with their ice cream.' There is one slim hope for the future: Nissan unveiled its new zero-emission, electric ice-cream-van prototype, which tweets customers its location rather than playing chimes.

NO PUBLICITY IS BAD PUBLICITY ▸

Carlsberg announced that its beer tasted like 'a puddle of fetid camel's piss'.

After 46 years of telling people it was 'probably the best beer in the world', Carlsberg changed tack and suddenly announced that it was, in fact, 'Probably *not* the best beer in the world'. The firm launched a £20 million campaign criticising all the beer it had been selling until that point, and saying that now they'd

Heinz released a
hybrid ketchup-and-
mayonnaise product in
Canada that it called
Mayochup, not realising
that in the indigenous
Cree language this
means 'shitface'.

realised its shortcomings, they'd changed the recipe. The vice president of marketing announced: 'We lost our way. We focused on brewing quantity, not quality; we became one of the cheapest, not the best.' As part of the campaign, the firm also publicised people's tweets about the old stuff, which claimed that it was like 'the rancid piss of Satan', 'a puddle of fetid camel's piss' or 'a urinal cube that has been in the trough for a week'. When Carlsberg asked for permission to use the first of these lines, the tweeter responsible replied, 'I am confused as to how you will use my quote regarding Carlsberg as the rancid piss of Satan in an effective advert but, by all means, feel free.'

The city of Vienna also tried a reverse-advertising trick when it attempted to lure tourists by drawing attention to all its one-star reviews. The campaign, called 'Unrating Vienna', aimed to show that online comments are not necessarily the best way to find out about a city. So billboards went up featuring reviews for (among others) the State Opera ('the orchestra does not even try'), Schönbrunn Palace ('have a pint instead') and the historical Hofburg Palace ('boring'). The Leopold Museum, which contains one of the world's largest collections of Austrian modern art, was covered in a huge projection of a one-star review, which just said: 'paintings are disgusting'.

NOBEL PRIZES

The most controversial Nobel Prize of the year was awarded in a fictional TV show.

After 12 years and 279 episodes, one of America's most-loved comedy shows, *The Big Bang Theory*, finally ended its run. The denouement of the nerdy sitcom saw two of its protagonists, husband-and-wife team

Amy Farrah Fowler and Sheldon Cooper, finally achieve their life's aim: winning the Nobel Prize for Physics for a theoretical discovery in super-asymmetry. Actual Nobel laureates pointed out, however, that if the story had played out in real life, another pair would probably have won the prize, because they had already stumbled across the same theory in an experiment, though without understanding its significance, and the Nobel committee usually favours whoever finds a result first. The laureates also argued that the committee prefers experiments to theory.

The final episode's storyline revolves around the conflict between the two pairs of scientists fighting over an award that can only be given to a maximum of three people. *Vulture* magazine, which interviewed the former (actual) prize-winners to get their views, reported that while most said the committee would favour the experimental pair, one laureate pointed out that the most likely real-life outcome would be that the Nobel committee would wait for one of the scientists to die, then give the award to the remaining three.

—————— ▼ ——————

Every autumn, the Ig Nobel Prizes are given to scientists whose work makes the judges 'laugh . . . then think'. This year's winners included: a team from France who measured the temperatures of the scrotums of postmen; a team from Japan who estimated the daily saliva consumption of a five-year-old, and a multinational group of scientists who looked at how, and why, wombats produce cube-shaped poo.

NORTH KOREA ▶

Votes in the North Korean election took two days to count, even though there was only one name on every ballot paper.

Most of the world's dictators love a good show-election, but very few come close in their sheer audacity to North Korea's Kim Jong-un. Of the 687 politicians who stood in the vote for Supreme People's Assembly, 687 had been approved by Kim's Workers' Party. All 687 ran unopposed. Voters turning up at the voting station were given a ballot paper with a single name on it, and simply took the paper and placed it in a ballot box. They didn't

NORMANDY LANDINGS

6 June marked the 75th anniversary of the D-Day landings, codenamed 'Operation Neptune' . . .

The 'D' stands for 'day'. It's a military term still used today to refer to the day of an attack when the date is unconfirmed or secret. It means you can refer to the days preceding and after it as, for example, D-Day-1 or D-Day+1, and it makes sense even if the date changes (the army also uses 'H-hour' to refer to the time). Other languages have equivalents, such as Jour-J (French), Lá L (Irish) and Dan D (Slovenian).

The Allies tried to convince the Germans an attack would take place in Pas-de-Calais, rather than Normandy, by setting up a fake military camp, complete with plywood ships and inflatable tanks. They sent out misleading radio signals about 'FUSAG', an army of elite US troops supposedly being stationed there. In reality, FUSAG was fictitious, but the Germans believed the ruse and amassed most of their forces in the wrong place as a result.

The BBC, under the government's instruction, ran a competition for the best photos and postcards of France sent in by members of the public. They then passed these on to the army so they could get a better idea of the layout of the beaches in advance of the invasion.

Lord Lovat, a Scottish commander, ordered his personal piper, Bill Millin, to play the bagpipes on the front line during the landings. Millin duly obeyed, serenading the soldiers with 'Highland Laddie' and 'Road to the Isles'. He survived, though his pipes were injured by shrapnel. When he spoke to captured German snipers later, they told him the only reason they hadn't shot him down was that they'd assumed he had gone mad.

In preparation for the landings, mini-submarines carried soldiers to the Normandy coast, so that they could swim to the beach, scoop up sand in condoms, and bring it back for anaylsis to check the ground would be suitable for troops and tanks.

'Hobart's Funnies' were specially modified tanks deployed by the Allies. They included: the Swimming Sherman, which had a huge canvas skirt that allowed it to float on water as well as roll along the ground; the Bobbin Carpet Layer, which unrolled a length of reinforced carpet ahead of it to help vehicles traverse the soft sand; and the ARK (Armoured Ramp Carrier) that transformed into a bridge for troops to walk over if they encountered a ditch.

have to put a cross in a box, or write anything on the ballot. The reason the count took such a long time was probably because officials were combing ballot papers for signs of dissent. According to North Korea analyst Fyodor Tertitskiy, anyone who dared not vote for the single candidate – by, for instance, crossing out the name – would probably have ended up being declared insane by the secret police.

Voting is compulsory in North Korea, and it's a show of patriotism to turn up early, so the queues that formed first thing in the morning were massive. The turnout was 99.9 per cent – up from 99.7 per cent in the last election five years ago. The official news agency said that the missing 0.1 per cent of the electorate were 'working abroad or in oceans'.

NORTH MACEDONIA (NÉE MACEDONIA) ▶

North Macedonia stopped flying its original flag because it has a Vergina on it.

A Vergina is an ancient symbol that looks like a sun with sixteen triangular rays. When the Republic of Macedonia won its independence in 1992, it adopted the emblem on its flag, much to the annoyance of Greece, which pointed to the fact that the Vergina is actually an ancient Greek image. It was first discovered by archaeologists in the Greek town of Vergina, and the oldest Greek craft lager is called 'Vergina beer'.

But it was the new country's name that annoyed Greece the most. The name 'Macedonia' is derived from the ancient Kingdom of Macedon, whose territory brushed the south of the Republic of Macedonia, but largely coincided with modern-day Greece: the most famous resident of the Kingdom of Macedon was Alexander the Great, who was born in the Greek city of Pella. The

Greeks felt that by taking the name, the Republic of Macedonia was not just stealing part of its culture, but also one of its most famous sons. In the end a compromise was found; the country is now called 'North Macedonia' and its citizens will be known as 'Macedonians', but the North Macedonia government was forced to admit explicitly that it has no connection to the ancient people of that name.

As part of the agreement, all depictions of the ancient-Greek Vergina had to be removed from display in North Macedonia; Skopje Alexander the Great Airport was renamed simply Skopje Airport; and officials in both countries met to agree the content of each other's school textbooks. Food and drink proved a bit more tricky. Winemakers in both countries make 'Macedonian wine' and refused to compromise about their names; and makers of the traditional 'Macedonian halva', a flour-based confectionery, also argued over their branding. There was no controversy, thankfully, over who would be allowed to make Vergina beer.

NOT FROM AROUND HERE...

For the New Zealander who's big in Australia, *see* **Aussie Election**; and for the Englishman who's big in New Zealand, *see* **World Cup, Cricket**.

NOTRE-DAME

A French priest risked life and limb to rescue Notre-Dame's communion wafers.

Father Fournier, chaplain of the Paris Fire Brigade, said that as soon as he was called to the Notre-Dame fire, he realised his priority was 'to preserve above all the

the bells!

real presence of our Lord Jesus Christ' – the wafers and wine, or Blessed Sacrament, which, to Catholics, are literally the body and blood of Christ. He therefore rushed into the cathedral as burning beams fell to the floor and drops of molten lead rained from the ceiling, 'retrieved Jesus' and, while still inside the cathedral, used the consecrated bread and wine to bless it. In his view, 'It was probably both this and the excellent general manoeuvre of the firefighters that led to the stopping of the fire.'

Fournier saved many more of the building's sacred contents, including the purported Crown of Thorns that Jesus wore on his way to be crucified; a supposed relic of the True Cross; and a nail said to be from the crucifixion. Volunteers formed a human chain, which Fournier helped to co-ordinate, and passed artefacts in order of their relative sacredness from one person to the next to get them out.

Two months after the fire, the cathedral reopened. Only about 30 people were allowed in for the first Mass to be held there, and, as this photograph shows, the priests, canons and the Archbishop of Paris all had to wear builders' hard hats.

Part of the reason why the fire was able to take hold was because, when the smoke alarm initially went off, those sent to investigate it mistakenly went to the roof of the adjacent 'sacristy' building, rather than the main structure. It was half an hour before the source of the fire was properly located. Donald Trump's tweeted suggestion that firefighters should drop water on the fire from 'flying water tankers' was rejected by experts, who pointed out that the force of this could cause the whole structure to collapse.

Offers of help flooded in. Air France promised free flights to anyone involved in the reconstruction, and more than one billion euros in donations were pledged for the repair, mostly from millionaires and billionaires (including Europe's richest person), though only 9 per cent of this had materialised more than three months later. Many of the wealthiest would-be donors who had promised to help out either went completely silent or refused to release the cash before knowing what it would be used for. According to Notre-Dame's press officer, they didn't want it used 'just to pay employees' salaries' during the clean-up.

Fortunately, no one was killed in the fire. Even the 180,000 bees that live there survived and probably had quite a good time of it, since when they sense smoke, bees gorge on all their honey until they've eaten themselves into a stupor. But considerable damage was nevertheless caused, particularly to part of the original 856-year-old cathedral roof, made from more than 5,000 oak trees. The spire, which had been added in the 19th century during restorations inspired by Victor Hugo's *The Hunchback of Notre-Dame*, also collapsed. The day after the fire, various editions of the 1831 novel, in which Hugo had drawn attention to the building's state of disrepair at the time, occupied the first, third, fifth, seventh and eighth slots in Amazon France's bestseller list, with a book on the history of Gothic architecture coming sixth.

▼

Thanks to the video game *Assassin's Creed*, a historically accurate restoration of Notre-Dame may well be possible, because a senior architect for *Assassin's Creed Unity*, which is set in Paris, spent two years studying and re-creating the building, down to the last stone.

NUCLEAR MELTDOWN ▶

Iran gave the US the silent treatment.

▼

When two oil tankers were attacked in the Gulf of Oman, one of Obama's former advisers questioned the official US line that Iran was responsible for this act of piracy. He was ridiculed in Congress by Republican Dan Crenshaw – a man who always wears an eyepatch.

In retaliation for the US's decision to pull out of the nuclear deal agreed with President Obama in 2015 and reimpose crippling sanctions, Iran broke its side of the bargain and enriched the uranium it holds, above previously agreed levels. At a meeting in June, Iran's Supreme Leader Ali Khamenei assured Japan's prime minister Shinzo Abe that this shouldn't be taken as an indication that he wanted to develop nuclear weapons. He added, however, that he wasn't going to say that directly to Trump, because, 'I do not see Trump as worthy of any message exchange.' In fairness to Khamenei, Trump takes things quite personally, too: according to leaked comments made by the former British ambassador to the US, Sir Kim Darroch, the US president abandoned the nuclear deal for 'personality reasons' – essentially, to spite his predecessor.

Under the terms of the original deal, Iran's level of uranium enrichment was capped at 3.67 per cent. When the agreement was broken off, it started enriching it at 4.5 per cent (in other words, 4.5 per cent of the uranium atoms in its stockpile were the type that could be used in nuclear bombs). Since the level required to make weapons is actually 90 per cent, the country has some way to go. It's not even close to 2015 levels, which were up to 20 per cent.

The reimposition of US sanctions may be deeply damaging to Iran's economy, but it also threatens that of countries such as France, Germany and the UK, whose companies the US has sought to ban from trading with the Islamic republic. To circumvent this, a system called INSTEX has been set up – essentially a bartering scheme that seeks to bypass US sanctions by avoiding any cash changing hands between Iran and its trading partners. For instance, if a European company needs to sell 10 apples *to* Iran, INSTEX will find another company that needs to buy something of equal value *from* Iran – say, 20 oranges. The company buying oranges then pays the European company selling apples, rather than paying the Iranian orange-sellers. At the other end, the Iranian company buying apples pays the orange-sellers, rather than paying the European apple-sellers. The oranges nevertheless still go to Europe, and the apples still go to Iran. If this sounds complicated, it is, and the arrangement has taken more than a year to set up. But it does mean that everyone still gets paid, and receives their goods, without money having to enter or leave Iran. And the great thing is that President Trump need never know about it.

IN WHICH WE LEARN . . .

Who made a Petty mistake, whose partners are in the dog house, what bacteria just can't get over, and why you should never offer an olive branch to a songbird.

OBRADOR, LÓPEZ ▶

Mexico's president went from working from home to living at work.

Andrés Manuel López Obrador has a reputation for frugality. One of his first moves as president was to take a 60 per cent pay cut, and he later turned the lavish presidential palace (it's 14 times bigger than the White House) into a cultural centre. Obrador initially remained in his modest home on the outskirts of Mexico City, but eventually the pressure of the commute became too much and he moved into an apartment of another palace, the National Palace, which is also where he works. Living close to the office makes a lot of sense, given that at 7 a.m. every single day Obrador holds a 90-minute press conference.* Twitter and YouTube personalities are also invited to these press events, because he believes 'blessed social media' helped to elect him.

Over the years Obrador has had a number of nick-names, including The American, The Commander, The Rock and the Large Freshwater Gar, but now he's mostly known as AMLO, after the initial letters of his name. His fans are known as AMLOvers, and there are a lot of them. With approval ratings as high as 80 per cent at the start of the year, Obrador could well be the most popular politician in the world. At weekends he tours the country to speak to the people, and important decisions can be made at these assemblies.

AMLO travels to these events economy-class, having promised to sell the presidential plane (along with helicopters and bulletproof vans) to pay for anti-migrant measures that he agreed with Donald Trump. What cheap flights offer in value, though, they lose in terms of peace and quiet; on one flight this year, Obrador was loudly serenaded by a fellow passenger, who sang,

*Compare this to the White House, where Sarah Huckabee Sanders reduced press conferences to about one a month, then cancelled them entirely, except in exceptional circumstances; journalists noticed that the White House press podium had gathered a layer of dust by June.

—————— ▼ ——————
Obrador cancelled a multimillion-peso transportation project, after asking the audience to vote with a show of hands. When they voted against the infrastructure plan, he said they would spend the money on a hospital or improved water system instead – asking them to vote, again with their hands, on which of those two they would prefer.

'Obrador is a great presidente and will always be able to count on our support, *sí señor*!' When the plane landed, the passenger gave the president an encore.

Obrador's frugality trickled down throughout the country's civil service. He fired the 100 most well-paid members of the treasury, cancelled a much-needed new airport that was already one-third of the way through construction and, to save energy, some government workers are no longer allowed to charge their phones at work. The one place he was happy to spend money was on baseball. It's Obrador's favourite sport and, despite being 65, he still likes to play when he has time. He loves baseball so much that he appointed a minister for baseball, who is tasked with having between 60 and 80 Mexican players playing in Major League Baseball over the next six years.

OBSTACLE COURSES ▶

Scientists developed an obstacle course for sperm.

The team from the University of Toronto developed a microscopic race between 100,000,000 sperm as a way to identify the top 1,000 to be used in IVF treatments. They all had to swim along a very thin corridor (tricky for sperm to negotiate, as they usually swim in a corkscrew motion, though they can also 'slither' when necessary), the theory being that the fastest would be better at swimming through a woman's reproductive tract. Since another experiment this year established that women's reproductive channels contain lots of 'pinch points' to weed out weaker candidates, this theory makes a lot of sense. And it's certainly a better method of selection than the current one, which involves looking through a microscope to establish which are the best swimmers.

IVF is becoming ever more necessary as fertility rates among men continue to drop. Over the last 80 years it's been estimated that sperm quality across the planet has plummeted by 50 per cent. Environmental contaminants may well be to blame.

Another micro-obstacle course to have been developed in 2019 targeted individual bacteria. E. coli have a move called 'swim and tumble', which they deploy to avoid poison or to seek out food – but all previous studies have only looked at the way they move in unencumbered environments, rather than real-world ones. So scientists from Carnegie Mellon, the University of Pittsburgh, and the Salk Institute for Biological Studies built a series of microscopic chambers with obstacles in them, to slow them down. Although the obstacles were only one-hundredth of a millimetre high, the researchers found that bacteria did in fact change their behaviour to get round them. It's thought that if we can learn how they swim under pressure, we might be better placed in future to fight the infections they spread.

OK ▶

For the 'OK' asteroid that almost caused the collapse of civilisation, *see* **Armageddon**; and for the 'Ok' glacier that foretells Armageddon, *see* **Civilisation, Collapse of**.

The world was flush with toilet news this year . . .

A MAN IN BELGIUM BROKE THE RECORD FOR THE LONGEST ANYONE HAS SAT ON A TOILET. HE LASTED 116 HOURS, ALTHOUGH AS THE TOILET HE WAS SITTING ON WAS NOT PLUMBED IN, HE WAS ALLOWED A FIVE-MINUTE BREAK EVERY HOUR, IN CASE HE NEEDED TO GO TO A REAL ONE.

SOME UK CINEMAS INCLUDED AN INTERVAL IN THEIR SCREENINGS OF THE THREE-HOUR FILM AVENGERS: ENDGAME TO GIVE PEOPLE A CHANCE TO GO TO THE LOO.

A SET OF PUBLIC TOILETS IN HULL WAS ADDED TO LONELY PLANET'S 'ULTIMATE UK TRAVEL LIST' OF THE 500 TOP DESTINATIONS IN THE COUNTRY.

HULL'S OTHER SIGHTS, THE HUMBER BRIDGE AND WILBERFORCE HOUSE MUSEUM, DIDN'T MAKE IT ONTO THE LIST.

Police in Tennessee warned the public to stop flushing meth down the toilet, as it might end up downstream where alligators live and create 'methgators'. When the statement was taken too seriously, they had to follow it up with:

'Let us be perfectly clear: the methgator was a humorous illustration used to highlight the dangers of flushing drugs down your toilet. Alas, the methgator is not real. Let's say that again: THE METHGATOR IS NOT (at this time) REAL'

A GOLD TOILET was stolen from Blenheim Palace. Maurizio Cattelan, who exhibited the loo at the birthplace of Winston Churchill said: 'WHO'S SO STUPID TO STEAL A TOILET?' If melted down the artwork would be worth more than £4 MILLION

OLIVES

Olive-harvesting robots are sucking more than two million birds off trees every year.

The agricultural machines pluck the fruit off the trees by night. Unfortunately in the process they suck in and kill the songbirds that are roosting there. According to a new study, they kill 96,000 birds a year in Portugal alone, while in Andalusia they accounted for 2.6 million bird deaths a year until the practice was banned there.

This is a good reason to dislike olives; and, as it turns out, many people do. For the first time they have overtaken Brussels sprouts as the most-hated food in Britain. A staggering 37 per cent of people dislike olives enough to refuse them completely, according to a survey conducted by HelloFresh. Sprouts came fourth, while gherkins and seafood were second and third, and mushrooms were sixth. The study found that almost all British people are fussy eaters: only one person in ten said they were willing to eat whatever was put in front of them.

In good news for British olive-haters, Italy's olive harvest plunged by 57 per cent, due to freak weather. Things got so bad that one scientist predicted Italy might have to start importing olives, as it couldn't provide for itself. The crisis led to protests, with thousands of Italian farmers demanding government aid and wearing *gilet arancioni*, or orange vests, in a nod to the French *gilets jaunes* movement. All of which makes Waitrose look ultra-prescient: in spring the company stockpiled six months' worth of olives. However, this wasn't due to them predicting a bad harvest – they were just worried that certain goods from Europe might be harder to come by after the end of March, when Britain was scheduled to ██████.

ON THE BLINK

Robots had their jobs taken by humans.

A Japanese hotel that's partly staffed by robots had
to sack more than half of them for being incompetent.
The Henn na – meaning 'strange' – hotel employed
243 automatons to perform functions like checking
in customers, mixing cocktails, storing luggage and
answering guests' questions. But their record was not
impressive: the humanoid and dog-oid dancers in the
lobby constantly broke down; the concierge bot couldn't
answer basic questions, like the opening hours of
nearby tourist attractions; and the bellboy bots (bell-
bots?) could reach only about a quarter of the hotel's
rooms, and kept getting stuck trying to pass each other
in the corridors. One guest was incessantly woken up in
the night by an in-room assistant asking him to repeat
what he'd just said, because it mistook his snoring for
speech. The under-performing robots were given the
boot and replaced with humans.

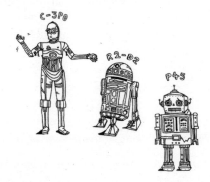

In other faulty news:

▶ Consumer watchdog *Which?* found that many of the
   leading fitness trackers miscalculate how far you've
   run. One of them, for example, underestimated a
   marathon by 11 miles, meaning that the user would

have had to run 37 miles to register 26. Separate research found that every fitness tracker on the market overestimates the number of calories burned during exercise, some by more than 50 per cent.

▶ A toll machine near a casino in Kansas started spitting out money instead of taking it. To make matters worse, when the toll authority realised what was happening and sent a message to alert their staff, so that the equipment could be fixed, they accidentally broadcast it to members of the public instead, so everyone knew where to go for free money.

▶ Shoppers in Cardiff got stuck in a lift that kept accelerating to the top of the shaft and then plummeting back down seven floors, non-stop, for 40 minutes. They likened the experience to being in a horror movie. By way of compensation, the shopping centre offered them free parking permits.

▶ And an enquiry into a complaint made by a man in Dubai that his PlayStation game was faulty concluded that it was the man who was malfunctioning, not the game: it turned out he's just terrible at playing it.

OOPS ▶

A Dutch fighter jet shot itself in the face at 15,000 feet.

The jet pilot was taking part in a training exercise, when he fired off some cannon rounds. An unexpected level of air resistance slowed the rounds down, with the result that he actually ended up flying into them (he was unhurt, but had to crash-land). Friendly fire accidents during training aren't that unusual: in 2016, a Norwegian fighter pilot accidentally fired a round of gunshots at his own control tower during an exercise, instead of at the intended target.

In other 'Oops' moments from the year:

▶ The British Museum realised that a 'vase' it's had on display for 30 years is actually a mace it had exhibited upside down. What appeared to be the vase opening was, in fact, the aperture into which a long handle usually fits on a mace, so that it can be used to club enemies. A cuneiform inscription on the top of the mace (or bottom of the vase) references the world's first-known border war, to which this object was witness.

▶ A hiker in Texas called the emergency services, believing she was being stalked by a growling wild pig. When the Parks & Wildlife authorities arrived, they found her taking refuge up a tree, along with a fellow walker. The source of the 'growling pig' noise was soon established: it was actually cars driving over a nearby rumble strip.

▶ Two men in Florida who tried to break into an ATM with a blowtorch ended up welding the hinges shut instead.

▶ Singer Cardi B publicly thanked one 'Tom Petty' for the bouquet of flowers in her dressing room, following her Grammy win – not realising that the Tom Petty in question was the rock star, who died in 2017, and that the card on the flowers just featured a quote from one of his songs.

▶ An international wheelchair tennis event in Australia had to be moved after it turned out they'd accidentally built the court on a slope.

▶ And a woman who ordered a cake with a picture of Mariah Carey on it was presented with one that featured an image of Marie Curie; another woman who ordered a Moana cake actually got one with a picture of marijuana; and a child nicknamed 'lizard' received a birthday cake iced with 'Happy Birthday Loser'.

OR ARE YOU JUST PLEASED TO SEE ME?

Things mistaken for guns this year included a banana, a sex toy and a didgeridoo.

Commuters at Melbourne's Flagstaff station panicked when police in body armour, and carrying assault rifles, stopped a train during rush hour, following reports of a man acting suspiciously with what appeared to be a rifle. He turned out to be a trumpet player whose case had been mistaken for a rifle bag. During the panic, busker Will Austin was also searched by police, who thought his didgeridoo might have been a gun. There was a silver lining. Austin's subsequent Facebook post about the incident, in which he used the Aboriginal name – *Yidaki* – for his didge, went viral, providing, as he put it, 'a little bit of cultural education'.

In other 'jumping the gun' news:

▶ Canadian police were called out following a report of a man waving a firearm, only to find someone waving a broom at squirrels in his garden.

▶ Police dashed to a school in Maryland to discover that a 'man with a gun' was, in fact, a man with a barbecue lighter.

▶ Two schools in Colorado were temporarily closed due to a woman seated in a nearby car with an eyelash-curler that witnesses mistook for a weapon.

▶ An Uber driver in Connecticut, who was masturbating in his car, reached for what police thought was a gun as they approached. It was actually a sex toy.

▶ And a man from Bournemouth attempted to rob a bank with a banana. Laurence Vonderdell brandished the piece of fruit concealed inside a carrier bag at a cashier in a Bournemouth bank, informing them, 'This is a stick-up.' He later handed himself in to police and was sent to prison for 14 months.

OVERREACTIONS

A sleepy Norfolk town spent £1,700 on terrorist insurance.

Thetford council decided that it was money well spent, because events such as the Thetford Gaming Convention were expected to attract up to a thousand people and could, they thought, be a target for ISIS. Many residents weren't so sure. 'Surely the council would be better off spending the £1,700 on something useful like a roundabout,' said one, while local farmer Mark Maloy, weighing up the possibility of a terrorist attack in Thetford, concluded, 'There's more chance of being kicked to death by butterflies.'

A much smaller sum of money provoked an even more disproportionate response in India. Ismail Khan was first arrested in 1978 for allegedly stealing 20 rupees (roughly 20p) from the pocket of a man standing in front of him in a bus queue. For the next 26 years he protested his innocence until, in 2004, he stopped bothering and a warrant was issued for his arrest. He was finally taken into custody in April this year. After three months in prison he had the original charges dropped, on the condition that he didn't take part in any illegal activities (which there's no evidence he did in the first place) in the future.

In other unusual insurance news, Aviva revealed that among the oddest claims it had received over the past year was one for damage to a car caused by a horse mistaking it for another horse and trying to have sex with it. There was also a claim for a mobile phone that had been smashed by a monkey, and one for damage to a shed created by a burglar who'd accidentally locked himself in it.

OUR SURVEY SAID...

Time to take the No Such Thing As A Fish *Surveys Survey. See how you compare with the hundreds of thousands of people around the world who were polled on the following seven questions...*

1. Do you think dad bods are the new six pack?

YES ☐   NO ☐

A: 51 per cent of the 2,217 Americans who were surveyed about this answered 'yes'; 65 per cent said they thought dad bods were at least attractive.

2. Who do you think would make the best prime minister of the UK?

BORIS JOHNSON ☐   NIGEL FARAGE ☐

MICHAEL GOVE ☐   RORY STEWART ☐

JEREMY CORBYN ☐

A: A survey of 2,000 adulterers on the website Illicit Encounters revealed that 32 per cent of them think Nigel Farage would make the best PM. Boris Johnson came second with 24 per cent, Michael Gove scored 11 per cent, Rory Stewart nabbed 4 per cent of the vote and Jeremy Corbyn managed to clock up just 1 per cent.

3. Do you find yourself actively avoiding the news?

YES ☐   NO ☐

If 'yes', why?:

☐

A: If you answered 'yes' to this one, you: a) probably shouldn't be reading this book; and b) are in step with 35 per cent of UK news consumers, who also said they were actively avoiding the news. Of those people, 71 per cent used the referendum about ▮▮▮▮ as their main reason for steering clear.

4. Do you believe in supernatural powers?

YES ☐   NO ☐

A: 71 per cent of (self-defined) atheists voted 'yes', according to a survey conducted by the Understanding Unbelief project. It also found that 12 per cent of atheists believe in reincarnation, 20 per cent believe in life after death, and about one-third of all the atheists polled believe that some events are 'meant to be'.

5. Who do you kiss more, your partner or your dog?

PARTNER ☐   DOG ☐

A: 52 per cent of those polled admitted to kissing their dogs more often than their partner. And 61 per cent of the dog-snoggers added that they kiss their pet on the mouth. 52 per cent also said that, given the choice between sleeping with a dog or a partner, they'd rather get into bed with the dog.

6. Should Arabic numbers be taught in school?

YES ☐   NO ☐

A: In this survey, conducted by polling company Civic Service, 3,624 people were asked: 'Should schools in America teach Arabic Numerals as part of their curriculum?' 2,020 respondents didn't seem to know that all the numerals in 2,020 are Arabic (along with 1, 3, 4, 5, 6 . . . you get the idea) and said they should be banned. The survey was designed to show how people will answer a question without first understanding it.

7. How much money would it take for you to give up your very best friend?

£0 – 100,000 ☐   MORE THAN £200,000 ☐

£100,000 – 200,000 ☐   I'D NEVER GIVE THEM UP ☐

A: Women are more prepared than men to give up their best friend, if this survey of 2,000 people in the UK is to be believed: they will accept an average of £106,000, whereas men hold out for £180,000. Scousers are the least loyal, being willing to sacrifice their bezzie for just £62,000, while Glaswegians are the most devoted friends: they won't do it for anything under £200,000.

IN WHICH WE LEARN . . .

Why Russia didn't get its new pop tsar, who signed up to Prince-tagram, who doesn't like the Queen's face, why it's so hard to find the Duchy of Cornwall, and which robots got a Royal Flush.

PARENTAL MISGUIDANCE

Russians interfered in a vote . . . for a kids' TV talent show.

Ten-year-old Mikella Abramova was initially declared the winner of popular TV show *The Voice Kids* in Russia, having secured 56.5 per cent of the phone-in vote – more than twice the runner-up's vote share. Suspicions were raised on social media, however, both because of the unusually high number of votes cast and the fact that she's the daughter of a pop star and a millionaire banker. On investigation, it emerged that a large proportion of her votes had been texted-in by bots. The scam would have been far too costly for most people to orchestrate, but was not – as many people noted – unaffordable for Mikella's parents. Although organisers named no names, the result was cancelled.

In other parts of the world, parental cheating was conclusively proven. *Desperate Housewives* star Felicity Huffman, who fittingly played a controlling, overprotective mother in the show, was one of 50 people to be charged over a major scam that involved parents committing fraud to get their children into university. Those convicted had given millions of dollars in bribes to a sham charity, controlled by consultant Rick Singer, that offered various dubious services – for example, faking a student's exam results (often without their knowledge), or getting an extremely clever impersonator to sit an exam on their behalf (and even mimicking their handwriting). Some of the parents had faked evidence of their children's sporting achievements by photoshopping their faces onto athletes' bodies. Huffman herself was handed a 14-day jail sentence.

A high school in Texas introduced a dress code . . . for parents. Parents of students at the James Madison High School in Houston were told they weren't allowed to turn up wearing pyjamas. Or leggings. Or low-slung trousers, low-slung shorts, short dresses, low-cut tops, shower caps or hair curlers.

PAYOUTS

A civil servant in Northern Ireland was awarded £10,000 for having to look at the Queen's face.

——— ▼ ———
In America, a woman who slipped on a fallen 'wet floor' sign in a casino was awarded $3 million. In the UK, by contrast, a Network Rail report about payouts revealed that a passenger who slipped on some ice was awarded a measly £10.

Lord Maginnis recounted in the House of Lords how Lee Hegarty, a senior civil servant in Northern Ireland, received £10,000 compensation a few years ago after complaining about having to walk past a large portrait of the Queen each day at his workplace. The Northern Ireland Office refused to confirm or deny the story, but if it was true, hopefully Hegarty wasn't too offended at having to count through thousands of pictures of the Queen's face when he collected his payout.

Compensation was also offered, rather less contentiously, to Terry Brazier, a 70-year-old from Leicestershire, who received £20,000 after his local hospital circumcised him by mistake. He had actually gone in for a bladder procedure and was unaware of where the knife had ended up, partly because the local anaesthetic meant he couldn't feel much below the waist, and partly because he'd been busy chatting to the nurses during the operation. Brazier said, with considerable cool, that the removal of his foreskin came as 'a real surprise'.

PIGEON FANCYING

The 'Lewis Hamilton of Pigeons' was sold by Mr Ferrari.

The number of pigeon fanciers in the UK has fallen from 60,000 in 1990 to only 21,000 today. But the hobby is growing elsewhere in the world: there are at least half a million colombophiles in Taiwan, and hundreds of thousands more in mainland China. As a result, the prices of elite racing pigeons are really taking off.

Even so, many were surprised when auctioneer Jorgi Ferrari officiated over a bidding war that led to a pigeon called Armando selling for €1.2 million. Armando may have been described as 'the best Belgian long-distance pigeon of all time' and the 'Lewis Hamilton of Pigeons', but, at four times the level of the previous record, the price he achieved still exceeded expectations. His racing days, however, are now over: he was so expensive that he can no longer be expected to fly competitively, as he might get lost – or worse. Instead he'll spend the rest of his life servicing female pigeons. Seven of Armando's descendants have already sold for more than £120,000, so while paying £1.2 million for a bird might sound like a lot, it may turn out to be something of a coo.

PIGS

This little piggy went to market, *see* **Year of the Pig**; this little piggy went to space, *see* **Launches**; this little piggy chased a woman up a tree, *see* **Oops**; this little piggy got inked, *see* **Tattoos**; and this little piggy brought the English accent all the way home, *see* **Brits Abroad**.

PLANETS

For Freddie Mercury, *see* **Queen, The**; for Venus razors, *see* **Apposite**; for Flat Earth FC, *see* **Name Changes**; for Bruno Mars, *see* **Clamping Down**; for Jupiter, Florida, *see* **Apposite**; for a Saturn V rocket, *see* **Apollo 12**; for Uranus, Missouri, *see* **Uranus Examiner**, and for Operation Neptune, *see* **Normandy Landings**.

PESKY PESTS

THE PENTAGON WAS ACCUSED OF WEAPONISING TICKS

The US House of Representatives ordered the Pentagon to
reveal whether it tried to use ticks as biological weapons.
Conspiracy theorists claim that Dr Willy Burgdorfer, who
discovered the bacterium that causes Lyme disease, also
worked for the US military. They believe that the illness,
which affects more than 300,000 Americans every year,
was the result of an experiment whereby infected ticks
were dropped on communities to see how diseases
spread, with a view to using the tactic in wartime.
The main problem with the theory is that ticks have
been causing Lyme disease since the 19th century,
and scientists only worked out what causes it in the 1980s.

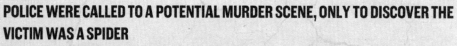

POLICE WERE CALLED TO A POTENTIAL MURDER SCENE, ONLY TO DISCOVER THE VICTIM WAS A SPIDER

Neighbours called the police in Perth, Australia, when they heard a man repeatedly
screaming, 'Why won't you die!' and a child crying in the background. It turned out the man's
comments were being directed at a spider and that he suffered from extreme
arachnophobia. The incident report concluded: 'No injuries sighted (except to spider).'

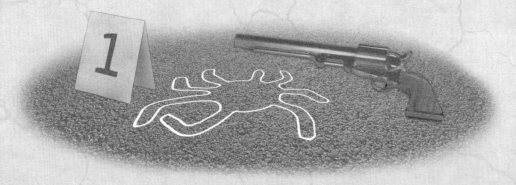

CHIRPING CRICKETS WERE MISTAKEN FOR A 'SONIC WEAPON'

In 2017, more than half of the staff at the US embassy in Havana complained that a mysterious noise was causing them to suffer from headaches, nausea and other illnesses. Many speculated that the embassy was being targeted by an acoustic weapon, but a 2019 study by the University of California, which closely matched the mystery noises with audio files from their insect database, concluded that the 'sonic weapon' was most probably the mating song of local crickets. The investigation continues.

THE UK REALISED IT IS FACING A WORMAGEDDON

A study by the National Environment Research Council found that 42 per cent of British fields have poor earthworm biodiversity and 16 per cent have no deep-burrowing worms whatsoever. Over-cultivation, excessive ploughing and pesticides have been blamed. It wasn't all bad news for worms, though: while many have gone missing, some new ones have been discovered, including a species found on the Shetland Islands that has one pair of eyes on its head and another on its bottom.

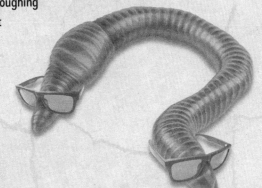

POKER-BOTS

Scientists built a card-playing robot that is so good it could destroy the poker industry.

Microsoft is developing a bot called 'Super Phoenix' that it hopes will master the ancient Chinese tile game Mahjong which, like poker, often involves dealing with incomplete information. Super Phoenix is currently at '10th Dan', a rank held by only 0.0054 per cent of human players. The next step is to reach Tenhou, the highest rank in the game, which has been attained by only 13 human players in history.

There have been AI poker players before. But Pluribus, developed by scientists in the US, is the first machine to be able to play multiple humans in a six-player game of No-Limit Texas Hold 'em, bluff against them and win. In a trial game, it defeated some of the world's best professional players over the course of thousands of hands. Noam Brown, one of the developers, said that the source code would be kept secret because of the risk of a 'serious impact on the online poker community'. In other words, professional players would go bust and everyone would stop playing. Even today poker players are playing fewer high-stakes games online, because of the odds that they may be up against a machine without knowing it.

One reason poker has previously been so hard for AI programs to play is that the game requires the machine to know how to bluff, how to call its opponents' bluff and how to vary its playing style so that other players don't know whether the AI itself is bluffing. One person who'd played against Pluribus said, 'The stamina of it, the consistency of it, these are things I've been trying to achieve my entire career . . . seeing this thing be perfect at it was pretty overwhelming.'

The poker-playing robot technology might prove useful in real-world situations such as business negotiations or cyber-security. Earlier in the year it was announced that a slightly older poker AI called Libratus had been bought for use at the Pentagon, for potential use in war-games and strategic planning. So even though it may not be playing much poker, Pluribus might soon be getting work in a nuclear command centre near you.

POLITICAL DRAMAS

Hollyoaks *was partly written by the government.*

Hollyoaks – maybe the greatest Channel 4 6.30 p.m. soap currently on air (all right, the only one) – briefly turned out to be a hotbed of officers from the government's deradicalisation programme, Prevent. They acted as advisers to the show over a plotline that involved one of the main characters getting involved in far-right violence. The national coordinator of Prevent said he would be 'delighted to receive approaches from other soaps' to help them with similar themes – so there's every chance that we'll see some of the fertiliser used in *Emmerdale* being made into a bomb, or the Rover's Return being used for dead-letter drops.

In Egypt, things have gone rather further: 15 out of 24 dramas on Egyptian TV this year were made by Synergy, a firm linked to the intelligence services, and programme-makers have been ordered to come up with scripts that explicitly praise the military and promote conservative family values. Shows therefore tend to feature heroic policemen foiling terrorists, battling corruption and definitely not destabilising the autocratic government of President Sisi. (Sisi has previously manip- ulated soaps for his own benefit – back in 2013 when he was a general, he cancelled popular soap operas during Ramadan to increase the turnout for his street demon- strations supporting the army.)

And in Iran, some hardliners have used state TV to attack other bits of the government. *Gando,* a series all about spies and spying, was financed by a small cultural institute linked to the country's Revolutionary Guards. It was broadcast on Iran's national television network (which is backed by the same hardline elements) and seems to have been written to accuse the centrist government of being bureaucratic and corrupt. The

▼

Some non-governmental groups are writing their own drama shows to get their point across. The new Brazilian soap opera, *Aruanas*, written with the help of Greenpeace, glam- orises environmental campaigners battling to save the rainforest. Twenty-three million people watched the first episode.

government announced it might sue the producers for its 'lies and libels', which is the equivalent of the Metropolitan Police suing over the latest plot of *Line of Duty*.

Meanwhile the media-regulation authority in Pakistan ordered programme-makers to stop writing storylines involving conflict with mother-in-laws. Unfortunately it's not because they're tired of old-fashioned sexist gags, but because they regard the plots as covering too many feminist issues, and lacking sufficient men.

POO

Scientists in New Zealand recruited a troupe of super-duper 'super poopers'.

A faecal transplant can be a life-saving operation for patients who have dangerous gut conditions, or whose internal 'microbiome' has been depleted by illness. But you can't just transplant any old faeces into a patient who needs the operation. It turns out that some people's faeces are just better than others – specifically, those that are full of the good bacteria that can help other people's guts recover when they're transplanted across. The people blessed with such faeces are known to medicine as 'super poopers'. Research by the University of Auckland suggests that the more species of bacteria in the faeces, the better, although they also acknowledge that it's much more complicated than that, and that there's no 'one stool fits all' solution.

Faecal transplants are proving so popular that Australia suffered a poo shortage. Poo transplant clinics have sprung up across the country and some are taking donations, but the demand for high-quality stools is so high that the poo banks issued an urgent call for new donors to top up their supplies. Once you make a deposit in the bank, the stool is turned into a pill, referred to – by some Aussie doctors, anyway – as a 'crapsule'.

POT / KETTLE

A Kenyan MP turned up drunk to deliver a speech about alcohol abuse.

A meeting was convened for constituents and local politicians in Kenya's Nakuru county to discuss the increasing sale and consumption of home-brewed alcohol and work out how to tackle it. When MP Kuria Kimani turned up, people noticed that he was acting oddly. He insisted on taking a route to the venue that involved assistants lifting him over a fence, after which he plummeted out of sight on the other side of it. The audience's fears were confirmed when he stumbled up to the podium and slurred his way through an incoherent speech. A furious onlooker described him as 'drunk out of his wits', and Kimani was quickly ushered away by his staff when meeting attendants started threatening to beat him up for his shameful behaviour.

In other hypocrisy news:

▶ After Brazilian president Jair Bolsonaro spent much of his campaign promising a clampdown on drugs, his own presidential plane was found with 39 kilos of cocaine on board. It was being smuggled by one of his military personnel, Sergeant Manoel Silva Rodrigues, who was travelling on the plane at the time. It was doubly ironic because Bolsonaro has often emphasised the integrity and professionalism of his armed forces.

▶ Quebec's education minister was accused of double standards when he proudly tweeted a photo of himself with Pakistini activist and youngest-ever

Nobel laureate, Malala Yousafzai. Malala always wears a headscarf in public, but Quebec bans teachers from wearing religious symbols in schools.

▶ President Duterte of the Philippines signed a 'safe spaces' law to penalise various acts of sexual harassment, such as wolf-whistling, cat-calling and telling sexual jokes. He himself is famous for giving speeches full of sexual jokes and references, including one last year which argued that female communist guerrillas could be shot in the vaginas to render them 'useless'. In 2018 he kissed a woman on the lips in front of a cheering crowd, suggesting that she should tell her husband it was a joke.

▶ And Prince Harry criticised the dangers and addictiveness of social media, and the lack of human connection online, one day after he and his wife set up a record-breaking Instagram page. The profile was the fastest-ever to reach one million followers. It also made one enemy: driving instructor Kevin Keiley, the previous owner of the couple's handle, @sussexroyal. He said his permission hadn't been sought; he just woke up to find the royal couple using it.

PRIDE ▶

Munich Zoo marked 50 years of LGBT Pride by celebrating its bisexual lions.

Keepers at the German zoo led tours which took in those of its animals that exhibit homosexual behaviour, while teaching visitors about animal sexuality: 8 per cent of male lion sex, for example, is same-sex (females exhibit lesbian behaviour, too, but only in captivity). And homosexuality is also common in other zoo favourites, such as giraffes, snakes and penguins. Staff at London Zoo went one better, erecting a banner that read: 'Some penguins are gay, get over it.' They should know: the zoo is home to three gay penguin couples – Ronnie and Reggie, Nadja and Zimmer, and Dev and Martin – who all live happily together on a fake beach.

The whole of June was set aside for Pride events around the world, to commemorate the 50th anniversary of the Stonewall riots, which inspired the first Gay Pride march a year later. During that month, Iceland allowed people who didn't identify as male or female to legally change their gender to 'X'; Botswana decriminalised homo-sexuality; New York announced it would build the US's first statue honouring trans rights; and YouTuber Elijah Daniel bought every building in the tiny Michigan town of Hell and made a law banning any flags there, except for the rainbow Pride flag. The US women's football team won the World Cup during Pride week, after which their captain, Megan Rapinoe, told the viewing public: 'Go gays! You can't win a championship without gays on your team, it's pretty much never been done before. That's science right there . . . so yeah, to be gay and fabulous during Pride month at the World Cup is nice.'

Not everyone was quite so progressive, though. Members of an Italian far-right party tried to stop the country's Pride march, and when they were unable to do so, organised a prayer in a churchyard in Brianza – only to be chased away by nuns. And in Massachusetts a so-called 'Straight Pride' event was set up in protest against Gay Pride. Its organisers called the police in a panic when they received suspicious packages in the mail, only to discover, when one of the envelopes was opened, that it was filled with glitter.

PROTESTING ▶

A man in Kazakhstan was detained by police for holding a placard with nothing written on it.

In a bid to test how the notoriously anal Kazakh police would respond, Aslan Sagutdinov held up a wordless white piece of card and said nothing at all. Even so, officers in the northern city of Oral arrested him and bundled him into a police car. When he asked why he was being detained, they said, 'We'll sort that out later.' He was released without charge.

In other protest news:

▶ A thousand people were hired to attend a rally in Kiev against the practice of hiring people to attend rallies.

▶ In an attempt to show their movement was peaceful, Algerian protesters, whose marches led to the resignation of President Abdelaziz Bouteflika, came back the next day and cleaned up the streets.

▶ The controversial Westboro Baptist Church protested against Danica Roem, the first transgender person to be elected to the Virginia General Assembly. By way of a counter-protest, a group of heavy-metal fans stood alongside, playing the kazoo to drown them out. The church members were so annoyed they gave up their protest and went home.

PUTIN, VLADIMIR

For online censorship, *see* **Error 404**; for offline censorship, *see* **F***king Bad Language**; for hiding from a ship, *see* **GPS**; for making Italy shipshape, *see* **Roman Ruins**; and for a marine mammal's moniker, *see* **Russian Spying**.

PUTTING YOURSELF ON THE MAP

The Cornish tourist office demanded that weather forecasters stop standing in front of Cornwall.

The Cornish patsies met officials from the Met Office and the BBC to complain that their TV weather presenters always stand to the left of the British Isles when doing reports, thus obscuring Cornwall and the Scilly Isles. They argued that visitor numbers to the region were suffering as a result, and requested that forecasters take a step to the side. They also requested that presenters stop lumping Cornwall in with the rest of 'the south-west' in their forecasts – their argument being that often when the rest of the south-west is wet and cloudy, Cornwall is actually dry and sunny. This claim might raise a few eyebrows among those who have ever been on holiday in Cornwall.

Two Icelandic mayors were also worried about the weather wiping their region off the map. Jón Páll Hreinsson and Guðmundur Gunnarsson complained that if you look for their towns on Google Maps, all you

When Hurricane Dorian threatened the US, Trump said it would hit Alabama – a claim rubbished by meteorologists. To press home his point, Trump showed a map of the hurricane's projected path that he'd changed with a marker pen to show Alabama in the firing line. Defacing weather maps is illegal, but Trump's team still capitalised on the furore by selling branded marker pens.

can see from the satellite images is snow. They worry that this presents a misleading impression of the areas – which are often dry and snowless – and might deter tourists. They campaigned to have Google Maps change the images of their towns, arguing that it's especially unfair because rival towns had their satellite photos taken during the summer, and so look more appealing by comparison.

IN WHICH WE LEARN . . .

*How noise pollution is affecting birds'
biology, who had 'automatic chemistry'
with Donald Trump, and who was
mourned by the world of physics.*

QUANTUM ENTANGLEMENT ▶

Physicists took the first-ever photo of a particle reacting to something that hadn't happened to it.

──────── ▼ ────────

Quantum entanglement may help us to create a new kind of radar by using the fact that if two particles are paired, when something happens to one, it changes the other. So if a plane flies past the first particle, you should be able to detect it with the second. This year, a team in Austria demonstrated for the first time that this works in practice (though currently only under lab conditions).

To do this, scientists from the University of Glasgow first had to create two sets of light particles, or photons, that were inextricably linked, thanks to a concept called 'quantum entanglement'. When two photons are linked like this, whatever you do to one of them will simultaneously happen to the other, no matter how far away they are from each other. It's a bit like having a twin brother in Australia whose expression changes every time you change yours. Einstein didn't like it – he called it 'spooky action at a distance' – but experiments have consistently shown the phenomenon to be genuine.

Having created the sets of particles, the Glasgow team placed them in different locations in the lab. One lot of particles was left alone, while the other was then passed through a material known as β-barium borate that caused them to change, ever so slightly. The scientists then took photographs of both groups of photons using a camera that took 40,000 photos per second, at a temperature of −30° and in pitch darkness; and sure enough, the two sets of snaps looked identical in a way that was too unlikely to be caused by luck alone.

It's a bit like going on a roller-coaster and having your photo taken, while at the exact same time your twin in Australia is having their photo taken as they sit quietly in a café. Thanks to this 'spooky action at a distance', both you and your twin would be wearing precisely the same slightly embarrassing, wide-eyed, screaming expression.

QUARKS ▶

The world lost a big personality who found the smallest things.

Physicist Murray Gell-Mann showed promise early on, winning an under-12s spelling bee when he was just seven. He went on to scale even dizzier heights, gaining a scholarship to Yale aged 14 and following that up, 25 years later, with a Nobel Prize in Physics. This was for his theory that protons and neutrons are composed of smaller particles, the fundamental building blocks of everything: quarks. Gell-Mann thought the sound 'kwork' was right for his new particle, but hadn't decided on a spelling until he read James Joyce's novel *Finnegans Wake*, which contains the sentence 'Three quarks for Muster Mark!' Gell-Mann settled on that, though he pronounced it to rhyme with 'pork', not 'park'.*

*'Quark' was certainly an improvement on the suggestion made by Gell-Mann's colleague and rival Richard Feynman. He proposed calling it a 'Quack'.

Gell-Mann's work finally made sense of what's known as the 'particle zoo', the mysterious mess of subatomic particles that scientists were struggling to classify. But the breakthrough might never have occurred if his father had had his way. Keen for Murray to pick a career that might make some money, he suggested engineering. Murray replied that he'd rather starve, and that if he ever designed anything, it would be guaranteed to fall down. In the end the two of them compromised on physics.

Among Gell-Mann's many other interests outside physics was ornithology. He even made a significant contribution to the discipline, developing the Rapid Assessment Program with two friends while on a birdwatching trip with them. This is a way of calculating the biodiversity of endangered ecosystems, which is still used in conservation today.

In addition Gell-Mann was a skilled linguist, speaking (to different levels of proficiency) English, French, Spanish, Italian and Danish. He also spoke enough Swedish to be able to use it in part of his Nobel Prize acceptance speech (he said that he achieved this by converting his Danish into Swedish, 'sometimes with some success and sometimes with much less success'). It's quite likely that he spoke other languages, too. One journalist reported how, when they were in a restaurant together, Gell-Mann called over a waiter and corrected the spelling of a Hungarian word on the menu.

All in all, despite the ups and downs of his life, Gell-Mann was a strange and charming man, from top to bottom.

QUEEN, THE ▶

A thousand toilet rolls were intercepted on their way to the throne.

A German company sent the paper to the palace as a gift for the Queen to ensure she wasn't caught short, if the UK suffered any kind of supply problem due to ▮▮▮▮. But the luxury loo rolls didn't make it to Her Majesty, instead being donated to a secondary school in Croydon.

Not only did the Queen not get her bog roll, she didn't get her cheeseburger pizzas either. Domino's Pizza fell for a prank, and tried to deliver £46 worth of pizza to 'Elizabeth' at Buckingham Palace. The driver was stopped by armed police, who did at least radio through to the control room to check whether the Queen had actually ordered a pizza.

One thing the Queen did receive at Buckingham Palace was the President of the United States. Trump said of his first State Visit that he had established an 'incredible' rapport with the Queen and that 'we had automatic chemistry . . . There are those that say they have never seen the Queen have a better time, a more animated time. We had a period where we were talking solid straight, I didn't even know who the other people at the table were, never spoke to them.' The banquet was incredibly ornate. It took a team of three officials eight weeks to unpack the cutlery and crockery, and it took five days to set the table. The food included halibut, watercress mousse, asparagus spears and chervil sauce, though one suspects Trump might have been just as happy with £46 worth of cheese-burger pizza.

—— ▼ ——

Following the success of the Freddie Mercury biopic *Bohemian Rhapsody*, Queen the band is now richer than the actual Queen.

Celebrating the 125th anniversary of . . .

THE WORLD'S FIRST AUTOMOBILE RACE, which ran from Paris to Rouen in 1894. The winner wasn't the first car to pass the finish line, but the one deemed the safest, most efficient and most cost-effective to operate. 102 vehicles registered; only 21 even made it to the starting line.

BILLBOARD MAGAZINE. Today, it's a famous entertainment publication, known for its spin-off Billboard Hot 100, America's main music chart. But Billboard started out as a magazine about actual billboards. Featured columns included 'The Bill Room Gossip' and 'The Indefatigable and Tireless Industry of the Bill Poster'.

THE ERADICATION OF AN ENTIRE SPECIES OF WREN, thanks to a single cat. Tibbles had arrived with her owner, the lighthouse keeper, and promptly started killing wrens and bringing them to him as presents. He sent specimens to naturalists in England, who confirmed that he had discovered a new species. Sadly, by the time that message reached him, his pet had made sure that the Stephens Island wren was not only a new species, but also an extinct species.

KINETOSCOPE, whose first parlour opened in New York. It was essentially a cinema, but rather than hosting a single screen for punters, it charged them 5 cents to look through a peephole at their own private movie. The parlour contained five of these Edison kinetoscopes, each showing a different film, so if you wanted to see the full set it would cost you 25 cents. The same year the parlour opened, Thomas Edison released the oldest-surviving motion picture, *Fred Ott's Sneeze*. In the gripping five-second movie, Edison's assistant, Fred Ott, is seen taking a pinch of snuff and sneezing comically.

PUSHBALL, a sport created by an American who reckoned that spectators found the ball in football too small and difficult to see. And so he came up with pushball, where the ball was 6 feet wide, made from the hides of nine horses and took two and a half hours to inflate. A horseback version developed, which proved surprisingly popular in the UK for about 30 years.

THE EGG-AND-SPOON RACE. All the participants in the first-known race to take place had to balance an egg on a spoon in one hand, while simultaneously punting a boat along a river with the other.

QUIET ▶

Residents of an Italian town had to keep quiet for an entire month so that a violin could be heard.

Britain's Department for Transport is introducing 'noise cameras' that can measure the sound levels of passing cars and then use licence-plate recognition software to identify those with illegally loud engines.

Cremona is famous for its musical instruments, in particular the violins and cellos made there by Antonio Stradivari. However, as instruments age, they become more delicate and may at some point have to 'go to sleep' for ever, as experts put it. The authorities therefore agreed to record the sounds of four of the most famous stringed instruments the city possesses, so that future generations will be able to hear them long after the objects themselves are no longer functional. The recordings were scheduled to take place in the city's auditorium. But there was a big problem. Because the instruments had to be recorded with highly sensitive microphones, there was a danger that the background noise of the city might get picked up as well. Even the sound of a single car engine, or of a woman walking past the building in high heels, might have ended up being recorded for posterity, alongside the Stradivarius.

So the city authorities launched an ambitious attempt to shut everyone up. They cordoned off the cobbled streets around the auditorium, and the mayor asked citizens to avoid any sudden and unnecessary sounds, for the five full weeks that the recordings were scheduled to take. To avoid faint electrical buzzing, every lightbulb in the concert hall was unscrewed. When a barista in a nearby café accidentally dropped a glass and smashed it, meaning that the sound of the glass ended up on the tape, the police popped in to shush her. Happily, aside from this hiccup, the noise ban worked, and future composers will be able to sample these recordings, to create new music using instruments that can no longer be played.

Elsewhere, noise pollution continues unchecked. A study by Queen's University Belfast found that human noise pollution is preventing birds from communicating properly: even when they try to chirp aggressively, other birds can't hear them. And birds themselves can cause problems – specifically on the French island of Oléron, where a rooster called Maurice became the centre of a court battle when his human neighbours complained about his morning calls. Maurice's owner, Corinne Fesseau, pointed out that cockerels just do what they do. The complaining neighbours said it was much too loud and that the area was supposed to be tranquil. Cockerel-owners turned up to show support outside the court, and the legal to-doodle-doo took three months to resolve – in Maurice's favour.

QUITTERS

A Slovenian MP resigned after stealing a sandwich.

While talking to a committee about what he felt to be the country's over-reliance on CCTV, Darij Krajcic relayed an anecdote about a 'social experiment' that he had conducted. He'd been in a supermarket, waiting to pay for a sandwich, but on realising all the staff were chatting amongst themselves and ignoring him, he eventually just walked out without paying. Initially the other MPs on the committee laughed. Opposition law-makers, however, drew attention to the grave nature of his crime and he was eventually forced to step down.

Other quitters of the year included:

▶ Bill McLeod, who became a civil court judge in Harris County, Texas, at the start of the year, but accidentally resigned in April after announcing his intention to run for the state Supreme Court. Article 16, Section 65 of the Texan constitution states that any such announcement from a judge means automatic resignation.

▶ The King of Malaysia abdicated for the first time in the country's history. Sultan Muhammad V of Kelantan gave up the throne, following rumours that he had married a Russian beauty queen. Arguably, though, this wasn't such a big deal, because in Malaysia the monarchy rotates between nine royal houses, with the monarch changing hands every five years.

▶ The entire governments of Burkina Faso and Mali, and every single member of the Sri Lankan parliament, resigned their roles at one time or another.

▶ And Jony Ive, the designer of the iMac, iPod, iPhone and iPad, resigned from Apple. Ive owns or part-owns more than 1,000 other patents, including three lanyards, two shopping bags and a toilet.

QUIZZES ▶

The Book of the Year 2019 contains a number of quizzes: for a speling test, *see* **Bees, Spelling**; for 🫤, *see* **Emojis**, for pitting yourself against the people, *see* **Our Survey Said . . .**; for a sp0t the difference, *see* **Spot the Difference**; and for cryptic clues, *see* **X-Word**. And for the answers, see page 358.

IN WHICH WE LEARN . . .

*Which reptiles are sinking, why Rome
is stinking, how robots can be of service,
and which robot will be in a cervix.*

RADIOACTIVE ▶

A museum in the Grand Canyon discovered it had left three buckets of radioactive uranium sitting out, exposed to the public, for almost 20 years.

This became public in February thanks to a rogue email sent by health-and-safety officer Elston 'Swede' Stephenson. Apparently, three paint buckets brim-full of radioactive uranium ore had been stored next to a taxidermy exhibit for 18 years, one of them so packed that it wouldn't close properly. It was calculated that visitors who paused at the nearby exhibit would have received a dose that exceeded recommended safety standards within 30 seconds; children passing nearby would have had an unsafe dose within about three seconds – such children, in fact, could have received 4,000 times the recommended safe dose. (Fortunately, these recommended doses seem to be very conservative, and unless museum visitors were actively licking the buckets, they would probably have been fine.)

The buckets were only discovered to be radioactive because the son of a National Park employee, who happened to be a Geiger-counter fan, brought one to the museum's collection room, where it went haywire. The tins were eventually removed in June last year, by the highly unscientific method of staff wearing dishwashing gloves pushing them with a mop handle. Once the staff had dumped the uranium ore into a nearby mine, they then returned the paint buckets to the building.

There was a radiation scare in Oklahoma, too, where a driver who was pulled over because his licence plate had expired was found to be transporting some whisky, a rattlesnake and a box labelled 'uranium'. Not only that, but the car turned out to have been stolen. As one police officer noted, 'the uranium is the wild card in that

RAPINOE, MEGAN

<u>Name:</u>
Megan Rapinoe

<u>Gender:</u>
Female

<u>Job:</u>
Professional footballer

<u>Salary:</u>
A lot less than male professional footballers

<u>Reason for being in the news:</u>
During the Women's World Cup, Megan Rapinoe was interviewed by a reporter from '8 by 8' magazine and was asked, 'Are you excited about the prospect of going to the White House?' Rapinoe replied, 'Pfft, I'm not going to the fucking White House.' When later asked about the outburst, Rapinoe showed only slight contrition, saying, 'I stand by the comments that I made about not wanting to go to the White House, with the exception of the expletive. My mom will be very upset about that.'

Donald Trump responded with a tweet saying, 'I am a big fan of the American Team, and Women's Soccer, but Megan should WIN first before she TALKS! Finish the job!' In the end, Rapinoe did finish the job, winning the World Cup for the US, along with the golden boot for top scorer in the competition, and the award for Player of the Match in the final. She could hardly have answered the president in a more clinical way. Immediately after the World Cup, one polling company found that Rapinoe would beat Trump in a presidential election.

Rapinoe is no stranger to controversy. In solidarity with the Black Lives Matter movement, she refuses to sing the national anthem before matches (although she did once score a goal, grab a pitch-side microphone and belt out a rendition of Bruce Springsteen's 'Born in the USA'). And she is a member of a group that is pursuing a lawsuit against the US Soccer Federation on the grounds that the women's team earns less than the men's, despite being massively more successful and bringing in more money. During the World Cup final American fans chanted, 'USA! Equal Pay!'

situation'. When officers asked the man what he thought he was doing, he told them he was hoping to make a 'super-snake'. Unsurprisingly, he was arrested.

But at least there is a place where that uranium can now safely be stored. A company called Deep Isolation managed to drill a hole into the Earth a mile long, put a fake barrel of radioactive material at the bottom and then retrieve it. Their suggestion is that if radioactive waste can be buried in shale seams 2 miles down – effectively, reverse-fracking – the radioactivity will be contained for many millions of years.

REINVENTING THE WHEEL

You can now be pulled over for drink-driving by your own car.

Volvo is developing a new vehicle that will have cameras and sensors on the inside and outside, enabling it to spot when drivers appear to be drowsy, distracted or under the influence of alcohol or drugs (it detects, for instance, whether they have their eyes closed for an extended period of time). Once the car has determined that it's being driven by an unfit motorist, it takes evasive action – cutting its speed or even pulling over to the side of the road, so that the driver is unable to cause an accident.

The battle against drink-driving is getting smarter and smarter. Convicted French drink-drivers are now being asked to fit breathalyser-controlled ignition locks to their car, which only work if the driver is fit to drive. To reduce the chances of them cheating, they have to blow into the breathalyser again, several minutes into their journey.

Across the motor industry, firms are competing to outsmart each other with technology. If you're driving

Hyundai unveiled a prototype for a car that can walk. The 'Elevate' operates like a normal automobile, but if it encounters an obstacle up to 5 foot high or long it can step over it by deploying four mechanical legs. The plan is to develop vehicles that can negotiate difficult terrain - for example, in areas hit by natural disasters.

through snow, it might pay to be in a Volvo – the company announced that its cars will soon be warning each other about slippery roads, thanks to automatic detection systems, which measure when the friction on the road is unusually low, then notify other drivers in the area. On the other hand, if the worst happens and you do have an accident, a Hyundai might be even better; the firm is planning a system that will measure the forces on a driver's body in a crash, work out in which ways they're likely to be injured, then contact the emergency services and tell them what is likely to have happened to the driver.

There's good news for taxi passengers, too. Google has invented a new tool that can tell you if your driver is going the long way round. If they depart from the optimum route by more than 500 metres, you will be alerted. With any luck, this information will help passengers who are being ripped off, as well as the (hopefully) smaller number who are being kidnapped.

REPTILE FALLS ▶

Dead alligators were dropped into the sea in the name of science.

Sometimes researchers drop wood into the ocean to see what turns up to eat it, after it has sunk to the bottom. It's a practice known as a 'wood fall' and is designed to shed light on the workings of ocean ecosystems. This year Louisiana scientists Craig McClain, Clifton Nunnally and River Dixon went a step further with their 'reptile falls', which involved dropping three dead alligators into the Gulf of Mexico. The first feeders, which turned up within 24 hours, were giant, pink, football-sized deep-sea woodlice. The scientists thought the bugs might struggle to penetrate the alligators' tough outer exterior,

REINCARNATION

(OR: CRAP ANIMALS TO COME BACK AS)

BY DAN SCHREIBER

Reincarnation used to be very straight-
forward: you died and then came back
as, say, a badger. But these days there's
paperwork. For over a decade, Buddhists
in China have had to apply to the government for approval to
reincarnate. And this year the Chinese government ruled that it will
be responsible for finding the next incarnation of the Dalai Lama – a
matter usually left to a committee of High Lamas in Tibet. The move
prompted the current Dalai Lama to threaten to reincarnate outside
Tibet, away from the Chinese authorities. It's possible, therefore, that
one day we might have two people claiming to be the Dalai Lama – a
Lama-approved one and a Chinese knock-off.

Now, I don't know how this reincarnation business works, but if the
Buddhists are right, we're all coming back as something. You might
think this is nonsense, but I'm not so sure. Buddhists can do some
pretty remarkable things. FACT: you can dry a wet towel by throwing
it over a meditating monk. They're actually able to raise their body
temperatures at will, as scientists discovered in Northern India.
(Warning: this does not work on all monks. And always, always ask
permission before hanging your damp socks on one.) Frankly, if they
can do that kind of wizardry, I'm inclined to believe what they say
about reincarnation.

My only issue with the concept is that I had assumed we might have a
say in what we returned as, but it turns out that we don't. And, having

thoroughly read the news this year, a worrying thought has dawned on me: there are a lot of crap animals to come back as.

I particularly pity anyone who was reincarnated this year as a mouse in Harvard. Scientists there have been feeding them extracts of marathon runners' poo to make them run faster. Yes, you read that correctly. Stool samples were taken from 87 marathon runners, a week before and after their events, and tested for changes in microbe levels. The mice were then fed an isolated strain of bacteria from the poo, before being put on a treadmill. Mice that received the bacteria ran 13 per cent faster than those that hadn't – though perhaps they were trying to escape the scientists.

It was also bad news for those who came back as seagulls. Until now they've been able to steal chips from humans, no matter how many times they've been shooed away. However, new research has shown that all humans may need to do to stop the birds from taking the food is to stare them in the face. That's the whole point of being a seagull kyboshed. No wonder gulls are so pissed off! (see **Birds, Angry**).

It's not even safe to come back as something as simple as lichen these days! This is thanks to a shocking new predator: the horny New Zealander. Botanists have warned Kiwis against consuming what's been called 'sexy pavement lichen', after discovering it was being sold online as a natural alternative to Viagra in places like China. On the plus side, if you are eaten to death, you'll at least have another chance to come back as something a bit better.

Whatever you reincarnate as, I hope it's something as loved as a Thai King's dog (see **Vajiralongkorn**) and that you return before any other government starts imposing their own strict reincarnation laws. And to those who think I'm being overdramatic and that it would be impossible for a government to actually track down someone who had illegally come back as, say, a moth, I have eight words for you: tell that to the Turkish bee, my friend (see **Capital Punishment**).

but in fact they made a beeline for the soft flesh of the armpits and got stuck straight in. In normal circumstances they can go without eating for five years, so this all-you-can-eat 'gator buffet should sustain them for many years to come.

As well as providing a banquet for giant pink woodlice, the researchers speculated that their 'reptile falls' might provide clues about ancient food webs. Alligators are very similar to prehistoric ocean beasts such as plesiosaurs, which would have died and sunk to the bottom of the oceans in great numbers. So if underwater life is attracted to the former, it may be that ancient sea-critters feasted on the corpses of the latter.

RHINOS

To help cure their fear of flying, rhinos were given emotional-support humans.

Like many of us, rhinos don't really like flying. They are very nervous animals and easily get spooked by any change in circumstances. So when two male and three female eastern black rhinoceroses needed to be moved from a zoo in Czechia to a new home in Rwanda, their minders made sure they were flight-ready. For months they fed the rhinos in the crates in which they would be transported, in order to get them accustomed to their temporary homes, and cuddled them to keep them calm. The transfer was a success – the largest transportation of rhinos from Europe to Africa ever to happen.

Meanwhile, in America, scientists at San Diego Zoo are developing a robot that can sail through a rhino's cervix. A female rhino's reproductive system is incredibly complicated – it's been described by Barbara Durrant, director of reproductive sciences at the San Diego Zoo, as 'like Lombard Street in San Francisco, where it's just back and forth, back and forth' – and this makes artificial insemination very tricky. So roboticists and biologists have come together to create a snake-like bot that can crawl through a rhino's reproductive tract and transport a fertilised embryo into the animal's uterus. If it works, it could help reverse the sharp decline in the world's rhino population – although they'd probably appreciate a cuddle afterwards.

ROBOTS

South Korea's new robotics museum will be built by robots.

The Seoul Robot Science Museum will open in 2022, but the first exhibit will be launched in 2020, when robots will mould and assemble the building itself (granted, humans will have quite a lot of input at the 'design' stage). Not only that, but the entire concrete land-scape around the building will be 3D printed too.

In other robotic news:

▶ Amazon tried out special robot-repelling belts and braces to stop their staff being run over by robots.

▶ The University of Pennsylvania developed a robot that can crawl through your brain without hurting you. The four-legged 'crawler' is the smallest robot with computer circuitry yet. It's 70 microns across – the width of a very thin hair – and can crawl on legs just 100 atoms thick. The hope is that the robots will one day track the activity of neurons in the brain or deliver helpful bacteria to the digestive system.

▶ Roboticists at MIT built a 'Jenga-bot' that has taught itself how to remove blocks from a Jenga tower without the stack collapsing. At the moment it's only playing against itself, but humans may well find themselves losing to it before long. It's a more significant advance than it sounds, because it's a further step in the creation of robots that can manipulate real-world objects.

▶ Researchers from Google, Columbia, MIT and Princeton came up with 'TossingBot' – a robot that can accurately chuck bananas into a bucket. Throwing objects of different shapes and sizes is a huge challenge for bots, but if they learn how to do it right, it could come in very handy in future. For instance, they will be able to make automated warehouses more efficient, by tossing objects from one place to the other, rather than walking them to their destination.

▶ And the robotic bottom that Ford has long used to test its car seats for wear and tear has been improved. It now has sweat glands and can mimic the behaviour of a driver who is driving naked on a hot day.

ROCKALL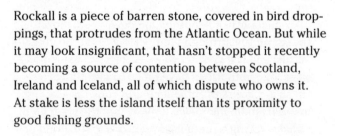

A diplomatic spat erupted over a tiny rock in the middle of the sea.

Rockall is a piece of barren stone, covered in bird droppings, that protrudes from the Atlantic Ocean. But while it may look insignificant, that hasn't stopped it recently becoming a source of contention between Scotland, Ireland and Iceland, all of which dispute who owns it. At stake is less the island itself than its proximity to good fishing grounds.

Given that a nation's territorial waters typically end 12 nautical miles from its coast, none of the countries has a particularly strong claim: Rockall is 160 nautical miles from Scotland, 200 nautical miles from Ireland and 380 nautical miles from Iceland. Furthermore, the

UN convention is that a state can lay claim to territorial waters only if the land in question is habitable, but the environment on Rockall is so unforgiving that nobody has ever stuck it out for more than a few weeks. The record is held by adventurer Nick Hancock, who spent 45 days there in 2014 during his optimistically named '60 days on Rockall' campaign.

Scotland's claim to Rockall dates from 1955, when its sailors first planted a flag on the extinct volcano and screwed a small plaque to its summit. Ireland claims a much longer association with the rock, as St Brendan is said to have visited it in the sixth century, although it should be noted that it's not altogether certain St Brendan actually existed. Irish premier Leo Varadkar summed up the futility of the situation in June when he suggested that everyone share fishing rights around Rockall, saying, simply, 'Rockall is a rock'.

ROMAN RUINS

Rome was plagued by a street gang who went around illegally mending things.

Rome's infrastructure is in a disastrous state. The city's roads contain 10,000 potholes; 1,000 tonnes of rubbish was left on the streets as temperatures hit the mid-30s Celsius; and last year there was a spate of exploding buses. The authorities have failed to sort things out, and so a network of activists has sprung up. The *Gruppa Artigiani Pronto Intervento*, or GAP, goes around filling potholes, fixing fountains and repairing broken roads, despite the fact that it's against the law, because it's done without official permission and involves lots of trespassing. After every operation, the group leaves its signature, along with leaflets attempting to recruit more Romans to the cause.

Meanwhile a different bunch of activists got to work publicising the garbage problem by posting pictures of piles of rubbish, to shame the government into taking action. Their Facebook page – *'Roma Fa Schifo'*, Rome is Disgusting – now has 200,000 followers. Other Romans launched an online competition for the most disgusting dustbin. One person who unexpectedly assisted the campaign was Vladimir Putin. People noticed that when he was invited to Rome, the bits of the city that he visited did at least get a light cleaning.

In the face of the continuing crisis, mayor Virginia Raggi called in the Italian Army to prune the city's trees, and deployed prisoners to fill potholes and clean up the city's parks. Perhaps in an attempt to shift responsibility elsewhere, Rome updated its local laws to stop tourists behaving antisocially. It is now illegal to touch a drinking fountain with your lips (which is going to be hard to enforce). Messy eating has also been banned, as well as walking round bare-chested and putting 'love-locks' on monuments or bridges. However, if the city continues to stink that badly, lovers won't be visiting much longer.

ROOM WITH A VIEW

The head of the Budget Suites hotel chain offered a room for £27,500 a night.

Hotelier Robert Bigelow may be used to dealing with travellers on American road trips, but his next project will be offering accommodation 200 miles above the surface of the Earth, in the International Space Station. Bigelow's hotel is slated to launch in 2021, and for a bargain £27,500 rate, residents will get food, air, medical kits, exercise equipment and use of the station's life-support systems and toilet.

If the price seems astronomical, it's worth bearing in mind that the ISS is orbiting the Earth at 17,000 mph, and so astronauts experience 16 sunrises and sunsets every 24 hours. In other words, you'll get 16 days for the price of one. There is no information yet on minibar prices.

RUNAWAYS

Eleven senators from Oregon ran off.

The magnificent eleven (or the dirty almost-dozen) are all Republican state senators, who walked out of the Oregon legislature in June and proceeded to go AWOL. They were protesting against climate-change legislation that the Democrat-controlled senate was hoping to pass, and were seeking to block it by ensuring there wouldn't be enough senators present for any bills to get through. For nine days nobody knew where they'd gone.

The Democratic governor instructed state police to track them down and bring them back so that the chamber could vote on the bill. But the police's jurisdiction only covers Oregon, so the senators simply fled into neighbouring states. One of them, Cliff Bentz, hid in Idaho, changing hotels frequently and using a 'burner' phone wrapped in tin foil. His colleague, Tim Knopp, no doubt regretted the fact that he'd left in such a hurry, informing the *Washington Post* (from a secret location) that he'd only packed two pairs of socks. Another senator, Brian Boquist, sent the ominous warning: 'If you send the State Police to get me, Hell's coming to visit you personally.' He later threatened violence, saying that the authorities should 'send bachelors and come heavily armed'. All the senators eventually came back, having killed off the climate bill.

Another runaway who came back was an Austrian man who handed himself in, 10 years after running away from prison. He had spent most of the last decade living on a beach in Tenerife, but said he'd had enough, because the Canary Islands 'aren't as nice as they used to be'.

RUSSIAN SPYING

Норвежцы сказали, что киты, которые плавали рядом с кораблями, были русскими шпионами.

The beluga whale was definitely lost, but whether or not it was a Russian spy will probably never be known. We do know that Russia has a marine mammal corps – in the past the Russian Army TV channel has broadcast a programme showing beluga whales being trained as 'underwater special forces'. But when this particular cetacean was found swimming in a Norwegian bay with a harness that had 'Equipment St Petersburg' written on it, some experts said it was just as likely to be a children's emotional-support animal as a Russian spy. Some swimmers who interacted with the whale were convinced it was a highly trained operative, however: diver Tom Ralph said the beluga stole a knife from another diver, then 'backed away about a metre and just sat there with this knife in its mouth'.

If the whale is a spy, then it has defected. And it seems quite happy in its new Norwegian home. It has entertained locals in return for 20 kilos of herring every day and, thanks to an online poll, got a new name, Hvaldimir – which is a contraction of the Norwegian word for 'whale' and the first name of Mr Putin.

IN WHICH WE LEARN . . .

*Why a medium spacesuit caused an
extra-large problem, where you can find
a belt made of seaweed, how to spot a
sockpuppet, why teenage boys' pants are
all on fire, who keeps 24 gerbils down
their trousers, and how a musician
saved a rare bird's genes.*

SAX APPEAL

New Zealand recruited a saxophonist to get endangered birds in a sexy mood.

The kakapo – a flightless, slightly dozy bird that is native to New Zealand – is desperately endangered, with just 142 adults holding out on three small islands that have been specially cleared of predatory mammals. Every new kakapo therefore counts, particularly as the population now faces a fresh threat from a fungal infection. So New Zealand's Department for Conservation called for a saxophonist to 'get our kakapo in the mood'. 'While the effect of saxophones on kakapo might not yet be scientifically proven,' the job ad read, '. . . we reckon it's worth a punt.'

The successful applicant, 23-year-old Piers Dashfield, duly set to work, recording tracks that were to be played to the parrots to encourage them to mate. His recording booth was kitted out 'with all sorts of things to make it romantic. The lights were dimmed, there were flowers and petals all around, a little bottle of wine, a framed picture of the kakapo.' He also received the unofficial title of New Zealand's Saxiest Saxophonist.

Conservationists called on science as well as saxophones to save the kakapo. They deployed 3D-printed 'smart eggs' that make noises, to train mothers in how they should behave when they have actual eggs to look after. They also used a sperm drone – known as the 'cloacal courier' – which flew male kakapo semen across the island to waiting females. A camera rig was placed in every nest, and every parrot was fitted with a transmitter so that conservationists could support them as necessary; and they were all given a tailored diet. To get the word across to the public, an 'advocacy' kakapo, named Sirocco, toured the country as an Official Spokesbird for Conservation. All this, and the saxophone music, seems to be paying off. This year 76 chicks were hatched, double the number in 2016.

SCIENTISTS HAVE DISCOVERED... ▶

Teenage boys are bigger bullshitters than girls.

This was the conclusion of a survey of more than 40,000 15-year-olds from all around the world. Asked if they understood a number of mathematical concepts (including some that don't actually exist), boys were much more likely to claim that they did. And of all the bullshitting boys, those in North America were the most bullshitty.

But not all studies resulted in such statements of the bleeding obvious. Scientists finally worked out what time it is on Saturn; discovered that astronauts who go into space are likely to have herpes flare up; and found that while it is theoretically possible to travel through wormholes, it would take longer than going to your destination directly, so it's not much of a shortcut. More down-to-earth studies found that just thinking about a cup of coffee can improve your focus and that severe constipation can cause amnesia.

Chimps were recorded using a stick to mash potatoes, and teaching each other the skill; young male bonobos were observed having sex while being helped out by their mothers, who acted as bodyguards; and the monkey word for 'eagle' was found to be the same as their word for 'drone'.

An entirely new species of human was found in the Philippines; a species of shipworm was discovered that eats stones and excretes sand; and scientists made the vital discovery that cats farm bacteria in their bottoms. Another team worked out that by 2030 planet Earth will produce at least five billion tonnes of poo, most of which will come from cattle. Joe Brown, professor of environmental engineering at Georgia Institute of Technology, said, 'It's a huge problem. Animal

SAUSAGES

By ANDREW HUNTER MURRAY

Careful readers of the previous two Books of the Year may have noticed the large – some would say unhealthily large – number of sausage stories included. In 2017, there was the unmanned drone sausage-delivery system. In 2018, there was the butcher who escaped his own locked freezer using a sausage as a battering ram.

My colleagues are now resigned to my insistence on covering the big sausage news each year. (Please note: 'big sausage news' just means the biggest stories about individual sausages, rather than news stories specifically about very big sausages.) But this year they have decided it should be solely my responsibility. So I am delighted to present the year's top sausage scoops, unmediated by the others and their cruel anti-sausage agenda.

← Don't believe any of this. Andy insisted on writing this page by himself, and actively refused any suggestions to tone down the madness.

First, North Yorkshire was promised – then cruelly denied – a sausage-based tourist attraction. Hambleton council approved the construction of 'Sausage World' by Yorkshire's Heck Food, which offered fun for all the family: founder Andrew Keeble boasted, 'We have a machine that can produce 1,300 sausages a minute. It's like a Gatling gun.' Obviously, this would have been amazing, and I would have been first in line for a season ticket, but tragically Sausage World was one of the casualties of ▮▮▮; it will no longer qualify for an EU grant. The fight isn't over yet – the firm will try to raise money in other ways, an executive told 'Meat Management' magazine. (Also, anyone who doesn't like the sound of 'Meat Management' magazine should probably skip the rest of this article and frankly I'm surprised you made it this far.)

Heck was responsible for another of the year's sausage stories, when the firm – already an expert in dealing with large, pink tubes of offal – received a visit from Boris Johnson during the Tory leadership contest. Bojo was presented with a special 'Boris banger' and was draped with a string of sausages. But some people were furious, pointing out the irony of the firm welcoming Johnson when half its workforce consists of immigrants from Eastern Europe, many of whom may be affected by ▮▮▮▮. An anti-Heck campaign was launched – or, as Teesside Live called it, a 'Boris banger boycott backlash'.

Elsewhere, the humble sausage was under threat. Politicians in Germany – the epicentre of world sausage news – considered a proposal to strip sossies of their tax privileges. Most products are taxed at a VAT rate of 19 per cent, but for meat products it's 7 per cent: effectively, German sausages are state-subsidised. This year the powers-that-be considered raising the VAT on meat, but the prospect of hiking the price of a packet of sausages by 29 cents was ultimately deemed too radical and the idea was abandoned (I therefore halted my sausage-pricing protest outside the German embassy).

If you still think the world of bangers is dull and stodgy, bear in mind that there's always something new on the sausage horizon. This year, for example, Australian scientists started developing sausages made of maggots and locusts, which are much more sustainable than traditional recipes. This will please campaigners like Carolien Niebling, a Dutch designer who has spent several years saying we should be nieb-ling on more ethical alternatives and written a book called 'The Sausage of the Future'.

Tragically, this book went to press before the annual jamboree of UK Sausage Week kicked off, so we're unable to tell you what won in the categories of Traditional Sausage or Innovative Sausage. And there's so little room left that I can't tell you about the Marks & Spencer 'Love Sausage'. Or the square-sausage Aldi–Lidl controversy.

OK, that's enough sausages, thanks, Andy.

Wait! Or the Great British Sausage Surplus. Or the ~~sausa~~ *seriously.*

waste is going up because, as populations and wealth increase, there's a bigger demand for protein . . . nobody is talking about this.' Perhaps it's about time we all took a leaf from a North American teenage boys' book and start talking bullshit.

SCOOTERS

The man who invented the adult scooter did so because he was hungry for a sausage.

2019 was a big year for scooters. Not just because countless so-called adults took to zipping around cities on them, but because it marked the 20th anniversary of the invention of the adult scooter. Swiss businessman Wim Ouboter had often ridden scooters as a child (he was inspired to do so by his sister, who had one leg shorter than the other and so found it easier to ride a scooter than a bicycle). Later in life he found himself living near a sausage shop that he liked, which was too far away to walk to, but not far enough away to justify a car journey. So, partly to solve this conundrum, he launched the adult scooter in 1999.

Ouboter became a micro-scooter millionaire, but even he couldn't have predicted how things would develop. This year the descendants of his prototype have been rolled out in dozens of cities across the world, spreading anarchy and injury wherever they go. Studies revealed that e-scooters get caught up in accidents 44 times as often as motorbikes and 22 times as often as cars, and that one user in three is hurt on their first go. French surgeons reported a surge in demand for orthopaedic operations, linked to scooter usage.

As if that wasn't bad enough, some e-scooter software developed bugs. The rental firm Lime announced in an official statement that riders should be extra-cautious, because of a technical issue that could cause 'sudden excessive braking during use' – particularly when scooters were being ridden downhill at top speed.

Some authorities launched a crackdown. France, whose capital is now home to 25,000 *trottinettes*, made it an offence to ride on a pavement or a main road. Denmark's police took on intoxicated scooter-riding Danes, arresting 28 people in a single weekend (four stoned and 24 drunk). Berlin's authorities fined one rider every four minutes. And Munich's police arrested nearly 100 riders in just four weeks, including one man who crashed his scooter into a police car. A spokeswoman for the German Council on Traffic Safety told a newspaper, with great understatement, that 'In our view, the launch of e-scooters in Germany isn't going particularly well.' Unless the firms behind them start showing some control, sales may start going downhill – fast.

When Hurricane Dorian was heading towards Florida in September, e-scooter firms removed all the scooters they could from the region, to avoid the risk of a lethal 'scooternado' – a storm of unmoored scooters, whipped up into the hurricane and then ejected.

SEAWEED

Mexico was menaced by the Wide Sargasso seaweed.

Australia's scientists found a new use this year for a native pink seaweed called Asparagopsis. Researchers at the University of the Sunshine Coast have discovered that if the seaweed is fed to cattle, the methane produced in their gut falls by 99 per cent. Were it to be fed to every cow in Australia, the country could cut its greenhouse gas emissions by 10 per cent.

In the first half of the year alone, 650,000 tonnes of the monster seaweed washed up onshore in the country's Yucatan peninsula, where it promptly started to rot, releasing hydrogen sulphide (which stinks like rotten eggs) and driving away visitors and tourists. Things got so bad that the state of Quintana Roo declared a state of emergency.

Until 2010, the seaweed (named sargassum) was mostly found in the Sargasso Sea, which got its name from the fact that early Portuguese sailors noticed it was full of the stuff. But since then it's been spreading further and further, and now it's taking over the Atlantic. The 550-kilometre-wide mat that swamped Mexico was only a small part of a larger system, more than 8,000 kilometres wide, which stretched all the way from the Gulf of Mexico to West Africa. Last year the Great Atlantic Sargassum Belt, as it's called, weighed more than 22 million tonnes. This year the sprawling island weighed the same as 200 fully loaded aircraft carriers.

Sargassum is usually a good thing – it is a valuable habitat for various animals and, in small doses, can nourish beaches. But when large quantities of the stuff get washed up, it leaks heavy metals and acid back into the water as it rots. This smothers corals and sea grasses, as well as corroding plumbing and causing breathing problems for sunbathers with asthma. The huge blooms are due to (surprise, surprise) humankind. Deforestation, excessive use of fertiliser in the Amazon and rising sea temperatures all create the perfect conditions for a seaweed kraken.

SELFIES

For the poppy-razzi, *see* **Apoppylypse**; for a beautiful lake with #NoFilter, *see* **Influencers**; and for taking photos with a camera-fern, *see* **Zoos**.

SHARP SHOOTERS

For accidentally shooting a pool worker, *see* **Iguana Invasion**; for accidentally shooting your own plane, *see* **Oops**; and for accidentally shooting yourself in the testicles while hiding drugs in your anus, *see* **Unusual Suspects**.

SHEEP DIP

A music festival was told that its pink sheep were in baa-ad taste.

Every year the Latitude Festival in Suffolk releases a flock of pink-dyed sheep onto its grounds to join the human revellers. But this time around PETA (People for the Ethical Treatment of Animals), the RSPCA and many social-media users condemned the practice, on the grounds that it's cruel to the animals. Latitude pointed out that they use a water-based, completely harmless dye, and that the sheep are used to being dipped in other substances, such as insecticides, anyway. Animal-rights campaigners countered with the additional complaint that the sheep might be upset by the music, which is perhaps more plausible (Stereophonics were headlining).

In other animal-dyeing news, Clacton suffered an outbreak of blue cats and dogs when eight sacks of ink powder broke in a fire. The blaze and smoke carried the blue powder through the air of the seaside town, where it settled on its furry residents. Across the Atlantic, two alligators turned orange in South Carolina after spending the winter hibernating next to rusting drainage pipes; and an 'exotic' orange bird that was brought into Tiggywinkles animal hospital in Buckinghamshire turned out to be a seagull covered in curry powder.

SHERLOCK CLONES

Scientists in China made a copy-cat of a cop's dog.

'Huahuangma' is a seven-year-old Kunming wolfhound known as the 'Sherlock Holmes of police dogs' because of her success in cracking dozens of murder cases. In fact she shows such a good nose for catching criminals that scientists have cloned her, in the hope of creating a new breed of sleuthing pooches. The first clone, Kunxun, was born this year and immediately showed 'a good aptitude on sniffing, detecting and adapting to unfamiliar environments'. China's Ministry of Public Security hopes eventually to have an army of mass-produced police-dog clones.

Meanwhile, in New Orleans, Holmes and Watson were back together and on the alert for the sign of 'Fore!', as golfers Bubba Watson and J. B. Holmes joined forces in a pairs competition, the Zurich Classic. It's not just in their names that the two resemble the fictional detectives. While Dr Watson described Sherlock's cocaine habit as his 'only vice', Bubba admitted to using CBD, the non-psychoactive chemical found in marijuana, to deal with pain and inflammation. And, like his namesake, J. B. Holmes keeps a skull in his home – his own. He revealed that he was rushed to hospital in 2011 for a structural defect in his head. He keeps the bone that was removed as a reminder that there's more to life than golf.

SHOW MUST GO ON, THE ▶

A man attending Phil Collins's 'Not Yet Dead' tour died and then came back to life.

As the veteran musician performed in Napier, New Zealand, a member of the crowd suffered a cardiac arrest. Fortunately a bystander spotted this and immediately started giving him CPR, which he continued to do until paramedics arrived and took over. The man, who had 'clinically died' in that moment, was successfully resuscitated, although he did have to miss the end of the concert.

In other 'show must go on' news:

▶ When singer-songwriter Lewis Capaldi needed the toilet mid-performance, he took the microphone with him and gave a running commentary, even as he was urinating (the sound of which could be heard in the background).

▶ Cellist Yo-Yo Ma paused his gig because too many people were coughing. He invited those feeling unwell to leave the venue, and for the rest to collectively clear their throats.

- Rapper Cardi B found her underpants were too far up her bum, mid-show, and so she announced to the audience, 'I'll be right back, I gotta take this wedgie out my ass.'

- R&B star Nelly cut off a song to tell the audience, 'That ain't no grown-man shit', after someone in the crowd somehow managed to loosen his laces as he walked across the stage.

- The Who frontman Roger Daltrey told members of his audience to stop smoking cannabis, because he was allergic to it. When the audience laughed, he said, 'I'm not kidding. Whoever it is down there, you f***ed my night, I'm allergic to that shit and my voice just goes.'

- Celine Dion put her whole concert on hold while a fan went to the bathroom. She explained onstage that, given what he would have paid for the ticket, it wasn't fair for him to have to miss a moment of the show.

- Bob Dylan complained that too many people were using their phones to take photos and videos of him onstage. The singer paused during 'Blowin' in the Wind' to tell the audience to stop. Immediately afterwards he tripped over a speaker and almost fell over. We know this thanks to the person who filmed it on their phone and posted it on Instagram.

- And 2019 marked 50 years since The Beatles played their last concert, an impromptu gig on the roof of Apple Music HQ, which was stopped by the police after 42 minutes, following noise complaints. We're still waiting for that one to resume . . .

SHUTDOWN ▶

The FBI ran out of money to buy drugs.

When Donald Trump and Congress failed to agree a deal for funding the US–Mexico border wall, a 35-day government shutdown followed – the longest in US history. It left the FBI with extremely limited staff and funds, meaning that agents posing as drug users in undercover operations sometimes didn't have the cash they needed to buy drugs and keep up the pretence of criminality.

But that wasn't the only unexpected consequence of the shutdown. In devastating news for hipsters, craft brewers were unable to make new beers because the staff from the Alcohol and Tobacco Tax and Trade Bureau, whose job it is to approve labels, were on involuntary leave. Coastguards were also told not to come to work, but were given a helpful 'tip sheet' on how to cope when they weren't being paid. It recommended 'holding a garage sale, babysitting, dog-walking or serving as a "mystery shopper"'.

Space was another casualty of the shutdown. The Hubble Telescope went unrepaired after a breakdown (journalists who emailed NASA engineers for a comment received the reply: 'I am in furlough status and unable to respond to your message'). And the world lost contact with a 100-foot-long space-balloon art project that was supposed to open up into a diamond shape when it got to space. A lack of federal communications staff meant that engineers couldn't give the green light to unfurl it, and it therefore floated away into space without ever assuming its intended shape.

The shutdown was, however, good news for animals. When a lack of coastguards forced the closure of public beaches, a group of about 60 elephant seals took up residence on one stretch of sand on a Californian beach

America's Joshua Tree National Park was vandalised during the shutdown due to a severe lack of law enforcement rangers. Ancient trees were chopped down, and delicate vegetation at iconic sites was destroyed by vehicle traffic. One former superintendent of the park said it could take up to 300 years for the park to fully recover from the 34-day hiatus.

265

and proceeded to give birth to 35 pups there. Even when visitors returned, the seals were reluctant to leave. Meanwhile, at the Smithsonian's National Zoo, giant pandas Tian Tian, Mei Xiang and Bei Bei were able to enjoy a little privacy when the funding cut-off caused the panda cam to be switched off.

Finally, and perhaps most ironically, a shutdown caused by Trump's insistence on greater border security led to the cancellation of a State Department conference on border security.

SIGNS ▶

To stop American road signs being stolen, the number 69 was replaced with 68.9.

Historically, it's been 'Route 66' signs that have been the most stolen on American roads, but recently Sex and Drugs have joined Rock 'n' Roll as the top reasons for theft. Milestones, including the number 69, therefore tend to disappear, as do those with the number 420 (an internationally recognised reference to cannabis). To combat the theft problem, Department of Transportation spokesperson Beth Bousley said that instead of replacing 69 signs with 68.9, and 420 signs with 419.9, they might simply miss out the offending markers.

In other inauspicious sign news:

▶ A Tennessee movie theatre that sits across the road from a church changed its sign for the movie *Hellboy* to *Heckboy*.

▶ A supermarket in Wales mistranslated its Welsh signage for alcohol-free beer, so that it appeared to offer 'free alcohol'.

▶ Sydney lavished £3.2 million on New Year's Eve fireworks, but failed to spot that a large sign, projected onto Sydney Harbour Bridge, spelt out '2018' rather than '2019'.

▶ And a psychologist in Chelmsford who was fined for driving in a bus lane won her appeal, after successfully arguing that the road had too many signs for her brain to process.

SISTERHOOD, THE ▶

The first ever all-female spacewalk was cancelled because NASA didn't have a spacesuit that fitted.

Astronaut Anne McClain completed one spacewalk wearing a medium-sized suit. Since, however, she trained in both medium and large sizes, she thought she'd be fine to wear the larger size for her second spacewalk, when she was due to be accompanied by fellow astronaut Christina Koch. But as the day approached, she realised she didn't feel comfortable wearing the bigger size, and because Koch needed the only available medium-sized suit, McClain decided to give up her spot to a man.

In more successful sisterhood news:

▶ A British Army reservist became the first woman in 90 years to descend the Cresta Run toboggan track in Switzerland. Women had been banned since 1929 following medically unsound claims that the run could cause breast cancer.

▶ The Académie française, guardian of the French language, finally agreed that every job title should have a feminine version. Now female researchers, authors and firefighters, for instance, can be known as *chercheuses*, *autrices* and *sapeuses-pompières*.

▶ For the first time ever, a woman was invited to take part in the 800-year-old British practice of swan-upping, the annual survey of the Queen's swans.

Karen Hammond joined 18 male uppers in their skiffs as they boated up the Thames, counting swans.

▶ And giant inflatable breasts were installed on rooftops across London as part of a campaign to de-stigmatise public breastfeeding. Similar breasts were also installed on Amsterdam's canals on International Women's Day, in a bid to desexualise women's chests. The breasts were named Ms Saggy, Ms Tiny, Ms Weird, Ms Fake and Ms Hairy.

SKY PENIS ▶

The US Air Force denied that its pilots had deliberately drawn a penis in the sky.

The image, formed by the planes' contrails, was unmistakable from the Earth, but officials said it was simply an inadvertent cock-up. Apparently the planes had been flying in parallel, and had then been instructed to practise engaging in a dogfight, before suddenly being instructed to hold off. According to the official response, they therefore had to 'hook to reposition before then beginning the fight again, causing them to hook once more'.

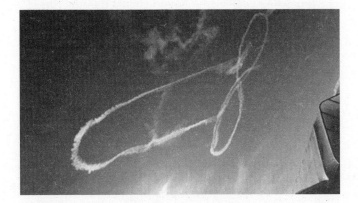

The story broke just weeks after it emerged, thanks to a Freedom of Information request, that pilots had deliberately drawn a phallic symbol in the sky in 2017. The transcript of their conversation read:

Pilot 1: You should totally try to draw a penis.

Pilot 2: I could definitely draw one. That would be easy. I could basically draw a figure eight and turn around and come back. I'm gonna go down, grab some speed and hopefully get out of the contrail layer so they're not connected to each other . . .

Pilot 1: Balls are going to be a little lopsided.

Pilot 2: Balls are complete. I just gotta navigate a little bit over here for the shaft.

Pilot 1: Which way is the shaft going?

Pilot 2: The shaft will go to the left.

Pilot 1: It's gonna be a wide shaft.

Pilot 2: I don't wanna make it just like three balls.

Pilot 1: Oh, the head of that penis is going to be thick.

SMALL PRINT ▸

The only person in the world who always reads Terms and Conditions won $10,000 for doing so.

We're all guilty of clicking on the box that says we've read the T&Cs, without having actually done so. After all, who has time to read all that small print? Donelan Andrews of St Petersburg, Florida, has the time – that's who.

Travel-insurance website Squaremouth decided to bury a competition in their small print. Their view was that no one would find it, and that after a year they would be able to donate the prize money of $10,000 to charity – and issue a cautionary tale about how careless we are when taking out policies. However, they reckoned without Ms Andrews, who spotted the clause hidden in the 4,000-word document just 23 hours after it was made public. Andrews is a self-declared nerd, who said, 'It's always been a passion of mine to be consumer-aware and, particularly, not to be taken advantage of.' When compiling exam papers in her job as a school teacher she would often hide a bonus in the instructions, to see if her pupils were paying attention – 'circle question number five three times and get 10 extra points', for example. Squaremouth handed over the prize money to her, and donated an extra $10,000 to the aptly named charity 'Reading is Fundamental'.

Let that be a lesson to all of you: ALWAYS read the small print.

SMOKING ▶

Hawaii considered a smoking ban for anyone under the age of 100.

The debate over smoking bans is complicated. Libertarians say that people should be able to poison themselves however they like, while public-health campaigners think the government should intervene more to save lives. Many US states have compromised by increasing the age at which you can legally buy cigarettes. In 2016, Hawaii was the first to make the minimum age 21, and New York became the 17th state to do so in November. But Hawaii is now planning to go a whole lot further.

Democrat politician Richard Creagan proposed a new bill that would see the smoking age rise to 30 in 2020, 40 in 2021, 50 in 2022 and 60 in 2023, before reaching

Scientists at the University of Stirling studied the idea of printing health warnings such as 'smoking kills' along the sides of individual cigarettes. Smokers who were asked about the proposal confirmed that such warnings would definitely put them off.

100 in 2024 (presumably, if you look like you're in your late nineties, you'll have to bring some ID). Smokers in Hawaii can at least be assured that their state has the highest life expectancy in the whole US, with the average resident expected to live to 81.5 years of age. The irony is that if this new cigarette law is enacted, life expectancy will increase and more Hawaiians will therefore be able to celebrate their 100th birthday with a packet of fags.

SMUGGLING ▶

The owner of The Smuggler's Inn hotel was charged with people-smuggling.

The Smuggler's Inn was also the scene of a crime in 2012 when police arrested three people there for smuggling drugs in a car which had the licence plate 'SMUGLER'.

The inn is in Washington State, just metres away from the Canadian border. In the past the owner, Robert Boulé, has played up the smuggling theme – every room is named after a famous criminal. But this year Boulé may have taken his amusing theme too far: he was charged with 21 counts of 'inducing, aiding or abetting' seven people who were trying to enter Canada illegally.*

On the other side of the world it wasn't people being smuggled, but animals. One woman who was seen walking awkwardly through a Taiwan airport was stopped and found to have 24 gerbils strapped to her legs. She claimed she'd bought them for friends, but the authorities believe she was on a dummy run, testing the airport's inspection procedures for rather more lucrative goods the next time round. In the UK, Jeffrey Lendrum, a bird-egg smuggler, pleaded guilty after being caught at Heathrow with 19 rare eggs stuffed inside socks and strapped to his chest. And a Canadian man was fined C$15,000 (£8,800) for smuggling almost 5,000 leeches in a reusable grocery bag inside his hand

272

luggage on a flight from Russia to Canada. Leeches are a protected species because they are over-harvested in the wild.

Perhaps the least competent smuggler to be apprehended was a Colombian man who was arrested in Barcelona airport while attempting – extremely conspicuously – to smuggle half a kilo of cocaine under his wig. CNN called him a 'cocaine bigwig', and the *New York Post* said the criminal would have 'hell toupée'.

SOCKPUPPETS

An investigation into an astrology app's reviews found that you can't read anything in the stars.

The *Daily Telegraph* was one of many publications to look into the murky world of online reviewers and find how surprisingly easy it is to pay people to give fake five-star reviews. They were able to buy flattering, fraudulent reviews for an astrology app, as well as talking people into giving five stars for Brighton's West Pier, which burned down in 2003.

Many of the articles on this practice – often known as sockpuppetry – cited a website called Fakespot, which uses AI to work out whether reviews are real or not. Fakespot says that around 34.6 per cent of reviews on Amazon are untrustworthy, and that for some items, such as Bluetooth headsets, it's more than 50 per cent.

Amazon admits that it has a problem, but says these fake review figures are implausibly high. It's tough to know who to believe. After all, the websites that rate other websites can also be gamed. Fakespot has a rating of 2.5 out of 10 on Trustpilot; which in turn has a rating of 1.5 out of 5 on reviews.io.

Donald Trump's former lawyer, Michael Cohen, should know all about this. When challenged by *The Wall Street Journal*, he admitted asking a tech expert to fix two online polls for Donald Trump: one on America's top business leaders, and the other on 2016 presidential candidates. He also asked the expert to set up a fake Twitter account called 'Women for Cohen', which posted comments about how good-looking he was. The account was supposedly for 'Women who love and support Michael Cohen. Strong, pit bull, sex symbol, no nonsense, business oriented, and ready to make a difference!' He paid for the work with $12,000 cash and a boxing glove once worn by a Brazilian mixed martial-arts fighter.

SONGS, BERDY

The president of Turkmenistan performed a soft-rock song named after his favourite horse.

Gurbanguly Berdymukhamedov was joined by his 14-year-old grandson on keyboard and backing vocals in a rendition of the song, which is called 'Rovach' and boasts such lyrics as 'You are like the morning dawn / You are like a sacred form.' It was broadcast on Turkmen TV, complete with what appeared to be a guitar solo performed by the president himself (although it was hard to tell if he was actually playing). How much his people enjoyed the song is unclear, but since Berdy won his last election with 98 per cent of the vote, he's presumably not worried about getting an adversely critical reception just yet. He often performs on the state TV channel on national holidays – he's mad about music – and because lots of people are banned from travelling on those days, his ratings are pretty good.

As well as being keen on songs and stallions, Berdy likes bikes. Soon after the release of his latest song, he put out a video that showed him riding a bicycle while shooting a pistol at cut-out targets (apparently hitting bullseyes every time). And to mark World Cycling Day, his government arranged the longest-ever single file of bicycle riders. This isn't the first time he's tried to break a bike record – last year he got 3,246 people to ride simultaneously, in order to set a record for the largest-ever cycling lesson. In the midst of all this, Berdy still found time to

SPOT THE DIFFERENCE

1. This year, scientists took photos of the most massive and most minuscule things ever (*see* **Holes, Black; Quantum Entanglement**) – but despite one being infinitely more enormous than the other, the pictures look remarkably similar. See if you can work out which is which.

 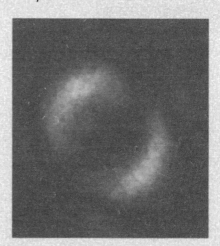

2. Until the rules changed this year, Guinness World Records had very specific rules about what counted for the 'fastest marathon run by a nurse' (*see* **Marathons**). Which of these was closest to their idea of a nurse's outfit?

 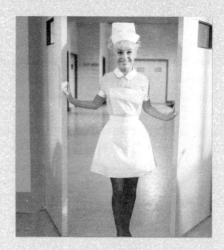

3. The world's press thinks former Ukrainian prime minister Yulia Tymoshenko has a spooky resemblance to Princess Leia (*see* **Mimics**). Can you use the Force to determine which is which?

4. When Vladimir Putin travels he does so disguised as an airport (*see* **GPS**). Can you see through the Russian president's cunning camouflage and work out which of these is the real landing strip?

promote his own son to a role as deputy governor of a whole province.

Just a month later Berdy vanished from the public eye, prompting speculation among the repressed people of Turkmenistan, and rumours in the foreign media, that he'd died. However, when more than a month had passed, he turned up again, featuring in thrilling new footage, first of him pointing at a bus shelter, and then of him driving a rally car round a flaming crater called 'Hell's Gate'.

SONGS, BIRDIE ▶

The Galapagos Islands saw the Origin of a New Species.

—— ▼ ——

Scientists have found that birdsong can make squirrels relax. If the creatures hear, say, a predatory hawk followed by the sound of song-birds chattering (which means the birds think they're safe again), they take their cue from them and relax faster.

The finches on the Galapagos are some of the most important birds in scientific history: they inspired Darwin's ideas on evolution. Over the last 50 years the islands have been invaded by parasitic maggots, which nibble away at the birds' beaks, leaving holes that alter the pitch of the finches' mating songs, to the point where females don't respond to the calls of the males. Even stranger, some confused birds have sex with the wrong species, creating new hybrids in the process. At least one species is likely to be hybrid-ised out of existence, thanks to the tiny maggots.

Britain also faces a bird problem: there are now 40 million fewer of them than there were 50 years ago. To highlight their plight, and to promote the work of the Royal Society for the Protection of Birds, folk musician Sam Lee, who performs concerts in which he duets with nightingales and other songbirds, released a single consisting entirely of birdsong. It was an unexpected hit, making it to number 18 and becoming the third-highest new entry in the charts that week, after Stormzy and Taylor Swift.

STEEP, A BIT

The first lady of Israel spent more than $10,000 a year on takeaways.

Sara Netanyahu was accused of misusing public funds for ordering $96,000 worth of takeaway food between 2010 and 2013. She eventually pleaded guilty to a lesser charge of spending $50,000 on the takeaways and escaped jail, partly because the 'public humiliation' that she had already suffered from the case got taken into account.

The Israeli press often depicts Ms Netanyahu as a 'Marie Antoinette' figure who has an eye for the finer things in life, but even she would surely baulk at the bunch of 24 grapes that was sold in the central Japanese city of Kanazawa for 1.2 million yen (£8,800). The 'ruby red' grapes are prized for their juiciness, high sugar content and low acidity, and farmers only allow a certain number onto the market each year, to keep demand artificially high. The buyer, Takashi Hosokawa, owns a hotel, and said he would offer them as a surprise gift to his guests.

Actually there was one even more expensive collection of grapes on offer this year: the ones that were turned into a €30,000 bottle of wine. Bordeaux winemaker Liber Pater's 2015 vintage apparently has 'hints of crunchy black forest fruits, with silky tannins and long fine finish'. We haven't tried it, but judging purely by the description, it appears to be very similar to 'Toro Loco', available for £3.99 at Aldi.

STEEP, VERY

The Men of Harlech won an uphill battle to claim the world's steepest street.

The record for the world's steepest street used to be held by Dunedin, New Zealand, which boasts a road that

SQUAD, THE ▶

'The Squad' is the name given to four Democratic Congresswomen who hit the headlines when Trump tweeted they should 'go back and help fix the . . . crime infested places from which they came'. All of them are American.

1

2

① RASHIDA TLAIB

One of only two Muslim women ever to sit in Congress, and the oldest of 14 siblings. Hours after being sworn into office, she said publicly, in reference to Trump, 'We're gonna go in there and we're going to impeach the motherfucker.' She's repeated that sentiment a number of times since. Before she was elected, she was once thrown out of a public meeting where Trump was speaking, for heckling him.

② ILHAN OMAR

The other of just two Muslim women ever to sit in Congress. She brought about a change to an almost 200-year-old rule in Congress before she even took office, successfully campaigning to have the ban on hats in the House – in place since 1837 – lifted, so that she could take the oath of office in her headscarf. The ban was lifted on the day she was sworn in. Omar was born in Somalia and spent four years of her life, from the age of eight, in a refugee camp in Kenya. She then moved to the US and went on to work as a reporter, highlighting problems with the legal system. She claims she once shouted 'Bullshit!' in court when watching a jury sentence an elderly African American woman for stealing a $2 loaf of bread to feed a hungry child.

③ ALEXANDRIA OCASIO-CORTEZ, aka AOC

The youngest woman ever to sit in Congress. She averages more retweets than any politician other than Trump; in a single month she generated more online interactions (i.e. retweets and likes) than CNN, ABC, MSNBC, NBC and *The New York Times* combined. The Democrat Communication Committee tasked her with giving the rest of them lessons on how to use Twitter well. In an attempt to discredit AOC, the *Daily Caller* website published a fake nude picture of her. She denied the image was of her, and was vindicated when a foot fetishist stated that the feet on display didn't belong to the Congresswoman. When asked how he knew, the wikiFeet user said, 'I've sucked enough toes in my life to recognise when something doesn't look right.'

④ AYANNA PRESSLEY

The first black woman ever elected to Congress from Massachusetts. Pressley credits her mother, Sandra, as the inspiration behind everything she does. When Ayanna worked on John Kerry's presidential campaign, Sandra became a 'second mother' to the team and used to make them bags of sweets called 'Sandy's Candies'. She also used to wear a hat at her daughter's meetings that read 'Mama Pressley'. When she died, 300 people attended the funeral, and when Ayanna later got married and the pastor asked, 'Who gives this bride', 10 women stood up, each holding a photo of Pressley's mother.

at one point achieves a gradient of 35 per cent (in other words, you climb one metre vertically for every three metres you move horizontally). Each year the people of Dunedin celebrate by releasing 75,000 chocolate balls down the hill, in a race called the Running of the Balls.

But recently Dunedin faced a challenge from the town of Harlech (population about 1,400) in north-west Wales. Residents, led by local man Gwyn Headley, claimed their own street, Ffordd Pen Llech, was even steeper at points – it's so steep that if you drop a brick on the ground, it will roll; and if you park your car, it can slide downhill even with the handbrake on. So they launched a campaign to 'put Harlech on the map', contacting the council, hiring surveyors and notifying Guinness World Records that they were going to try and take the record.

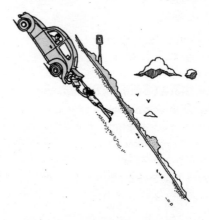

Guinness imposed some stringent requirements. Before Harlech's claim could be verified, the town had to demonstrate that the street was commonly used by the public; that it was fully paved; that it had buildings running along either side of it; that it was accessible to vehicles; and that a blueprint of it existed (this last requirement proved tricky, because the street was built before blueprints were invented). Some residents of Dunedin were so concerned by the challenge Harlech posed that they suggested resurfacing their own street to make it even steeper. But it was no good. When Guinness eventually issued their pronouncement, it was the Welsh street and its steepest gradient of 37.45 per cent that took the crown. Headley was triumphant, telling the *Guardian*, 'I feel utter relief and jubilation. I feel sorry for Baldwin Street and the New Zealanders, but steeper is steeper.' The people of Harlech celebrated by holding the steepest street party in history. They didn't release 75,000 chocolate balls, but they did roll some Maltesers down it. It's a start.

STOCKPILING

Switzerland stopped panic-buying in preparation for the Second World War.

The country set up emergency coffee reserves after the First World War, to make sure it was ready for any bean shortages in the event of a Second World War. The reserves have been maintained ever since, and 15 different companies involved in the coffee industry, including Nestlé, are legally required to store enough of the beverage there to keep the country caffeinated for three months, in the event of a supply-chain breakdown. Now, however, the Swiss government has decided this is no longer necessary and has published plans to stop hoarding the beans in 2022. It announced that the drink is not considered 'essential for life' these days, adding that 'coffee has almost no calories and consequently does not contribute, from the physiological perspective, to safeguarding nutrition'.

A 600-tonne stockpile of toilet paper – 3.5 million rolls – was amassed by German importer Wepa in their UK warehouses in anticipation of ▮▮▮▮▮.

They weren't the only ones to stop stockpiling: mathematicians worldwide breathed a sigh of relief when it emerged that they no longer need to hoard chalk. After a video in 2015 revealed that the 'world's best chalk' company was going out of business, professors started panic-buying Hagoromo Fulltouch Chalk – which some have called the Rolls-Royce of chalk, and about which one mathematician said, 'It is impossible to write a false theorem with it.' Some academics ordered up to 15 years' worth. Fortunately, Hagoromo sold the recipe and the chalk is now being manufactured again, so it's available from all good chalkmongers.

STRAW, THE FINAL ▶

Florida's governor banned the state legislature from banning cities from banning plastic straws.

—— ▼ ——
When plastic straws are banned in the UK in 2020, it will still be legal for bars to keep them behind the bar and give them out if you specifically ask for them (presumably with a bit of a nod and a wink to the barman).

Plastic straws are being outlawed around the world, as they are widely thought to be a serious but easily avoidable pollutant of the Earth's oceans. There has nevertheless been some pushback, not least in Florida, where law-makers this year voted to stop individual cities from banning any kind of plastics. In response to *this*, however, Florida's governor, Ron DeSantis, argued that environmental laws are particularly important for his state's tourism industry, and that each city should be free to make up its own mind. He therefore exercised his veto and stopped the new law. But that wasn't the end of the matter. Just over a month later another law was proposed that would force all cities to ban straws. DeSantis vowed to block this law as well, so it seems likely that for the time being Florida will continue to be subjected to straw poll after straw poll.

The debate is more nuanced than you might think. Britain's straw ban will take effect in 2020 and is widely supported by the public, but some campaigners have argued that elderly and disabled people find plastic straws invaluable and will suffer if they become difficult to get hold of (though there will be exemptions for hospitals and care homes). Others point out that plastic straws make up only around 0.00002 per cent of all marine plastic pollution (in terms of weight). The reason we notice them more, they argue, is that they float, and so are more likely to turn up on beaches (the very fact that they do wash up onshore means, of course, that they're less hazardous to animals that live in the sea). Some have championed metal straws as a substitute for plastic, but people often steal them, which means that bars have to keep buying them in bulk, effectively making them single-use. And when McDonald's replaced its plastic straws with paper ones this year, they found that the reinforced paper couldn't be recycled, unlike their previous 100-per-cent-recyclable plastic straws.

Ostensibly for these reasons, but actually because it irritated his political enemies, Donald Trump's team claimed to have sold half a million dollars' worth of plastic straws – adorned with the slogan 'liberal paper straws don't work' – at his rallies. Luckily, the campaign team also confirmed that the straws are recyclable.

SUMO WRESTLERS

For standing in beautiful harmony, *see* **Chrysanthemum Throne;** for facial-hair indecency, *see* **Clamping Down**; and for a closely knit band, *see* **Competitions**.

SURPLUS, FRUIT

The president of Afghanistan gave the order: 'Let them eat watermelons.'

In 2018, Afghan farmers lost many of their crops to a devastating drought. This year, however, they enjoyed a bumper watermelon harvest. You might think this could only be good news – unfortunately, because the increase in supply was not matched by an increase in demand, all that happened was that the price of watermelons plummeted. At one stage you could buy a ton of them for just $11. Clearly, the only way out of the crisis was for people to eat a lot more watermelons. And so the country came together to do just that.

President Ashraf Ghani began the push when he ordered that the army buy thousands of watermelons for its soldiers. Doctors then did their bit by advising people to eat meals consisting of just bread and watermelons. Universities got students to buy watermelons at inflated prices so that they could get a grasp of basic economics. And watermelon-eating contests became popular. One champion watermelon-eater, Rahmatullah Quchqarzada, said, 'I have never eaten this much watermelon in my life, but people were cheering me on. And I didn't want to let down my father's name.' His father is a clerk with the Afghan government.

Oddly, the Philippines found itself in much the same situation when, after a run of unusually hot, dry weather, the country was left with about 10 million more mangoes than usual, forcing farmers to give bags of them away for free. Fortunately the government stepped in, organising a mango festival and offering cooking classes to teach people creative, mango-based recipes.

SURPLUS, NORMAN ➤

See **World, Around the.**

IN WHICH WE LEARN . . .

Who got a tattoo of a BBQ, who couldn't get away from the MMA, who was the greatest threat to OPEC, and why Donald Trump continues to spout BS.

TATTOOS ▶

Ariana Grande got a tattoo of a barbecue by mistake.

Since the National Museum in Rio de Janeiro burned down a year ago, 150 former curators, staff and students have signed up to get a tattoo of the museum, both to help them deal with the loss, and as part of the campaign to bring it back.

The Grammy award-winning singer posted pictures of a new tattoo on the palm of her hand, and told her fans that it was made up of the Japanese characters for '7 Rings', the name of her new song. Some people who saw the image, though, pointed out that while her new tattoo was indeed the character for 'seven' followed by the one for 'rings', it didn't mean what she thought it did. She'd left out a character that should have gone in the middle, without which 'seven' and 'rings' actually reads as '*shichirin*', which is a small charcoal grill. Grande, by the way, is a vegan.

She took it in good humour – 'huge fan of tiny bbq grills,' she told her fans – but then had the tattoo changed, writing on Instagram: 'RIP tiny charcoal grill. Miss u man. I actually really liked you.' Unfortunately the fix didn't work, either. She thought that by getting the Japanese symbol for 'finger' added, she'd done what was required to turn the small charcoal grill into '7 Rings', but because the characters were added in the wrong place, she ended up with a tattoo that read 'small charcoal grill finger'. She was reportedly offered a $1.5 million sponsorship deal with a tattoo-removal company.

While tattoos may have become more common in pop music, the Chinese government has started to take a dim view of them and has even banned its pop stars from flouting them. It also ordered its football team to play in long-sleeved shirts at the Asian Cup, despite the stifling heat of the UAE, where the tournament was being held, to hide any monstrous ink. On top of all that, the Beijing government has had male TV stars' earrings edited out, over worries that they make them look effeminate – the result is blurred ear lobes on TV.

Tattoos are not just for show, though. A team of scientists from Germany has developed permanent sensors that can be implanted into the skin, and that will change colour according to the patient's blood-sugar levels, or blood acidity. They've only been tested on pigs so far, but the day may be approaching when you decide whether or not to call 999 just by looking at someone's tattoo.

THAT'S (NOT) ALL FOLKS!

Conor McGregor threw in the towel, then 10 days later he threw it back out again.

On 26 March, the fighter tweeted the unambiguous words: 'Hey guys quick announcement, I've decided to retire from the sport formally known as "Mixed Martial Art" today.' This followed a six-month suspension for his part in a violent crowd brawl that occurred after one of his fights. Ten days later a second tweet appeared: 'I want to move forward, with my fans of all faiths and all backgrounds . . . Now see you in the Octagon [the name given to the Ultimate Fighting Championship ring].' It's not the first time he's reversed a career decision. He also announced his retirement in 2016, only to post a statement on Facebook two days later that ended: 'I AM NOT RETIRED.'

Another celebrity to un-retire himself this year was Andy Murray, who was given a tear-inducing goodbye ceremony at the Australian Open, where a video was played showing his career highlights as well as testimonies from many of his rivals. He won the doubles at Queen's Club five months later. And comedian Hannah Gadbsy returned to stand-up after her retirement show sold out on three continents, earned an Emmy nomination and was turned into a Netflix special. She justified it by saying, 'I'm left with the choice. I'll either be an idiot or a hypocrite, and I'd rather be a hypocrite.'

If comedians and sports stars find it difficult to retire, then musicians find it almost impossible. Twenty-seven years after his original retirement tour, the No More Tours Tour, Ozzy Osbourne planned to go back on the road with a tour called the No More Tours 2 (owing to an injury, this has now been postponed until 2020). Elton John toured his farewell show this year, after first claiming he was retiring from touring in 1977. And Kiss began a farewell tour in January, 19 years after their first official farewell tour. The show was widely praised for its striking set, but not by Mötley Crüe, who accused Kiss of stealing the stage set from *their* farewell tour in 2014. Mötley Crüe themselves signed a legally binding 'Cessation of Touring Agreement' during that 2014 tour, so they, at least, are officially prevented from going back on the road again.

THAT SUCKS ▶

For birds being sucked, *see* **Olives**; for being sucked into a hole, *see* **Macabre**; and for a bird being sucked into a hole, *see* **Holes, Glory**.

THE INDEPENDENT GROUP (TIG)

See **Change UK**.

THE INDEPENDENT GROUP FOR CHANGE

See **Indecisive Politicians**.

THIEVING BASTARDS

A Great (Model) Train Robbery took place in Kent.

Trains worth £25,000 were stolen from the Gravesend Model Marine and Engineering Society, whose headquarters are in Thong Lane. These were massive trains (for models, anyway), each powerful enough to pull along eight children. The members of the club said the thieves 'must have been built like the Hulk'.

In other thieving-bastard news:

▶ Police issued an appeal after 'a large amount of tweed clothing' was stolen from a steam-train rally in Derbyshire. A police spokesman said, 'If you have any information about this theft, or know of someone who has acquired a large amount of tweed clothing, please get in touch.'

▶ The police in Italy's Castelnuovo Magra got wind of the planned theft of a painting by Brueghel worth three million euros, so they replaced it with a copy and set up hidden cameras. The local priest and mayor were in on the deception, and the latter went on camera to publicly lament the 'theft'. Unfortunately the culprits weren't caught, but thanks to the subsequent publicity, they presumably now realise that what they took was completely worthless.

THUNBERG, GRETA

<u>Name:</u>
Greta Thunberg

<u>Occupation:</u>
Activist

<u>Middle Name:</u>
Tintin

<u>Experience at the World Economic Forum:</u>
Snowy

<u>Reason for being in the news:</u>
The 16-year-old Swedish environmental activist was invited to speak at the World Economic Forum, but unlike most other speakers, who flew into the Swiss city of Davos and stayed in luxury hotels, Thunberg took a 32-hour train ride and then camped out in the snow, in -18°C temperatures. She told delegates at the conference, 'I don't want you to be hopeful, I want you to panic. I want you to feel the fear I feel every day and then I want you to act.'

It's a message that she's consistently espoused since she started taking days off school to sit in front of the Riksdag parliament building in Stockholm, saying she'd do so until Sweden reduced its carbon emissions to those agreed at the Paris Agreement in 2016. She gave out leaflets saying, 'I am doing this because you adults are shitting on my future.'

When she was invited to appear at the Climate Action Summit in New York and the UN Climate Change Conference in Santiago, Chile, Thunberg again refused to fly, instead taking a zero-emissions solar-powered racing yacht across the Atlantic Ocean. It was a symbolic gesture only slightly compromised by the fact that a pair of sailors had to be flown over to America by aeroplane to get the ship back to Europe. Thunberg's activism has resulted in her being named by the OPEC oil cartel as its 'greatest threat'. She called that her 'biggest compliment yet'.

- For reasons that are not at all clear, 30,000 litres of iceberg water worth less than £7,000 were stolen from a Canadian distillery. An extremely puzzled boss told the BBC, 'It's not like there's a black market'; while another distillery employee, pointing out that the water had probably been contaminated during the theft, asked, 'Jesus, what are they going to do with it?'

- 15 per cent of all the vanilla in Madagascar was stolen. Vanilla is so fiendishly expensive – it's worth six times as much as it was five years ago – that Madagascan farmers are having to guard their crops with shotguns and hire guards to combat a wave of thefts.

- And one Massachusetts man came home to find that someone had broken into his house and stolen nothing at all. They had just cleaned it. He said, 'Nothing was damaged, nothing was taken . . . just arranged in a really creepy way.' Almost every room had been spruced up, and an elaborate origami rose had been made out of toilet paper.

TOTO

In the middle of the desert, one song is now playing on a loop . . . for ever.

The song is 'Africa' by Toto, and it is playing via an MP3 player and six speakers as part of an art installation set up by Namibian-German artist Max Siedentopf. Ironically, even though the song's best-known lyric is 'I bless the rains down in Africa', it's been put in the Namib Desert, parts of which get as little as 5mm of rainfall a year. Siedentopf has not disclosed the exact location, but for anyone wandering the 81,000 square kilometres of desert, it should become obvious when you're nearby.

The device runs on solar batteries, so it should theoretically keep playing for eternity. However, Siedentopf acknowledged that though he'd built the equipment for durability, it will eventually erode if it's not maintained, meaning that the song would stop playing in as little as 55 million years. He also admitted, 'Some [Namibians] love it and some say it's probably the worst sound installation ever.'

In other vaguely Toto-connected news, Cleveland's National Weather Service issued a 'small dog warning', urging dog owners to 'hold onto your pooch!' as 50-mph winds hit the city. Small dogs have been known to blow away in the past: in 2009 a 70-mph gust of wind in Michigan picked up a Chihuahua belonging to a woman called Dorothy and deposited it nearly a mile away.

TOURISTS ▶

Austria got 194 new US embassies, and they all serve fries.

US citizens in Austria who find themselves in trouble had their lives made much easier this year. The US embassy announced that any American visitor whose passport has been lost or stolen, or who is otherwise 'in distress', can visit the nearest McDonald's, which will offer them consular assistance by putting them in touch with the main embassy in Vienna. All 194 branches in Austria now have a 24-hour hotline to the embassy. (They're only quasi-embassies – the company clarified that the branches of McDonalds are still Austrian territory, so you can't claim asylum in a McDonald's.)

The authorities were forced to confirm that it wasn't much ado about McMuffin. It was a genuine attempt to help US citizens access help overseas. Not everyone was happy: the website Eater.com said the move was 'a bizarre downloading of a public service to a multinational corporation whose main speciality is applying heat to thin discs of ground meat'. The terrifying clown who symbolises the whole billion-dollar venture, President Donald J. Trump, did not comment.

TRUMP, DONALD

According to the Washington Post, *which rates Trump's claims on a 'Pinocchio scale', the president made 10,000 false or misleading claims in his first 828 days as president. They included:*

> *That he'd secured US troops in South Korea their first pay rise in a decade.* In fact they have received a pay rise every single year since 1961.

> *That Alexander Graham Bell was a great American inventor.* Bell was Scottish-born and spent his early life in Canada.

> *That wind farms cause cancer.* 'They say the noise causes cancer,' he said, as well as claiming that a wind farm would cut your house price by 75 per cent. The *Washington Post* pointed out that this claim is 'so bizarre that it's not even clear how you would fact-check it . . . How would that even work?'

That Twitter makes it deliberately hard for people to follow him. 'I've had so many people come to me, [saying] "Sir, I can't join you on Twitter." I see what's happening!' He is the 12th-most-followed person on Twitter on the planet.

That Japan's PM, Shinzo Abe, nominated him for the Nobel Peace Prize. Trump told reporters, 'He said "I have nominated you respectfully on behalf of Japan" . . . I'll probably never get it. That's OK.' The Japanese government refused to respond, perhaps because nominations don't become public for 50 years.

That his father was born in Germany. Trump has made this claim four times, most recently in April. Fred Trump was born in New York City.

That he hadn't called Apple CEO, Tim Cook, 'Tim Apple'. Trump tried two separate excuses for this slip of the tongue. First, he claimed that he'd actually muttered, 'Tim Cook, Apple' and that the media had misquoted him. Then he claimed that he'd said 'Tim / Apple' in order to 'save time and words'. The video is widely available online, and it's clear that he mistakenly used Cook's company name as his surname.

That he 'hadn't left the White House in months'. This was a quite extraordinary claim, made by Trump in an interview on Fox News, despite the fact that his trips to Iraq and Texas the previous month had been comprehensively covered by the world's media.

That homelessness in America 'started two years ago' and 'We never had this in our lives before in our country'. It's not clear why Trump thinks associating his presidency with homelessness is a good idea, but it turns out that he was blaming Democratic mayors for the problem.

TRANSIENT ANUS ▶

Biologists discovered an anus that disappears and reappears when its owner needs to defecate.

The anus in question belongs to the warty comb jelly, a jellyfish-like (though it is not a jellyfish) creature native to the Atlantic. Marine biologist Sidney Tamm was studying one under a microscope when he realised he couldn't find an anus – until, that is, the animal needed to defecate, at which point he noticed an opening conveniently appearing. Fortunately this happens every 10 minutes in larvae and every hour in the 5cm-long adults, so multiple observations were possible. Tamm realised that for each rectal evacuation, the gut would swell with waste until it touched the sides of the jelly. At that point, it fused with the skin tissue to form an anal opening that dilated and expelled the waste. As soon as this was done, the process reversed and the anus vanished.

Tamm admitted that he was very surprised by this 'transient anus', because 'all the scientific literature says that the anus is a permanent structure'. The transient anus is not known to exist in any other creature any longer, but he speculated that this may have been the original anus from which all subsequent ones evolved.

IN WHICH WE LEARN . . .

Who acts like a bogey-man on the golf course, how U2 can give you a birdie's eye view, who found a new sea under a sand wedge, which auction lots should have been left in a bunker, and who got arrested in an extremely un-fairway.

U2

The Cold War is helping 21st-century archaeologists find structures from 1000 BC.

During a period when tensions with the USSR were at their height, American Lockheed U-2 spy planes took thousands of pictures of the Middle East. Archaeologists who Desire to find ancient Assyrian features are now using those images to expose what they can't see when they Walk On ground level, due to their lack of Elevation. In many ways, the images are Even Better than the Real Thing, but this Window in the Skies does not always result in a Celebration. One group of archaeologists who are looking for a huge ancient canal are still struggling to locate it, as the site is now occupied by the city of Khabat, so they have to compare new maps with maps from Another Day, on which the Streets Have No Name. So, at the time of writing, they Still Haven't Found What They're Looking For.

UNDER PAR

When Greenpeace displayed a banner saying: 'Trump: Well Below Par', the president took it as a compliment.

Commander in Cheat, a new book by Rick Reilly, looked at Donald Trump through green-tinted glasses – comparing his nefarious tactics on the golf course with his record in the White House. Golfers pride themselves on their strict adherence to etiquette. Trump doesn't. He cheats so regularly – by kicking his ball into the shorter grass when he's in a tricky situation – that caddies at his Winged Foot Golf Club have nicknamed him Pelé, after the legendary Brazilian footballer.

The president claims to have won 18 club championships in his career (most clubs have an annual competition to crown that year's best golfer), but Reilly revealed that whenever Trump opens a new course, he simply plays the first round against a single, pliant opponent and calls that the first club championship. Trump is also vindictive. Against trees. For a while he kept a can of red spray paint in his golf cart and would mark with a cross every tree he hit, so that staff would know to chop it down. His lack of care for the flora goes hand-in-hand with his indifference to the landscape in general: this year Trump's Aberdeen course lost its status as a Site of Special Scientific Interest, following an investigation by environmentalists which revealed that it had done 'irreparable damage' to local sand dunes.

Trump also plays fast and loose with history. At the 14th hole of his Washington golf course there is a plaque commemorating an American Civil War battle

LOT: NOT A HOUSE

This was sold in Florida to first-time bidder Kerville Holness, who believed he'd successfully bought his first house for the shockingly cheap price of $9,100, when in fact he had actually purchased the foot-wide strip of land running down the driveway in front of the house. He was furious to discover not only that his bid was irreversible, but also that the real worth of the strip was just $50.

HAMMER PRICE: $9,100

LOT: A COMPUTER INFECTED WITH SIX OF THE MOST DANGEROUS VIRUSES IN HISTORY

The computer, which was created as part of an art project, was loaded with ILOVEYOU, WannaCry and other malware responsible for causing an estimated $95 billion of damage around the world. It was sold with a warning that it should never be switched on, and the buyer had to agree that if they intended to ignore this advice, they would not connect it to any computer network or the Internet.

HAMMER PRICE: $1.3 MILLION

LOT: HITLER'S PAINTING

An auction held in Nuremberg included five paintings by the former Führer, as well as other personal items, including a vase, a tablecloth and a wicker chair with a swastika on it. Under German law, public displays of Nazi symbols are illegal, so the auction house got round this by pixelating the offending parts in their catalogue. In the end, only the vase and the tablecloth found buyers. The auction would have been on a larger scale, had 63 paintings allegedly by Hitler not just been seized, due to suspicions that they were fake.

HAMMER PRICE: NOT SOLD

LOT: A GOLDEN BAKED BEAN

In 1995, Heinz hid 100 eighteen-carat gold beans in random tins across the UK to celebrate the 100th anniversary of the foodstuff. This year, one of those beans went to auction and was snapped up by . . . Heinz, who had failed to keep one for themselves and have been waiting 24 years for one to come on sale.

HAMMER PRICE: £750

that supposedly took place there. According to *The New York Times*, which consulted three historians about it, this is pure fiction. When confronted, Trump told reporters, 'How would they know that? Were they there?'

But no one can deny that Donald loves his golf. If he is re-elected in 2020, the total cost to the US taxpayer of his golf trips is likely to reach $340 million. And that's despite the fact that he's installed a $50,000 golf simulator in his private quarters at the White House. If you want to reach him, then the golf course is as good a place as any, which is why Greenpeace once got a paraglider bearing the banner 'Trump: Well Below Par' to fly over one. What they didn't realise is that in golf being 'below par' is exactly what every player is striving for – and Trump, of course, knows this. He said in response, when told of the intended insult, 'Beautiful, I WANT to be below par.'

UNDER THE SEA

Scientists found a new sea under the sea.

It was already known that there is fresh water below the ocean floor along the Atlantic coast of the US. But it only became apparent this year how much of it there is when researchers from Columbia University and the Woods Hole Oceanographic Institution established that the area is home to the biggest undersea, freshwater aquifer known. It stretches for 350 kilometres from New Jersey to Massachusetts and contains at least 2,800 cubic kilometres of liquid. The aquifer is believed to have formed after the last Ice Age, when large pockets of fresh water that ran off melting glaciers became trapped under layers of sediment.

In other under-the-sea news:

▶ Facebook announced it was in talks to lay a cable on the sea floor all around Africa, to provide Internet access across the continent. The provisional name of the cable is 'Simba'.

▶ The scaly-footed snail became the first species to become endangered due to deep-sea mining for precious minerals (the drilling takes place around hydrothermal vents – hot-water jets at the bottom of the ocean). The creature sounds adorable: at 4 per cent of its total volume, its heart is the largest (relative to body size) in the animal kingdom.

▶ A scientific observatory at the bottom of the sea suddenly disappeared. Divers sent to investigate why the Boknis Eck environmental monitoring station had stopped sending data, found all the equipment had vanished without trace. There's now nothing monitoring that stretch of sea for the first time in more than 60 years.

▶ A consignment of Nikes fell off a ship on the east coast of America last year and have since become of unexpected interest to scientists. Oceanographers realised that the shoes ended up responding to ocean currents in different ways, according to whether they were left or right shoes. More left shoes than right ended up in Newquay and – slightly more glamorously – more right shoes than left ended up in the Azores.

UNITED THE STAIRS ▶

For the boy wizard who lived under the stairs, *see*
Harry Potter and the . . . ; and for the Wikileaks man
who DEFINITELY DID NOT LIVE UNDER THE STAIRS,
see **Evicted**.

URANUS EXAMINER
BY DAN SCHREIBER

Sitting along the historic Route 66, six and a half miles east of Waynesville, Missouri is the small unincorporated town of Uranus. Founded just four years ago by self-proclaimed mayor Louie Keen, the roadside tourist destination boasts, among many other businesses, a fudge factory, an escape room (Escape Uranus), an axe-throwing centre (the Uranus Axehole), and a gift shop where 'I heart Uranus' t-shirts and 'Make Uranus Great Again' caps are popular purchases.

Last year, Louie expanded the Uranus empire when, following the demise of the county's only local newspaper, the 'Waynesville Daily Guide', he snapped up the defunct paper's editor and graphic design team. Keen then launched the 'Uranus Examiner', a publication that promised to 'Get to the Bottom of Big Stories'. Given that more than one in five local American papers have bitten the dust in the last two decades alone, the launch of the paper should have been celebrated. Unfortunately, just five issues into its run, following a flurry of controversy, the paper suspended publication. I spoke to the mayor of Uranus to find out what happened.

DAN: What exactly went wrong, Mayor?

MAYOR KEEN: Uh . . . it was the name. Waynesville's local mayor, Luge Hardman, publicly said 'I'm sorry. But the innuendo of that title puts my city up for public ridicule, and I will not be a part of it.'

DAN: To be fair, you can see why someone called Luge Hardman might want to steer clear of innuendo. What kind of influence did Mayor Hardman's comments have?

MAYOR KEEN: As a result, no one wanted to advertise with us, and the local schools and businesses shut down on us. A huge shame – I was just trying to fill a big gaping hole. Now there's over 50,000 people, if you include neighbouring counties, who no longer have a way of knowing what's happening in their local community.

DAN: So is that it for the 'Uranus Examiner'?

MAYOR KEEN: Absolutely not. We've already re-launched, with an all-new tagline 'Probing for news in Uranus deeper than ever before'. Take that, Luge Hardman. Right now, it'll only be published once every three months, but soon we'll go monthly. I'm planning on building up to a print run of 45,000 copies.

DAN: What can readers expect to see in upcoming editions?

MAYOR KEEN: There will be a lot about my big plans for 2020, which include setting up a zoological park, a wedding chapel and a motel. Pretty soon, people will be able to spend the night in Uranus, Dan. I'm also opening a Uranus brewery. We're bottling our own beer. And in the spirit of community, we'll be naming the first series of all beers after local towns in the county.

DAN: That sounds a nice break from the puns.

MAYOR KEEN: Absolutely. So, for example, our neighbouring county is Dixon, so we're going to have Dixon Uranus Beer.

DAN: Oh dear.

MAYOR KEEN: Then there's a town in the next county over called Licking. So we'll do a Licking Uranus Beer . . . there's even a town called Tightwad, if you can believe it.

DAN: Mayor Keen, thank you for your time.

The 'Uranus Examiner' is available to purchase at the Uranus Fudge Factory counter, Uranus, Missouri.

UNUSUAL SUSPECTS ▶

A naked Swedish police officer arrested a naked fugitive after recognising him in the sauna.

The details posted on Stockholm's Rinkeby Police's Facebook page were scant. We don't know, for instance, what distinguishing feature it was about the naked man that led to the officer recognising him; we don't know if the officer arrested the criminal straight away or left him to sweat; and we can only assume that he wasn't packing heat.

Amazingly, a similarly spontaneous, but less naked, arrest took place in Australia, where a detective who was hosting a press conference broke off to rugby-tackle a suspect that he noticed running behind him. Afterwords, Detective Senior Sergeant Daren Edwards dusted off his clothes and said, 'Suit was ready for a dry clean anyway.'

Other unusual suspects included:

▸ A suspected drug dealer in Manchester who left a rucksack stuffed with drugs on a tram – along with his full name and address.

▸ A man called Bud Weisser who was arrested for trespassing at the Budweiser factory in St Louis.

▸ A Canadian man who threw his speeding ticket out of his car window and was given a ticket for littering.

▸ A man who led police on a car chase in Michigan, only to be arrested when he stopped for petrol.

▸ A driver in New Jersey who was arrested for drink-driving and was then picked up from the police station by another person, who was also immediately arrested for drink-driving.

▸ A man in America who accidentally shot himself in the testicles while allegedly hiding drugs in his anus.

▸ The so-called 'Butt-Plug Bandits', who were on the run in New Zealand after stealing a bunch of adult toys.

▸ And a man in Australia who was arrested after trying to steal a hot pasta meal by stuffing it into his pants. He soon realised that the spaghetti was too hot, and had to pull down his trousers to stop his genitals burning. He left the store, but was soon captured, thanks to a trail of tomato sauce.

IN WHICH WE LEARN . . .

Why a chicken and a cat ended up in bed together, who can't sleep due to his own bells, who was Leyen low in London, who won a race while unconscious, and how Greggs woked-up its sausage rolls.

VEGANS ▶

*You can now eat a carrot made with meat and a
sausage roll made without any meat.*

What a time to be alive! The US fast-food restaurant
Arby's, whose slogan is 'We Have the Meats', has
invented the Marrot: a wad of ground turkey coloured
and shaped exactly like a carrot. The only bit that's not
meat is a bit of parsley sticking out of the top. And as
if 'Marrot' wasn't enough of an affront to the English
language, they also called it 'the world's first "Meat
Vegetable" or "Megetable"'.

In Britain the sandwich shop Greggs unveiled its new
vegan sausage roll, which is made from spiced quorn
wrapped in vegan pastry. And it sold like hot cakes,
much to the irritation of people who would never buy
anything labelled as vegan anyway. But before you rush
out to fill the freezer with the new pastry, be warned
that it should only be eaten as a treat. A single Greggs
vegan sausage roll contains half of your recommended
daily saturated fat; one-third of your recommended
salt; more calories than a McDonald's cheeseburger;
and palm oil, the farming of which was responsible for 8
per cent of the world's deforestation between 1990 and
2008. It doesn't, at least, have any animal products or a
nauseating neologistic name.

VENEZUELA ▶

*The Venezuelan economy is in such a bad state that
crime no longer pays.*

Venezuela's currency, the bolívar, is a mess. The government was accused of massaging the figures in April
when it reported that the inflation rate was *only*
130,060 per cent. It was actually around 1.3 million

VAJIRALONGKORN

Name:
Maha Vajiralongkorn, aka King
Rama X of Thailand

Full Name:
Somdet Phrachao Lukya Thoe Chaofa
Vajiralongkorn Borommachakyadit
Santatiwong Thevejthamrong Suboriban
Aphikhunuprakarn Mahittaladuladej
Bhumibol Nareswarangkrun Kittisiri-
sombunsawangwat Boromkhuttiyarajakuman

Other Titles:
Brother of the Moon, Half-Brother of the Sun, and Possessor of the
Twenty-Four Golden Umbrellas

Marital Status:
He married his former bodyguard just before his coronation, in a
ceremony where she lay prostrate at his feet and he poured sacred
water on her head.

Hobbies:
Used to dress his pet poodle, Air Chief Marshal Foo Foo (now deceased),
in formal evening attire and bring it to official events.

Reason for being in the news:
His coronation, which officially turned him into a living god.
Coronation gifts included a 'sword of victory'; golden slippers; a
crown that weighs 7.3 kilos, to represent the monarch's royal
burden; and a fly whisk made from Himalayan yak hair, symbolising
his duty to waft away evil.

To open the three-day event, courtiers collected holy water from 76
different provinces of Thailand, brought it to Bangkok, and poured
it over Vajiralongkorn's head. Next came the grand procession.
Since a large turnout is regarded as a mark of the king's
popularity, the royal family spammed millions of Thai people via
text message, urging them to attend.

After the coronation came the official housewarming party
(Ceremony of Assumption of the Royal Residence), during which a
chicken and a cat were placed on the royal bed. There was
speculation as to whether the animals pictured were alive or fake,
to which the palace responded: 'It should not be the focus whether
the animals were real or not.'

per cent. So in May, when inflation dropped below one million per cent for the first time in a year, it was scant consolation to Venezuelans, whose savings had already been lost and who found that money earned in one month was virtually worthless the next.

And spare a thought for the criminals. The country's gangsters complained that nobody was carrying money around with them any more, so there was nothing to steal. They also pointed out that with bullets selling at the equivalent of $1 a pop when the average monthly wage is only $6.50, it was getting too expensive to shoot people, too.

In 1980, Venezuela was the richest country in South America, and even today it has the world's largest proven oil reserves, but despite that, there were long queues at filling stations due to shortages of petrol. The collapse was down to a mixture of oil prices plummeting, American sanctions and gross mismanagement by the government. Some people were able to make the best of a bad situation, though. Bolívar banknotes may be worthless, but they are still a useful resource for artists who use them to make paper animals and, ironically enough, wallets.

VENGABOYS

The Vengabus is coming . . . back.

The Austrian government was brought down by the 'Ibiza Scandal' when the far-right vice chancellor, Heinz-Christian Strache, was caught on video in the holiday resort, trying to bribe a woman he believed to be the niece of a Russian oligarch. In fact she was part of a sting operation that successfully exposed Austrian government corruption.

While this may not have worked out very well for the politicians involved, it did wonders for the Vengaboys, because of the scandal's Ibiza-themed branding. Their 1999 song 'We're Going to Ibiza' experienced a surge in popularity, reaching number one in the Austrian music charts. The band was flooded with requests to gig there and ended up performing at an anti-corruption protest in Vienna – travelling there by Vengabus, naturally.

VICARS

A Welsh vicar tried to muffle his own bells.

Reverend David Parry, who preaches God's word at St Mary's Church in Conwy, North Wales and lives nearby, complained that the bells in the church's 19th-century clock tower, which chime every 15 minutes, 24 hours a day, were keeping him awake at night. He therefore wrote to the council requesting that they should be switched off at the end of each day, so that he and his family could get some sleep. In response, the council handed out questionnaires to 400 residents to see if they felt the same. As it turned out, almost no one else in the parish objected to the bells at all, so the Rev. Parry will probably just have to source some decent earplugs for now.

In Kent a slightly less sleep-deprived vicar launched an afternoon service on a Sunday, after realising that people weren't making the morning one because they had hangovers. Reverend Mark Montgomery said the service, which will take place twice a month in the local primary school, will give the more party-prone members of his flock a lie-in, so they can recover from the night before.

VISAS

Performances of a play about immigration had to be cancelled because the lead actor had the wrong travel documents.

The play was supposed to be performed at the 'Lost in Migration' conference in Malta to raise awareness about the suffering of people fleeing their home countries. However, Phosphoros Theatre Company, which produces plays starring refugees and asylum seekers, said their star Afghan refugee, Syed Haleem Najibi, had been barred from boarding the flight to Malta. Authorities at Heathrow said his travel certificate was not valid for entry into the country.

'Is this a Visa I See before me?'

Name:
Ursula von der Leyen

A.K.A.:
Rose Ladson

Reason for name change:
Threat from the Baader-Meinhof gang.

Who are the Baader-Meinhof gang?
Don't worry, you'll probably read something about them soon.

Reason for being in the news:
Von der Leyen was nobody's first choice for the role of president of the European Commission, but she managed to unite enough of the conflicting EU groups to scrape through, in a vote that Nigel Farage claimed had no legitimacy due to its tightness. It certainly was close. Von der Leyen got 54 per cent of the vote – just 2 per cent more than Nigel himself managed to secure in the 2016 referendum about ▮▮▮▮▮.

Von der Leyen grew up in a political family: her father was the state premier of Lower Saxony. For this reason the family was threatened by West Germany's far-left militant Baader-Meinhof gang (these days the Baader-Meinhof gang is best known for giving its name to the Baader-Meinhof effect: a term that describes an illusion whereby, after you first hear an unusual word, you seem to encounter it regularly). In fact the threat by the Baader-Meinhof gang was so great that von der Leyen had to go to London in the late 70s – and change her name to Rose Ladson – to throw the Baader-Meinhof gang off the scent.

Meanwhile another unfortunate migrant was convicted of lying to officials in the US, when his attempt to get a green card backfired. The man, who formerly played for the Liberian national football team, claimed to be married to an American citizen. However, when his supposed 'wife' handed her phone to the officers to inspect, so that they could check the marriage wasn't a scam, a new message popped up thanking her for 'the best sex ever'. Since the message did not come from the Liberian man, the marriage was called into question and found to be illegitimate.

VUELTA

Chris Froome won one of the biggest cycling races in the world while in intensive care.

Froome was competing in central France when he took his hands off the handlebars to blow his nose and was sent crashing into a wall by a gust of wind. He was knocked unconscious and broke a leg, elbow and hip, as well as bones in his chest and neck. However, while in his hospital bed he received news that the 2011 Vuelta a España winner, Juan José Cobo, had been disqualified for drug use, meaning that Froome was promoted from second to first in a race that had finished eight years earlier.

The Vuelta is one of the 'big three' races in the world, and so not only does this promotion mean that Froome has another title under his belt (added to his four Tour de France wins), but it means he technically became the first Briton to win a major cycling race – Sir Bradley Wiggins previously held the record, thanks to his 2012 Tour de France win, but of course we now know that Froome won in 2011. Thirty days later, after Cobo failed to appeal, the decision was made official.

IN WHICH WE LEARN . . .

Which England cricketer showed True Grit, how Zimbabwe spent a Fistful of Dollars, why Toni Morrison's publishers were Unforgiven, and which of the Magnificent Seven finally made it around the world.

WALL, BUILDING THE ▶

The US border wall was used for security . . . in Mexico.

The Mexican authorities revealed that at least 15 people have been arrested for stealing the razor-wire used to make the border and selling it to home owners in Tijuana who needed some homeland security of their own. The fencing was only installed in November last year, so it lasted fewer than six months before being nicked. It was sold off at the very reasonable price of $2.10 per home.

Trump's wall is in trouble. A statement by the US Customs and Border Protection agency confirmed that in the first 30 months of the Trump presidency, not a single new mile of 'wall' had been built along the US–Mexico border. The only new barriers were those replacing old bits of the border. While Trump did manage this year to secure $2.5 billion in unspent military funds for wall projects, he's still a long way (and a lot more money) from getting the entire border closed off. If it happens, it'll be the most expensive wall in the world, with estimates for its completion ranging from $8 million to $25 million per mile, meaning that the entire cost could end up being as much as $50 billion.

That said, there is some competition on the horizon for the title of the world's most expensive wall. This year it was revealed that Kenya's government spent $35 million on just 6 miles of wire fencing to protect the country against militants from neighbouring Somalia. (Given that the border between the two countries is 435 miles long, it's questionable how useful it is.)

Whether or not Trump's wall gets built, it's become very much a focus of American culture – and protest. Artist Cosimo Cavallaro, for example, has spent more than six

—— ▼ ——

When asked in a press conference whether the idea of a border wall was 'medieval', Trump replied: 'They say a wall is medieval, well a wheel is older than a wall . . . A wheel works, and a wall works.' Archaeologists quickly responded on social media to point out that walls actually predate wheels by around 5,000 years.

months building a 1,000-foot-long wall made of cheese on the US–Mexico border. When asked if his project wasn't a waste of effort, he pointed out, 'You see the waste in my wall, but you can't see the waste in [Trump's] $10-billion wall?' It's hard to say whether he's more interested in borders or in cheese, as he has previously made cheese boots, a cheese jacket and a cheese chair. Nonetheless, he is ploughing on, very caerphilly, and doing his bit to – in his words – Make America Grate Again.

There was at least one wall that did its job this year – a fake one that was installed in a Brooklyn subway to lure a persistent graffiti artist who had been spraying '#LoveTrump' all over Borough Hall station. Resembling a construction area, complete with a padlocked door, it certainly fooled the Trumpist tagger. When he arrived and started spraying, officials burst through the door and arrested him sooner than he could say 'big beautiful wall'.

The whole thing is such a sensitive subject that a baker in Washington was accused of racism for making joke 'Build That Wall' cookies for Valentine's Day. After a huge online backlash, he said, 'I guess the joke is on me.'

WAR ON PLASTIC ▶

A grocer discouraged plastic use by emblazoning his bags with incredibly embarrassing slogans; unfortunately, people started collecting them.

Among the slogans on bags dished out by Vancouver's East West Market were 'Dr Toew's Wart Ointment', 'Into the Weird Adult Video Emporium' and 'The Colon Care Co-Op'. Even worse, customers had to pay 5 cents for the privilege of creating the impression that they were warty perverts with colon problems. The shop's owner, David Lee Kwen, said he wanted to give his customers 'something humorous, but also something that made them think at the same time'. The plan, however, had an unintended consequence: customers began collecting the bags because they found them so funny. In response to this news, Kwen announced that he now plans to make canvas bags that sport the same embarrassing slogans.

—— ▼ ——

Ping Wang, a student in Sweden, and her supervisor Baozhong Zhang, created a new type of plastic from indole, the chemical that makes faeces stink. The good news is that the plastic doesn't smell at all, and can be recycled indefinitely. The bad news is that there are no plans at present to manufacture it on a large scale.

The war against plastic has a long way to go, as American explorer Victor Vescovo discovered when he made the deepest-ever dive in human history, descending nearly 11 kilometres to the bottom of the Mariana Trench – the lowest part of the ocean. He may have beaten the previous record by 11 metres, but he was still welcomed by plastic bags and sweet wrappers when he got there.

An even worse problem than drifting bags is microplastics – tiny molecules of plastic that make their way into the ocean, and even into the food chain, as larger items break down. A study done at the University of Newcastle in Australia found that humans ingest 2,000 pieces of microplastic each week, almost entirely from drinking water. Their total weight is 5 grams – the equivalent of a credit card.

WHALES

Japan resumed commercial whaling – which meant it hunted fewer whales.

A tour operator swimming off the coast of South Africa was swallowed by a whale while he was filming a shoal of sardines. He went down head-first, but luckily didn't make it past the gullet before the whale realised its mistake and spat him back out. He emerged still clutching his camera.

The country withdrew from the International Whaling Commission, resuming commercial whaling in its own waters for the first time in 30 years. At the same time it announced that it would no longer kill whales 'for research purposes' (widely interpreted as a cover for commercial whaling) in the Antarctic. The cap on the number of commercial whales it can kill was set at 227, significantly fewer than the 333 it killed the previous year in Antarctica. That allowance is split between 52 minke, 150 Bryde's whale and 25 sei whales, the last of which is an endangered species.

The whaling industry in Japan only employs about 300 people, but one of its centres is prime minister Shinzo Abe's constituency, which might explain why he prioritised this new policy. Those who live in whaling communities are proud of the tradition. After the first expedition under the new rules, fishermen and onlookers in the northern Japanese town of Kushiro celebrated by showering a captured 27-foot-long minke whale with celebratory sake.

WHEN IN ROM

A man on a pilgrimage found out that not all roads lead to Rome. Some lead to Rom.

Retired hairdresser Luigi Rimonti from Newcastle planned to make a pilgrimage to Rome to see some family and drop in on the Pope. He crossed the Channel without incident. However, a few days into his journey his satnav started to act up and he had to seek assistance from some workers at a petrol station. They helped him out by tapping 'ROME' into his navigation system – or at least they thought they did.

Realising, when he arrived at his destination, that what lay spread out before him looked nothing like Rome, Luigi stopped and got out of the car to read a road sign. Unfortunately, because he was on a slope and hadn't put the handbrake on properly, his car started rolling backwards, knocking him over and then dragging him along until it crashed into the road sign he'd been trying to read. This informed him he was in Rom, a pleasant German town about 1,000 miles north of his intended destination. It is, fortunately, very easy to tell the difference between the two. Rom's population is 800 and Rome's is close to three million. Rome wasn't built in a day; Rom arguably could have been.

Rimonti had to spend a week in hospital recuperating. His sons, who had insisted he use satnav in the first place, blamed themselves, telling the *Guardian* that he would probably have been fine if they'd just let him make his own way, 'like a penguin going home'.

WIGS

Zimbabwe's government spent £118,000 on wigs.

As Britain celebrated the 150th anniversary of the ending of the tax on wig powder (which had been imposed to fund war with France), a furious row broke out in Tanzania over a new 25 per cent tax on imported hairpieces. Wig-makers aren't happy, but the government claimed the move would promote natural beauty.

The *Zimbabwe Independent* newspaper reported that the bigwigs from the country's judiciary had kitted themselves out with 64 wigs at the hair-raising price of £1,850 each. Many questioned whether this should have been a priority, given the budget pressures on the judicial system. There was also some tearing of hair as to whether it's an outmoded way of dressing and a throwback to the colonial era, and so whether judges in Zimbabwe should actually wear wigs at all.

They are very nice wigs, though: made with horsehair in the traditional manner by a London firm. The manufacture of each one takes two weeks from start to finish and involves three people: a lace-maker, a weft-maker – a weft is a kind of yarn – and a dresser. The owner of the wig-maker, Stanley Ley's of Fleet Street, which supplied the order said, unsurprisingly, that he was delighted 'Zimbabwe are still keeping up the traditions of the English bar'.

WOFFORD, CHLOE ARDELIA

The world lost the Nobel laureate and Pulitzer Prize-winner who wrote her first novel because she didn't want to get kicked out of her writers' group.

Chloe Wofford published her first book relatively late in life – and under the wrong name. *The Bluest Eye* came out in 1970, but Wofford was upset when she received the first copies of the book to see the name 'Toni Morrison' on the cover. People had called her that since university, but it was just a nickname. Toni was short for Anthony, the baptismal middle name she took when she converted to Catholicism, aged 12 (after St Anthony of Padua), and Morrison was the name of the husband she'd divorced six years earlier. She was born Chloe Ardelia Wofford and, to her family, she was always Chloe. But from 1970 onwards she was, to the rest of the world, Toni Morrison.

She embarked on her first novel while she was working as the first black editor of fiction at Random House (the best publishing house out there, in our completely objective opinion) and raising two young sons. She had always loved reading, saying she found it a good way of getting out of doing chores when she was a child. As a member of a writers' club that she was reluctant to leave, because 'they served such good food', she soon realised she'd have to deliver something. She started getting up at 4 a.m. every day to write for an hour or two before her sons woke up, and she also wrote in the car if she got stuck in traffic on the school run, resting her notepaper on the steering wheel. Morrison didn't quit her publishing job until 1983, and even then she would regularly read the newspaper with a pencil in hand, so that she could copy-edit it as she went.

She had her detractors. One of her novels, *Paradise*, was banned in Texas prisons because, according to the authorities, it read as though it was 'designed to achieve a breakdown of prisons through inmate disruption'. But she also had many high-profile fans, including Marlon Brando, who used to call her up regularly and read extracts from her book, *Song of Solomon*, to her down the phone.

By the end of her life Morrison was acknowledged as one of the greatest-ever American novelists, winning a Pulitzer Prize for fiction in 1988 and the Nobel Prize for Literature in 1993. Two weeks after she accepted the latter, her house burned down, destroying almost everything she owned. Amazingly, though, it was such a cold winter that the water the firefighters used froze on several of her manuscripts, which saved them. She considered the Nobel Prize some consolation, at least, for the devastation caused by the fire – perhaps even more so because, as she once said in an interview, it was officially Chloe, not Toni, who received it.

WORLD, AROUND THE ▸

The youngest person ever to cycle around the world says he's 'not really a keen cyclist'.

We learned this when we interviewed 18-year-old Charlie Condell after reading about his record-breaking journey.* He told us he'd decided to cycle round the world after a chat with his dad in a pub (where most great decisions are made), during which he'd sketched out a plan to bike around Europe. It was only when his father suggested he 'stretch it out a bit' that Charlie decided he might as well circle the entire globe. He admitted that he hadn't done much cycling before, since he was really more a fan of running, rowing and climbing, and that he'd bought his bike just two weeks before setting off.

Unfortunately Guinness doesn't recognise Charlie's 'youngest person to cycle around the world' record because, understandably, it doesn't want to encourage younger people to attempt potentially dangerous records.

Frightening moments on the trip included waking up with a deadly green snake on his leg in Australia and being chased by a pack of farm dogs in Turkey, though the most inconvenient was probably getting his bike stolen in Australia. It was reported in the press that that bike was called Colin, but when we asked about this, he said it was a name he'd come up with on the spur of the moment, when a radio DJ had asked him about it: Charlie had met an eccentric man called Colin the night before, so it was the first name that popped into his head. Nothing he experienced on the trip has deterred him from future adventures: he now plans to travel round the world on a motorbike, visiting the countries he missed out the first time around.

While Charlie was pedalling his way across the globe, pilot Norman Surplus was flying round it in a gyrocopter – a flying machine that looks like a tiny, one-man helicopter. Norman really does have a nickname for his vehicle: he calls it Roxy, an anagram of its registration code, G-YROX. We spoke to him as well, and he told us that he actually started the trip back in 2010, but that for seven years Russia refused to let him fly in their air space, before finally relenting this year. (He was also strictly forbidden to fly over Iran, but couldn't resist looping 100 metres into its territory as he passed.)

At one point, sandwiched between two storms in Saudi Arabia, Surplus was forced to land Roxy in the middle of the desert and beg for bed and board from some extremely confused locals – the only people for hundreds of kilometres around. On another occasion he crash-landed into a lake in Thailand and got trapped beneath his vehicle underwater. He was then stuck in Thailand for three months while Roxy was fixed.

Norman was inspired to take on the challenge because he realised that of the 'Magnificent Seven' (as he categorises them) flying machines – aeroplanes, flex wings (e.g. microlights), airships, helicopters, rockets, balloons and gyroplanes – all but the gyro have completed round-the-world trips. The first gyro took to the air in 1923, Norman explained, and since then 'the world has waited for one of them to circumnavigate the globe'. And while all of our readers may not have felt those 96 years of suspense quite as acutely as Norman, we hope that you can now rest easier, knowing the wait is finally over.

WOODSTOCK

It's 50 years since almost half a million people gathered in upstate New York for a festival now regarded as one of the most significant cultural events of the 20th century...

The original Woodstock didn't actually take place in Woodstock. A month before it was due to start, local residents blocked it, so a new venue had to be found. Technically, therefore, it should be known as Max Yasgur's Dairy Farm.

Headline act Jimi Hendrix was supposed to close the festival on Sunday night. However, because of technical difficulties and bad weather, he didn't go on stage until 9 a.m. on Monday morning.

Guitarist Carlos Santana was so high on LSD when he played that he believed his guitar had transformed into an electric snake. He spent the whole set wrestling it.

While plans to throw a giant 50th-anniversary festival ultimately fell through, fans were still able to celebrate the milestone by purchasing a 38-disc CD box set containing virtually all the music from Woodstock 1969. Packed with 432 songs, *Woodstock – Back to the Garden* was released with a limited run of just 1,969 copies.

Announcements made from the stage over the course of the three-day festival included: 'Lisa Freytag, please meet Ron at the hospital right away', 'Kenny Irwin, please go to the information booth for your insulin' and 'Paul Andrews, Mike needs his pills and will meet you where he did yesterday.'

At one point, when storm clouds approached, the hippy crowd was urged by the organisers to 'think hard to get rid of the rain'. They therefore chanted, 'No rain, no rain, no rain.' It didn't work. However, the chant was recorded and subsequently became the opening track of side four of the official Woodstock vinyl.

When one food vendor, the Food for Love concession, found itself running low on burgers, it raised prices from 25 cents to $1. The crowd, sensing capitalist exploitation, burned the stand down. Learning of the food shortage, a Jewish community centre made sandwiches, which were then distributed by nuns.

There have been three subsequent Woodstock festivals commemorating the original. During the final hours of Woodstock '99, a peace organisation handed out candles to audience members to create a candlelight vigil. Unfortunately, the candles were used to set the audio tower on fire.

England's man-of-the-match in their Cricket World Cup Final victory over New Zealand was nominated for 'New Zealander of the Year'.

———— ▼ ————

One game between South Africa and Sri Lanka had to be suspended, when the grounds were invaded by a swarm of bees that forced the players to lie down on the grass to protect themselves. Amazingly, the same two teams had an identical experience two years earlier, and 10,000 kilometres away in Johannesburg. There's no evidence that the same cricket-hating bees were responsible for both attacks.

England's hero, Ben Stokes, who was born in Christchurch, New Zealand, said that he was flattered to be nominated, but that people should vote for the Kiwis' captain, Kane Williamson, instead. Actually, England's victorious team could have provided 'people of the year' for a whole host of countries. England's opening batsman, Jason Roy, was born in South Africa; its best bowler, Jofra Archer, is from Barbados; and its captain, Eoin Morgan, is Irish. Which made right-wing politician Jacob Rees-Mogg's tweet all the more baffling: 'we clearly don't need Europe to win,' he posted.

Morgan (who was wicket-keeper in two games for England, making him the original Irish Backstop) was asked by a reporter if the team had been helped by 'the luck of the Irish', but he pointed out that spinner Adil Rashid had said that Allah was also watching over them, and perhaps the diversity of the team was one of the things that raised them above former England teams.

A day after England's victory, Russia appeared to deny the existence of cricket when it published a list of officially recognised sports that included pétanque, draughts and mini-golf, but not 'the gentleman's game'. Alexander Sorokin, a member of the Moscow Cricket Sports Federation, said it must have been a mistake and that he was confident cricket would be included next year.

WORLD CUP, FOOTBALL

A bar that promised customers free shots for every goal the US scored in the Women's World Cup retracted the offer after the team beat Thailand 13–0.

American Social Bar & Kitchen in Miami publicised the promotion on social media, presumably not banking on the US achieving the tournament's biggest-ever win in their opening game. The bar managers frantically back-pedalled the day after the game, saying the offer wasn't meant to be taken seriously, 'especially when records are shattered'. Others were put out by the team's success, too, accusing its members of celebrating their 9th, 10th and 11th goals with unnecessary enthusiasm. Former Canadian player Clare Rustad called the team's antics 'disgraceful', adding, 'I think, as a Canadian, we would just never, ever think of doing something like that.'

The tournament garnered huge attention in the UK. England's Lionesses' semi-final match against the US, which they lost 1–2, was the most-watched TV show of the year, getting a bigger audience than the men's World Cup Final last year. It was the first time ever that the England women's team was composed entirely of full-time professional footballers. By comparison, more than one-third of the Scottish team still had full-time jobs alongside their football careers. The Scots trained for their matches by throwing a rubber chicken at each other. Sadly, that didn't help them make it out of the group stages. They were eliminated after a contentious penalty, when VAR spotted a fowl.

Lucy Bronze became the first ever English winner of the UEFA Women's Player of the Year. The defender's middle name is 'Tough'.

IN WHICH WE LEARN . . .

Why it would be a good idea for people to stop watching pornography on the Internet, and what's the least likely thing to happen in the history of the universe.

X-RATED

A pill called 'Big Penis' was taken off the shelves because it makes your penis bigger.

The supplement contained the prescription drug sildenafil, the active ingredient in Viagra, but the manufacturers failed to mention this in the ingredients listed on their non-prescription product. That's illegal. So Big Penis was banned by the US Food and Drug Administration.

Actually this kind of problem is a lot more common than you might think . . .

All 'erection-causing' energy drinks were banned in Zambia this year, while doctors in Papua New Guinea warned men against self-administered penis-enlargement surgery, amidst reports that they were injecting themselves with silicon, coconut oil, baby oil and cooking oil.

In other X-rated news:

▶ A Danish shot-putter turned politician put his election advert on Pornhub, explaining that 'you have to be where your voters are'. Unfortunately, his performance suffered and he ended up losing his seat.

▶ In Amsterdam, patrons of one cinema were able to experience '5D' porn. As well as involving 3D images, it featured bouncing chairs, blasts of air and jets of water, to give a fully immersive experience of, presumably, someone having sex aboard a North Sea trawler.

▶ A man in North Carolina had his television service cut off when he refused to pay for pay-per-view porn. He claimed his dog had ordered it by accidentally sitting on the remote control.

X-WORD

Here is The Book Of The Year 2019 cryptic crossword. All questions are related to the year's news. Answers can be found at the back of the book. Enjoy...

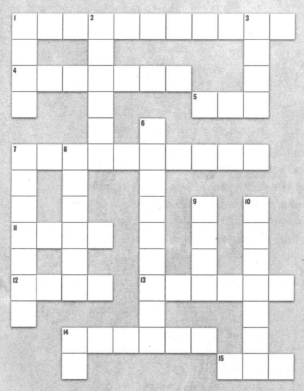

ACROSS

1. Sir Kim Darroch resigned after giving an unflattering assessment of him: he's a character, who doesn't wear trousers and smells like eggs. (6,5)
4. Lizards taking over Florida, disturbing us again. (7)
5. She announced her resignation before June. (3)
7. *Game of Thrones* writers made me confused, not hornier. (4,6)
11. What Andy Murray got in Australia and scored for the next five months? (4)
12. Alongside 14 ACROSS they shot for the Moon. (4)
13. Theresa May tried to organise withdrawal after initially being rejected. (6)
14. A Spanish chicken reached the Moon 50 years ago. (6)
15. I hear you are younger than previously thought? (3)

DOWN

1. Irish ▮▮▮▮ plans are discussed here, in the *Daily Mail*. (4)
2. World's most diverse site? (6)
3. Man (confused boy) thinks he dated Natalie Portman. (4)
6. Penis in pop star? She's gunna blow! (9)
7. Supermarket with a very large frozen section? (7)
8. 37 per cent of Brits think they're disgusting. So vile, so messed up. (6)
9. Tory minister to take charge? Not right now. (4)
10. She swore she would never go to the White House. (7)
14. Acting innocently to begin with, China is now using this to spy on its citizens. (1,1)

▶ And a French study worked out that the streaming of online porn worldwide uses up as much CO_2 as Belgium. We await the study that asks the world which it is most prepared to give up.

XENON ▶

Scientists witnessed the least likely event in the history of the universe.

All atoms are stable or unstable. The stable ones will stay that way for ever, while the unstable ones will give off energy until they find a stable state. This is known as decaying and is how radioactivity works. Some atoms are really unstable and decay almost instantaneously, but some unstable ones are very, very, very *nearly* stable, meaning that they hardly ever give off any radiation: one of these nearly-stable atoms is called xenon-124.

There's 3½ tons of liquid xenon sitting in a laboratory nearly a mile under the ground in Italy. Scientists were studying it for evidence that dark matter exists, but in the process they happened to observe one of the xenon atoms decaying. A xenon-124 decay is something that happens once every 1.8 sextillion years – that's about 130 billion times the age of the entire universe. It's the least-likely thing that anyone has ever seen happen, and it's fair to say it's the least-likely thing that's ever going to happen.

Or put it another way: the chance of scientists seeing that atom change in 2019 is about the same as the chance of you winning the main prize in the National Lottery three weeks running. Or predicting heads/tails correctly 70 times in a row. Or if you took all of the water in the Earth's oceans and put it into half-pint glasses, then chose one at random, of me doing the same and choosing the same glass. Stranger things do happen, though: three months later, England won the Cricket World Cup.

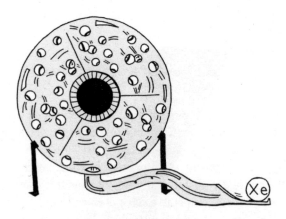

IN WHICH WE LEARN . . .

Why Ju-hong wants to be yo-ung,
why it's tough to age a yew tree,
why farmers are on YouTube, and what
makes the Pope go ewwwwwwwww.

YEAR OF THE PIG ▶

A Chinese company that tried to pay off its debts in ham announced that it was now running out of pigs.

The Chuying Agro-Pastoral Group, a pork and poultry producer, was in serious financial trouble last year, until the firm came up with a brilliant wheeze: it announced that it would clear £31 million worth of debts by paying bond investors . . . in ham. The ruse worked for a while – until earlier this year, when the company revealed that it had run out of money to buy pig food.

China is pork-obsessed. Some Chinese schools even give pupils pork to reward them for performing well (the size of the meat bag they get depends on how hard they've been working). The country is also economically very pork-dependent. But this year the Ham Dynasty took something of a hammering. China's pig farms have been devastated by African Swine Fever, a virus that is harmless to humans, but lethal to pigs – one in five Chinese pigs had to be culled. It got so bad that some cities started defrosting and eating their strategic reserves of frozen pork. The city of Jinan alone released 1,500 tons of it.

The industry suffered another big blow when the US seized one million pounds (450,000 kilos) of Chinese pork that was being smuggled into a New Jersey port in containers that ranged from noodle bowls to Tide detergent containers. More than 100 agricultural specialists and K-9 dog teams were involved in the operation and, in their war against illegal Chinese pork in general and African Swine Fever in particular, the authorities proceeded to incinerate all the meat, producing the biggest barbecue of the year, but without so much as a single sausage on offer.

YEW TREES

Most yew trees are younger than we thought.

Yews are some of Britain's oldest trees, but exactly how old they are has previously required a lot of guesswork. Now, however, a new, more accurate dating technique has been devised that looks not just at tree rings, but also at the girth of the trunk, and takes account of the fact that trees go through growth spurts. What it has revealed is that the oldest yews are at least 1,000 years younger than we thought. Indeed, the oldest tree in Britain, the Fortingall Yew, is probably 3,000 years younger than was once assumed: it's been downgraded from 5,000 years old to 2,000. Toby Hindson, a founder member of the Ancient Yew Group (which, as far as we know, has no plans to remove the word 'Ancient' from its name) told the *Daily Telegraph*, 'While 1,600 or 2,000 years old may seem low in terms of the inflated ages which many people have grown used to, it really still is extremely old.'

All of this age confusion is probably very stressful for the Fortingall Yew. And according to Neil Hooper, the Fortingall Tree warden, it was already pretty stressed.

He says that tourists keep snapping twigs off the tree or tying ribbons to its branches, and it doesn't like it. In fact there is some evidence that the yew may have changed sex, due to all the unwanted attention it's been receiving.

YOUTH ▶

A South Korean politician proposed making every single person in the country a year younger.

——— ❤ ———

A stone circle in Scotland, thought to date back 4,500 years, turned out to be from the mid-1990s. The circle at Leochel-Cushnie had been deemed a notable discovery by the Scottish authorities, but the former owner of the farm admitted this year that he had dragged the stones into place himself about 20 years ago, which makes the circle of stones roughly one-third the age of the Rolling Stones.

South Korea has an age system like nowhere else: according to the rules of 'Korean Age', a baby is one year old the moment it's born and it then gets a year older every 1 January. So a baby born on 31 December is two years old just a day later. New father Lee Dong-Kil told *The Japan Times* that he got lots of congratulatory messages when his daughter was born at 10 p.m. on 31 December. Then, two hours later, people texted again to congratulate the two-hour-old baby on turning two years old. When they're dealing with foreigners, the picture is similarly confusing: if you ask someone from South Korea how old they are, they will frequently give both their 'Korean age' and their 'international age'.

Reckoning that the way the rest of the world handles age makes a lot more sense, South Korean politician Hwang Ju-hong introduced a parliamentary bill to end the Korean system. Unfortunately, Korea's national assembly is currently in a state of gridlock, so Hwang may have to reintroduce his bill in a year (or two).

Someone else who may in reality have been slightly younger than her stated age was Jeanne Calment, reputedly the oldest woman ever, who died in 1997, supposedly aged 122. Russian researcher Nikolai Zak, however, is dubious. He suggests that Jeanne actually died in 1934, and that it was her daughter Yvonne (officially listed as having died that year) who survived until 1997, having swapped identities with her mother to avoid inheritance tax. That would make 'Jeanne' 99 when she died. Jeanne/Yvonne's family declined to comment.

YOUTUBE

Farmers can make much more money if they combine harvesting with vlogging.

Bloomberg profiled a number of farmers who are now making more money from YouTube than they are from their farms. One of them, Minnesota's Zach Johnson, also known as MN Millennial Farmer, makes five times more as a YouTuber than he does as a farmer. His most popular video consists of 11 minutes of him attempting to free a tractor stuck in the mud.

If you liked that YouTube news, you might also like . . .

▶ According to a survey conducted by LEGO, more British and American children aspire to be YouTubers than astronauts.

▶ A YouTube convention in Anaheim had a special parents-only area where they could sleep or drink wine.

▶ A dispute between two beauty vloggers turned ugly. Tati Westbrook has a beauty brand, and so when her friend James Charles posted an advert for a rival brand, the two fell out. Westbrook accused Charles of disloyalty, and the Internet agreed: Charles became the first YouTuber ever to lose more than a million subscribers in a single day.

YOU'VE GOT MAIL ▶

French cheese-makers put a Camembert into every French MP's letter box.

The gesture was made by traditional Camembert makers, the Association Fromages de Terroirs, in protest at the announcement that factory-made Camembert will in future have protected 'Appellation d'origine protégée' (AOP) status. Until now, only incredibly labour-intensive cheeses, produced using traditional methods in the region in which they were first developed, have qualified for the special label. A mere 5,000 tonnes of traditional Camembert are made each year, as opposed to 60,000 tonnes of the factory-made stuff.

In an attempt to get their whey, the terroirists launched a protest that involved stuffing a cheese into each and every parliamentary pigeonhole at the Assemblée nationale. They acknowledged that this might make parliament smell slightly worse, but argued that France must be rescued from becoming 'an ocean of cheese with the consistency of plaster'. There was a brief ceasefire last year, when producers of both types of cheese agreed to share the AOP status. But now the new president of the Association Fromages de Terroirs has decided to take up arms again. The cheese war rages on.

This wasn't the only postal protest of the year. During the Australian elections someone hollowed out a book entitled *Unpopular*, pooed in it and left it on the doorstep of ex-prime minister Tony Abbott. And in the US, an Ohio firm started a lawsuit against a company called 'Dicks by Mail', after an anonymous box containing confetti in the shape of penises arrived at their office. The firm thought it might have had something to do with a bomb threat they had had a few months before, and sued, alleging that the employees had suffered emotional distress when the parcel burst open with penile confetti. As they said in their suit, 'Nothing about the package warned it was a spring-loaded dick bomb.' However, after media coverage of the lawsuit, the anonymous sender came forward, explaining that his choice of a confetti penis cannon was entirely unrelated to the bomb threat – so they let it drop.

YUCK! ▶

The US Center for Disease Control warned hedgehog owners not to kiss their pets.

In the space of just a few months, 11 people across eight US states were infected with a specific strain of salmonella. All but one of them had had close contact with a hedgehog. Putting two and two together, the agency cautioned, 'Don't kiss or snuggle hedgehogs.'

In other yucky news:

▶ A study found that men's beards contain more germs than dogs carry in their fur. Nearly half of the 18 beards surveyed by the Hirslanden Clinic in Switzerland had bugs that could prove dangerous to human health – a significantly higher level than that found in the coats of 30 dogs.

▶ The Pope wouldn't let people kiss his fisherman's ring. Queues of fans often like to kiss the object, which is named after St Peter (who was a fisherman by trade), but at a Mass at the Holy House of Loreto in Italy, Pope Francis kept jerking his hand away from them. A spokesman said afterwards that he was worried about spreading germs down the queue.

▶ And the Internet became agitated when Fox News host Pete Hegseth said he hadn't washed his hands in 10 years, on the grounds that if he couldn't see germs, they couldn't be real. He later insisted he had been joking.

IN WHICH WE LEARN . . .

How the zebra got its stripes, how a German park got its pink lines and how a flyboarder flew across a border.

Z'S, CATCHING SOME

For songs to give you sleepless nights, *see* **Baby Shark**; for songs to make you soporific, *see* **Dick, Moby's**; for a ruff night's sleep, *see* **Our Survey Said . . .**; for sleeping peals, *see* **Vicars**; for deep-sea kippers, *see* **Zebrafish**; and for avoiding fake snooze, *see* **Zuckerburg, Mark**.

ZAPATA, FRANKY

A Flyboarding Frenchman flew from France to Britain.

Franky Zapata is a French engineer and an ex jet-ski champion who has spent years developing a jet-powered hoverboard (also known as a 'Flyboard'). This year he set himself the goal of becoming the first person to hover their way across the English Channel.

On his first attempt, timed to coincide with the 110th anniversary of Louis Blériot's cross-Channel flight, Zapata fell into the water halfway through, when choppy waves caused him to slip off the floating platform where he hoped to recharge his kerosene backpack. Ten days later, flanked by three helicopters, he made his second attempt, involving a slightly larger refuelling platform, and successfully made the crossing in 22 minutes, at speeds of up to 110 mph, and at an altitude of 15–20 metres.

As Zapata arrived in Kent, he burst into tears of joy and told journalists, 'It's crazy.' His chief assistant (and wife) Krystel said, 'I am so happy for him, and we can finally go on holiday.' Zapata flew back by plane the next day – only to get an email from the UK Border Force asking how he'd managed to leave Britain, given that they had no official record of him entering the country.

It wasn't his first triumph of 2019. Earlier this year Zapata flew around Paris for a military parade while carrying a rifle, in a bid to show that his invention could be deployed in war. He did admit, though, that the hoverboard is so loud that you'd miss out on the element of surprise. He's also talked openly about the risks involved. After his Channel crossing he said he had always dreamed of that moment, and that when you fly, 'you feel the turbulence and the air through your fingers', but during his maiden flight in his garage, three years ago, he nearly lost two digits in one of the turbines. And when asked what would happen if an amateur tried the board, he said, 'You would die. You would kill yourself in less than two seconds.'

Even maverick inventors, though, have to keep the neighbours happy. In his village, Zapata is only allowed to fly twice a week, and not before 10 a.m., between noon and 3 p.m., after 6.30 p.m., or on a Sunday or a Bank Holiday. Undeterred, he's now developing a flying car.

ZEBRAFISH ▶

When in mortal danger, zebrafish would rather get their end away than get away.

——— ▼ ———

Scientists from the UK and Brazil who gave zebrafish a mix of vodka and energy drinks found that the fish became less sociable, and more likely to indulge in risky behaviour.

Most species (including humans, the researchers were quick to add) will flee if confronted by a predator while they are mid-coitus, but thanks to the action of some pheromones in its brain, the zebrafish always prioritises love over war. Although only 4 centimetres in length, zebrafish are disproportionately important to scientists. They are easy to breed, are completely transparent, so that you can see their internal organs, and their genome is very similar to our own. This makes them the perfect animals to study if you want to work out what's going on inside the human body. Since they're used so regularly in science, we need to know everything about zebrafish, so the difference in decision-making when having sex was important to log.

Zebrafish may act differently from us in the bedroom in one sense, but in another, they've been shown to be very similar. It has recently been found that when they sleep they experience REM (rapid eye movement) periods, just as we do. Assuming that sleep only evolved once, it must have done so before we split from zebrafish, and this means that animals have been sleeping for at least 450 million years – and that sleep evolved in the sea. So we really have been sleeping with the fishes all along.

Zebrafish are surprising in other ways, too. Scientists discovered this year that alcohol helps them to remember things; that if they're born colour-blind, they can't find their food; and that they use quite complicated maths to ensure they stay in school(s). They're the first fish ever to have been observed 'giving up', too. When some zebrafish were put in a virtual-reality chamber that was rigged to create the impression that they weren't getting anywhere when they swam, they eventually abandoned the attempt and resigned themselves to just floating there.

ZEBRAS

In her first-ever scientific paper, an 85-year-old worked out why zebras have evolved stripes.

Alison Cobb first became interested in the subject a mere 80 years ago after reading Rudyard Kipling's *Just So Stories*, aged five. Kipling suggested that zebras got their stripes from standing in the 'slippery-slidy' shadows of tree branches all day. Cobb, who was sceptical about this, researched the matter further. In her first published academic paper, she concluded that the stripes evolved because as the black ones heat up more than the white ones, air turbulence is generated that gives the zebra a cooling breeze.

Other scientists floated an alternative theory. They dressed horses up in striped jackets and compared them to horses dressed up in plain jackets, to see if stripes repelled flies. What they found was that horseflies struggled to land in a controlled way on the stripes, either missing them completely or failing to decelerate properly, coming at them too fast and bouncing off. Of course both theories could be correct. Perhaps stripes evolved as a dual-purpose insect-repellent and breeze-generator.

ZELENSKY, VOLODYMYR

An actor famous for his fictional role as president of Ukraine became the real-life president of Ukraine.

Volodymyr Zelensky is a comedian and actor whose biggest role was in a hit TV series in which he played an ordinary man who accidentally becomes Ukraine's

In the TV show, the president played by Zelensky cycled to work every day. In real life, he walked from his house to his inauguration in May, high-fiving people who lined the route.

president. Very much not accidentally, he decided to ditch the role-playing and run to be the actual president this year. His party is called 'Servant of the People', named after the TV show, and he campaigned with the slogan: 'Vote for me, and I'll make your favourite TV show a reality.'

In the event, however, the TV star became uncharacteristically camera-shy on the campaign trail. He skipped a live TV debate with incumbent president Petro Poroshenko a few days before the election, leaving the president to stand next to an empty podium and speak for the whole 45 minutes. And he proved elusive when it came to interviews, though he did grant one to a journalist who beat him at table tennis at an election-night party. Even so, Zelensky beat the man whose confectionary empire has led to him being nicknamed the Chocolate King.

He also beat a man named Ihor Shevchenko, who had received a certain amount of attention for releasing a webcast called 'Do You Want to Become the Wife of a President?', in which he promised to select a wife from the hundreds of candidates he expected to apply. Shevchenko was knocked out in the first round of voting.

Following Zelensky's victory, he immediately called a general election in a bid to secure a parliamentary majority. Another candidate in that election was Svyatoslav Vakarchuk, lead singer of Ukraine's most successful rock band, Okean Elzy, who had also recently started a new party and whose campaign strategy consisted of performing gigs around the country. Zelensky initially met him to talk about the possibility of forming a coalition. Eventually though, comedy won out over rock, and Zelensky won a big enough majority to rule alone after an election cycle that was stranger than fiction.

ZOMBIES

'Santa's Village' had no reindeer because they'd all turned into zombies.

Zombie deer disease (also known as Chronic Wasting Disease) is the deer version of mad-cow disease, and it has hit the US quite badly. Symptoms include drastic stumbling, lack of coordination, listlessness, drooling, lack of fear of people and aggression.

The disease can be spread by fur or droppings (and aptly, given its name, through blood), so one of the best ways to contain it is to avoid moving the animals around. For this reason state officials in Alabama, which is currently free of the disease, announced that deer won't be allowed to cross state lines, and so for the first time in 15 years Santa's Village in Huntsville, Alabama, will have to do without Rudolph, Donner and Blitzen. How the authorities will stop the reindeer from flying over state lines has not been explained.

ZONES ▶

A German park tried to create a drug-dealer-only zone.

Berlin's Görlitzer Park is plagued by drug dealers, and repeated police missions have failed to clear them out. In a new strategy to cope with this, the park's manager set up a zone, designated by pink spray-painted lines, where drug dealers could operate, well away from the families and joggers who also want to use the park. It was a well-intentioned attempt to do something practical in the face of a problem that law and order has repeatedly failed to crack – but it also caused lots of controversy. The manager, Cengiz Demirci, tried to emphasise that 'This method has purely practical reasoning behind it', but to no avail. Mr Demirci was accused of being 'an agent of organised crime' and the idea was called 'an invitation to break the law'. And after all the controversy, the new pink zones didn't do any good anyway – local drug dealers completely failed to respect the line system.

Meanwhile a 'naked zone' in a park in Paris was being exploited by voyeurs. An area of the Bois de Vincennes has been set aside for public nakedness since 2017, but the naturists who use it say that 'perverts hiding in bushes' are spoiling their fun. 'It's a beautiful place,' said the president of the Paris Naturists' Association, 'and if we abandon it then they [the voyeurs] have won; except they haven't because then they wouldn't have anyone to look at.'

ZOOS ▶

A man whose name means 'dung' curated an exhibition of dung.

Miroslav Bobek, whose surname is a Czech word for a little lump of faeces, is director of Prague Zoo. The zoo has produced and sold elephant dung as manure for years, but now Bobek has decided to branch out and create a permanent exhibit of animal excrement. On display is everything from coprolites (fossilised faeces), to gorilla poo, to turtle turd, to the cube-shaped scat of the wombat. It's been organised to coincide with a new *Encyclopedia of Excrements* that the zoo is publishing.

In other zoo news:

▶ London Zoo now has a fern that takes selfies. Pete, a maidenhair fern, leaves biomatter in the soil as he grows, on which bacteria feed; the energy thus created has been harnessed to charge a battery; and the battery both powers and operates a camera set up next to the plant.

▶ In Nigeria, zoo-keepers and the media reported that $22,000 of cash that disappeared from the zoo's office had been taken and eaten by a gorilla. However, an official investigation came to a far more plausible conclusion: that the gorilla was innocent and the money had been stolen by armed robbers.

▶ A Texas zoo celebrated Valentine's Day by offering the public the chance to have cockroaches named after their ex-partners. The names were displayed in the zoo, and the unlucky cockroaches were then fed to hungry meerkats as a treat.

▶ And finally, a zoo in Australia doubled its population of endangered plains-wanderer birds with the help of a feather duster. The fathers of the species are usually the ones that rear the offspring, but at Werribee Open Range Zoo one father abandoned his chicks, forcing staff to improvise with a feather-duster substitute. According to the zoo's director, the hatchlings snuggled up into the duster for warmth and comfort, not remotely minding that it was an inanimate object.

ZUCKERBERG, MARK ▸

Facebook was fined $5 billion, but Mark Zuckerburg ended up $1 billion richer as a result.

Because of its involvement in the Cambridge Analytica scandal, in which a British political consulting firm harvested the personal data of millions of people's Facebook profiles without their consent, Facebook was given an enormous fine – but it was actually a lot less than people were expecting, so the Facebook share price went up by 1 per cent. This meant that within 30 minutes of the announcement that he had received a world-record fine, Mark Zuckerberg, who owns 28.2 per cent of the firm, became $1 billion richer.

Because Zuckerberg gets 10 votes for every share that he owns, his shares are more powerful than those owned by most other Facebook shareholders, giving him effective control of 60 per cent of any company vote. Not surprisingly, therefore, when shareholders held a vote in the spring to reduce his power, they were unsuccessful.

Some might question how he sleeps at night. But, actually, we know. That's because it was revealed this year that Zuckerburg has invented a way to wake up in a more controlled fashion. He invented the 'Sleep Box' for his wife, who would previously wake up in the middle of the night, worried that it was nearly time to get up and get the kids ready for school. Zuckerberg made a box that stays dark throughout the night, but then gently glows an hour before it's time to get up, so that you have a general idea of the time, without having to check your phone/clock.

▾

While Facebook users were encouraged to check their security settings, Zuckerburg spent millions on his personal security – $22.6 million in 2018 alone, according to the latest figures. The measures he took include getting bodyguards to sit near him, looking just like normal Facebook staff and organising a (rumoured) 'panic chute' – a secret tunnel from his office to the car park that he can use in case of emergencies.

IN WHICH WE LEARN . . .

*That a small circle can send
you round full circle.*

Readers looking for a story about a Chinese couple who ended up 1,310 kilometres away from their intended destination, you're as lost as they were. For where you need to be, *see* **Aa**.

ANSWERS

BEES, SPELLING

Seriously, you had to look up the answers? They were right there on page 18. As you're here, you might as well know what the words mean:

Auslaut (n.) the last sound of a word or syllable. So the auslaut of auslaut is 'laut'.

Palama (n.) the webbing on the feet of aquatic birds.

Cernuous (adj.) an adjective used to describe the way plants droop forward. 'You're looking very cernuous today, Andy'.

Odylic (adj.) describes a force or natural power thought to reside in certain individuals and things that underlie supernatural phenomena like hypnotism and magnetism. Dan probably believes in odylic ju-ju.

Erysipelas (n.) an acute febrile disease associated with intense edematous local inflammation of the skin and subcutaneous tissues caused by a hemolytic streptococcus. Clear?

Aiguillette (n.) that gold shoulder cord stuff soldiers wear to look smart. Seldom worn on the front lines due to the fact that it's extremely un-camouflagey.

EMOJIS

DEVOTE 25%   OF THE BUDGET   TO EDUCATION - BUHARI ALLOCATED JUST 7%   IN 2018   [VOMIT]

X-WORD

MANY THANKS TO . . .

To the Chief Gnome John Lloyd, and all at QI HQ: Anne Miller, James Rawson, Jack Chambers, Emily Jupitus, Joe Mayo, Liz Townsend, Natascha McQueen and Simon Urwin. Thanks for the facts, the ideas, the jokes and, in Joe's case, the terrified body (see **Birds, Angry**) that have been sprinkled throughout our book.

To Coco Lloyd, whose behind-the-scenes wizardry has made sure the good ship Fish stays afloat.

To Sarah Lloyd, show-runner extraordinaire, whose unflagging enthusiasm (and patience) have been vital ingredients in the Fish stew from day one.

To Alex Bell, the fifth Fisher, who has been riding sidecar with us all the way. Thank you for your brilliant ideas and for helping Andy to sneak a secret sausage into the book (for readers who didn't spot it, the hidden sausage can be found in the letter T).

To all at Penguin Random House: Henry Petrides, Konrad Kirkham, Katie Sheldrake, Sam Rees-Williams, Joanna Taylor, Mandy Greenfield and Lindsay Davies. Thank you for once again allowing us to be a part of your publishing family, and for all you've done to make this book a success both between its covers and out in the bookshops of the world.

To Elena Roberts, a seismic talent who no doubt will be running publishing one day soon. Thank you for not only taking on the seemingly impossible challenge you were tasked with, but managing to carry it out without killing one of us.

To Bean, Molly, Polina, Fenella, Wilf and all the other Ptaszynski, Murray, Harkin and Schreiber family members. Thank you for listening to us going on and on about our work. Much like a flyboarding Frenchman (see **Zapata, Franky**), we promise to take a holiday soon.

And lastly . . .

To Nigel Wilcockson, our intrepid publisher. We could not have asked for a greater leader to guide us on this expedition through the impenetrable jungles of 2019. Thank you so much for getting us through to the other side intact, and huge apologies for the forest of puns we forced you to hack your way through.

Okay, that's it, that's all of our facts (and all of our thanks), goodbye!

PICTURE ACKNOWLEDGEMENTS

Images are reproduced by kind permission of: ©Matt Crockett: Internal images of James Harkin, Anna Ptaszynski, Andrew Hunter Murray and Dan Schreiber. ©Darren Bennett: Illustration of Julian Assange's room in the Ecuadorian embassy (www.dkbcreative.com). Getty Images: Jean-Jacques Savin (Georges Gobet/AFP); Russian Orthodox priest blessing a tank (Stanislav Krasilnikov\TASS); Sea lion writing the name of Japan's new era (Kyodo News Stills); 'Rabbit' by Jeff Koons (John Lamparski); Archbishop of Paris leading the first mass held in the Notre-Dame (KARINE PERRET/AFP); Artists turn Venezuelan currency into handicrafts (Guillermo Legaria); Monty Python (Michael Ochs Archives); President Donald Trump (Nicholas Kamm/AFP); Carrie Fisher as Princess Leia (Lucasfilm/Sunset Boulevard/Corbis); Megan Rapinoe (Richard Heathcote). ©Colin Donihue: Study of lizard toepads in hurricane force winds. ©Carolina Waterfowl Rescue: Turtle shell repaired with bra clasps. ©Claire Wyckoff: Dick run route.©Bill Smith/Norwich Cathedral: Helter Skelter installation in Norwich Cathedral. ©Eric Tolentino/Jessica Anderson: Jessica Anderson running the London Marathon in nurse's scrubs. ©ZSL London Zoo: Penguins celebrating Pride month. Science Photo Library: Murray Gell-Mann (Estate of Francis Bello). ©Steffen Olsen: Huskies travelling across melted sea ice. ©Spanish National Police: Man caught with cocaine under his toupee. ©Max Siedentopf: 'Toto Forever' installation. ©Adam Gessaman: Sky penis. PA Images: Greenpeace protester flying 'Trump: Well Below Par' flag (John Linton/PA Archive). ©Alan Shaffer/Sarah Cavallaro: Cosimo Cavallaro building the cheese wall. ©East West Market: Plastics bags with embarrassing slogans. Alamy: National Standard of Mass, Kilogram (Science History Images); Franky Zapata demonstrating the Flyboard Air (Media Drum World); Woodstock, August 1969 (United Archives GmbH). Mary Evans Picture Library: A game of 'pushball' between Anerley and Crystal Palace, 4th October 1902 (The Illustrated London News). Shutterstock: Still from 'Carry On Doctor' starring Barbara Windsor, 1967 (ITV); Alexandria Ocasio-Cortez, Ayanna Pressley, Rashida Tlaib and Ilhan Omar (J Scott Applewhite/AP). ©McTear's/Ken McArthur Photography: Heinz golden bean. ©Tim Anderson/Channel 4: Conservative leadership debate. U.S. National Guard: East German students sit atop the Berlin Wall, November 1989 (University of Minnesota Institute of Advanced Studies). Wikimedia Commons: Black hole in Messier 87 (European Southern Observatory: CC BY 4.0); Glory hole in Lake Berryessa (Jeremy Brooks: CC BY 4.0); Karl Lagerfeld (Christopher William Adach: CC BY-SA 2.0); Yulia Tymoshenko (European People's Party: CC BY 2.0); Jair Bolsonaro (Fábio Rodrigues Pozzebom/Agência Brasil: CC BY 2.0); Doris Day; Keith Flint; Ekrem İmamoğlu; Tardigrade (Schokraie E, Warnken U, Hotz-Wagenblatt A, Grohme MA, Hengherr S, et al.: CC BY 2.5); Normandy Landings; Ibert Lemaître at the 1894 Paris-Rouen race; Billboard, November 1, 1894; Stephens Island Wren by John Keulemans; Edison Kinetophone; Egg-and-spoon race; Greta Thunberg (European Parliament: CC BY 2.0); Vladimir Putin (Пресс-служба Президента Российской Федерации: CC BY 4.0); King Rama X of Thailand (The Public Relations Department of Thailand: CC BY 3.0 TH); Ursula von der Leyen (© European Union 2019: CC BY 4.0); Jeremy the snail (Angus Davison: CC BY-SA 4.0) ©University of Glasgow/ Dr Paul-Antoine Moreau: Quantum Entanglement. Project Apollo Archive/NASA: Images of the Apollo 12 landing. Trevor the Duck-Niue Facebook page: Trevor the duck. ©Sent into Space: Image of the Spaceballs project that sent testicles into space. ©Dirk Ercken and Arturo Muñoz/Bolivian Amphibian Initiative: Romeo the frog. ©Google Street View: Kerville Holness's plot of land. Louie Keen: photograph of Mayor Keen.